WORKING WITH CONTRACTS

CONTRACTS

What Law School Doesn't Teach You

PLI Press's
Corporate and Securities Law Library

Accountants' Liability, by Dan L. Goldwasser & M. Thomas Arnold (B1-1348)

Corporate Law and Practice (2d ed.) (formerly *Understanding Corporation Law*), by Larry D. Soderquist, Linda O. Smiddy, A.A. Sommer, Jr., & Pat K. Chew (B1-1351)

Corporate Legal Departments (3d ed.), by Carole Basri & Irving Kagan (B1-1350)

Directors' and Officers' Liability, by Pat K. Chew (B1-1343)

Doing Business Under the Foreign Corrupt Practices Act, by Don Zarin (B1-1347)

Financial Product Fundamentals: A Guide for Lawyers, by Clifford E. Kirsch (B0-009H)

How to Draft for Corporate Finance, by Carolyn E.C. Paris (B0-00QE)

Investment Adviser Regulation: A Step-by-Step Guide to Compliance and the Law, by Clifford E. Kirsch (B1-1349)

Mutual Fund Regulation, by Clifford E. Kirsch (B1-3501)

The Securities Law of Public Finance (2d ed.), by Robert A. Fippinger (B1-1340)

Understanding the Securities Laws (3d ed.), by Larry D. Soderquist (B1-1345)

Working with Contracts: What Law School Doesn't Teach You, by Charles M. Fox (B1-3391)

Series Editor

Larry D. Soderquist
Professor, Vanderbilt University Law School
Of Counsel, Dinsmore & Shohl LLP
Nashville, Tennessee

PLI course handbooks on securities law topics are also available. Please ask for a catalog.

PLI PRESS
810 Seventh Avenue
New York, New York 10019
(800) 260-4754
fax: (800) 321-0093
www.pli.edu

WORKING WITH CONTRACTS

What Law School Doesn't Teach You

CHARLES M. FOX

PRACTISING LAW INSTITUTE
NEW YORK CITY

B1-3391

Library of Congress Control Number: 2002107004

ISBN: 1-4024-0158-2

To Lucy, Christina and Matthew with love.

About the Author

The author is a partner in Skadden, Arps, Slate, Meagher & Flom LLP, where he works on debt financings and restructurings and is actively involved in the firm's associate training programs. He spends much of his free time trying to understand why maturity, wisdom and devotion are of no use in improving the golf swing.

Preface

The author would like to thank his colleagues Elizabeth Bartolo, Linda Hayman and Phyllis Korff for their helpful comments on this book. Of course, the views and conclusions contained herein are the author's and do not reflect the positions of Skadden, Arps, Slate, Meagher & Flom LLP. The author welcomes feedback, criticism and musings at cfox@skadden.com.

Table of Chapters

Table of Contents

Chapter 4   Principles of Effective Drafting

Chapter 5   Drafting Techniques

Chapter 6   Review and Interpretation of Contracts

Chapter 7   Amendments, Waivers and Consents

Chapter 10 Miscellaneous Provisions; Miscellaneous Thoughts

Chapter 1

Introduction

§ 1:1   What Law School Doesn't Teach You

Linda, a new associate in a mid-sized law firm, gets her first assignment. She receives a call from a partner who tells her: "Our client, Unibanc, has a customer, Barnes Inc., that is considering a major acquisition of a company called Ashley Enterprises Corp. You're going to be working on the financing team with me and a senior associate. Come down to my office right away—we're going to rough out the closing checklist."

In the partner's office, Linda listens to the following discussion between the partner and the senior associate:

"This will be a syndicated loan with both a revolver and two or three term facilities. Barnes is currently financed by Minibank, so we'll need to review the existing credit facility, understand the prepayment provisions, and arrange to terminate all Minibank's existing liens and lien filings. Linda, that will be your job."

"Also, Ashley has twenty subsidiaries—we'll need to diligence them and make them a part of the credit package. One of them has an existing mortgage financing on its plant. Barnes wants to keep that financing in place because the pricing is cheap, so Linda, you'll need to review those agreements to determine whether there are any covenants that would prevent that subsidiary from executing a guarantee and security agreement."

"And speaking of guarantees and security agreements, why don't you take a first cut at drafting the guarantee that all of the subsidiaries will sign and the security agreement that the guarantors and the bor-

1

rower will sign. Bob will show you the precedents to use—the ones from the Romero transaction. All of the representations in the existing agreements will need to be modified to reflect the new parties."

Within the hour, Linda has the Minibank credit agreement, the subsidiary mortgage and the guaranty and security agreement precedents on her desk. She is doing her best to maintain her sense of confidence and optimism; nonetheless, her complexion has taken on a pasty green look.

Meanwhile, her next-door neighbor, also a first-year associate, is down in the library beginning work on his first assignment. He was told that the client was being sued for breach of a supply contract and was instructed to research and write a memorandum of law on the enforceability of a liquidated damages clause in the contract.

Why is this other associate in an entirely better mental state than Linda? Like many first-year litigation assignments, his assignment is something that *law school taught him how to do.* The case method of study familiarizes law students with the language and process of litigation. Legal research methods are taught starting in the first year of law school. Most law students are required to take a legal writing class, which inevitably includes only litigation-oriented writing projects—memoranda of law and briefs.

Conversely, law schools do a woefully inadequate job of preparing non-litigation lawyers—corporate, financing, commercial and real estate lawyers—to perform the most fundamental tasks that are expected of them. This is because much of what these practices entail does not involve "the law." Of course, there are strictly "legal" aspects of many transactions: a company making a public offering of equity must follow the securities laws; a merger of two corporations requires compliance with corporate laws; a secured financing must conform to the requirements of Article 9 of the Uniform Commercial Code. But these issues usually comprise a modest fraction of the time spent by transactional lawyers.

The law of contracts as covered by a first-year contracts class—offer and acceptance, consideration and the like—rarely poses any issues in sophisticated commercial transactions. The majority of a transactional lawyer's time is spent on structuring the transaction, advising the client on strategy, negotiating and drafting the contracts, orchestrating the closing, and throughout the life of the deal keeping the transaction organized and moving forward.

How is a new lawyer supposed to learn these skills? By doing and observing—in other words, "on the job" training. There is an awful lot that starting lawyers need to absorb before they become capable lawyers in their fields. However, the learning process for litigators is significantly easier because they start their careers knowing the necessary vocabulary and tools of their craft.

This book will provide the beginning transactional lawyer with an operative understanding of the vocabulary and building blocks of contracts. This will not solve all of the struggles of Linda or any other junior associate who is faced with the challenge of learning her craft, to one degree or another, by osmosis. Learning is an accretive process: the more one knows, the easier it is to learn, because there are reference points that new information can "stick" to. It's like a crystal. Once the seed of a crystal is formed, it grows quickly by accretion. I hope this book will provide the beginning transactional lawyer with some basic knowledge on which a larger set of skills can grow.

§ 1:2   The Role of Contracts

A long-term personal relationship (as anyone who has had one knows) is governed by a complex but unwritten set of rules. Certain behaviors are encouraged, some required, some forbidden. Disclosure is routinely necessary. Some actions are conditioned on the occurrence of other actions or circumstances. Wrongful behavior is punished and good behavior is rewarded.

All of the same dynamics are present in business relationships, the primary difference being that the rules of most long-term, and many short-term, business relationships are governed by written contracts. This is dictated by an interest in efficiency: although there is an initial expenditure of time and effort in creating the contract, the reduction in negotiation and disputes over the term of a well-written contract outweighs these initial costs. The process of contract formation also forces the parties to understand what they must give up to get what they want. This process results in more realistic expectations as to the risks and rewards of the transaction.

A contract creates a private body of law between its parties. Each party has the legal right to enforce the obligations and restrictions that the other party has agreed to. Many of the provisions of a complicated agreement go well beyond what clients consider the "business deal," and, as a result, some clients are prone to disregard these provisions as legal boilerplate. It is the responsibility of the lawyer to ensure that the client understands the impact that the contract will have on its business and its business relationships.

§ 1:3   Contracts: A Unique Type of Writing

Contract drafting is unlike other forms of writing that are familiar to beginning lawyers. The writing that we are exposed to on a day-to-day basis (even in law school) is almost entirely expository writing, the goal of which is to persuade or provide information to the reader. A contract is different: the goal of a contract is to describe *with precision* the substance of the meeting of two minds, in language that will be interpreted by each subsequent reader *in exactly the same way*.

This is no small order. A prerequisite for a precisely written contract is a clear understanding between the parties, which is often achieved only after significant effort. One of the lawyer's most important functions is to help her client think through all the relevant issues that lie beneath the surface of the client's business goals. Lawyers are trained to spot issues, and a good lawyer will protect her client's interests by spotting and analyzing all of the potential issues that arise in connection with each element of the transaction.

Each of these issues will then be the subject of a negotiation. The result of the negotiation may in turn give rise to additional issues to be negotiated and resolved. Then the outcome of each negotiated point must be reduced to language that each party (and its counsel) concurs accurately reflects their agreement. The process of drafting the appropriate language results in yet another negotiation between the lawyers, because there are many (perhaps even an infinite) number of ways to express any concept. Each lawyer will advocate wording that he believes most accurately reflects his client's understanding of the issue. These negotiations over language often demonstrate that points agreed to in principle still include areas of disagreement.

Ambiguity is the contract lawyer's enemy. Any term that can be interpreted more than one way can become the basis of a dispute, and eventually litigation, between the parties. Unfortunately, the qualities of the English language that make it a wonderful tool for poets—its rich supply of synonyms, its reliance on both latinate and germanic roots, its complex syntax and grammar—make it a challenge for lawyers to draft with precision and clarity.

§ 1:4   The Scope of This Book

This book:

- introduces the basic elements of all contracts (the "building blocks") and their functions;

- describes the lawyer's function in the drafting and negotiating process;

- examines specific drafting skills;

- discusses issues that arise in reviewing contracts, including due diligence issues;

- discusses amendments, waivers and consents;

- describes contract formalities;

- discusses some of the provisions typically found in financing and acquisition agreements; and

- provides a glossary of the language of contracts and basic transactional practice.

What doesn't this book do? It does not attempt to provide any substantive analysis or discussion of legal issues (one of its major premises is that a large portion of what goes into the drafting of a typical contract has very little to do with the "law" as we have learned it in law school). It does not purport to be a general guide to the practice of law for starting lawyers. It has nothing to add to the extensive literature on expository legal writing skills.

The author has practiced for 19 years as a financing lawyer with an emphasis on secured bank financings, many in the context of merger and acquisition transactions. As a result, there is a slight bias towards the agreements used in these kinds of deals. However, although the substance of contracts may vary, the language, tools and techniques of contracts do not. It is my goal to provide the starting lawyer with a comprehensive basic understanding of these common elements.

Chapter 2

Building Blocks: The Basics

---

§ 2:1   Introduction

Certain categories of provisions serve the same functions, regardless of the type or subject matter of the contract. These are referred to here as the *building blocks* of contracts. A lawyer who works with contracts must understand how each of these building blocks works:

- representations and warranties

- covenants

- conditions precedent

- remedial provisions

- definitions

What provisions in a contract aren't included in these categories? Provisions that set forth what the contract is *about*, referred to herein as the "operative provisions." For example, the operative provisions of a contract to sell the assets of a business would include a description of the assets, the calculation and method of payment of the purchase price, and the mechanics of transferring the assets. An asset sale contract containing only these operative provisions would be a very short document, legally enforceable, but not addressing many of the other important issues that buyers and sellers care about. What if there were a material problem with the assets that the buyer did not discover until the closing? A contract containing only the operative provisions would require the buyer to purchase the assets notwithstanding the existence of the problem. What if the seller caused damage to the assets or the business prior to closing? Same result. These are the kinds of issues that are addressed in the building block provisions—representations and warranties, covenants, conditions precedent, remedial provisions and definitions.

This chapter will provide a basic overview of the building blocks and their functions. Chapter 9 will provide a closer look at how building blocks are used to address specific legal and business concerns in the context of financing and acquisition agreements.

§ 2:2 Representations and Warranties: The Snapshot

Representations and warranties[1] are statements of fact made in the contract by one party to the other party as of a particular point in time. Their purpose is to create a "snapshot" of facts that are important to the recipient's business decision to enter into the transaction. The failure of a party's representations to be true will result in the other party having rights and remedies under the contract.

§ 2:2.1 *Representations: A Simple Case*

Let's look at a contract for the sale of the assets of a business, consisting of a plant that processes and dyes fabric. The buyer will want to know whether there are any environmental problems at the plant, because it may become liable for them under environmental laws. The buyer may have done an environmental examination providing a moderate degree of comfort that there are no environmental issues. However, it's possible there had been a hazardous waste spill that was not discovered in the environmental review. If, after the sale, that waste leaches onto an adjoining property, the neighbor may have a claim against the new owner for damages. This risk would be addressed by requiring the seller to make a representation in the purchase agreement regarding the absence of hazardous waste spills. If the buyer discovers before the closing that the representation is untrue, it would have the right to terminate the contract and walk away from the deal. Alternatively, if the spill is discovered after the sale closes, the buyer will have a claim against the seller for breach of representation. Typically, the buyer will also have an indemnity or damage claim based on the breach.

---

1. Although the terms are often used synonymously, there is a technical distinction between representations and warranties. A representation is simply a statement of fact upon which another party is expected to rely, while a warranty is a party's assurance as to a particular fact coupled with an implicit indemnification obligation if that fact is false. In a contract containing specific remedies for false representations and warranties (as is the norm), this distinction is not meaningful. In fact, it is typical for an agreement to label all such statements "representations and warranties," and practitioners tend to refer to them colloquially only as representations.

§ 2:2.2   *Smoking Out the Facts*

The process of negotiating representations has the effect of smoking out factual issues that might not otherwise be disclosed. Representations are a natural outgrowth of the principle of *caveat emptor.* In most commercial transactions, the parties are under no legal obligation to make any disclosure.[2] A party counteracts this principle by requiring disclosure of facts that may be relevant to its decision to enter into the contract. This is accomplished through the other party's representations.

Going back to our example, the buyer will ask the seller to make the following representation:

> Except as disclosed on Schedule C, Hazardous Materials have not at any time been released on or from any real property constituting part of the Purchased Assets.

When the seller receives the draft purchase agreement containing this representation, it has several choices:

- Tell the buyer it refuses to make the representation. The buyer will probably conclude that the seller has an environmental problem to hide, and will want the representation even more. Unless the seller has powerful negotiating leverage, this is a bad approach.

- Tell the buyer that it will give the representation "to the best of its knowledge," so that the representation is breached only if the seller fails to disclose relevant facts actually known to it. The buyer's reaction: "That doesn't do me any good if there was a spill at the property before you owned it."

- Give the representation after disclosing any responsive facts of which it is aware.

A party being asked to make a difficult representation will usually want to make complete disclosure in order to avoid liability. The disclosures may give rise to additional demands on the representing par-

---

2. However, as a general rule the securities laws do impose on issuers and sellers of securities an obligation to disclose all facts that would reasonably be expected to affect the decision of the other party to enter into the transaction. See also section 9:3.1[G] with respect to "10b-5" representations.

ty, however: the buyer in the example may insist on an undertaking from the seller to remediate the disclosed environmental conditions, or on a reduction to the purchase price to compensate the buyer for having to pay for the remediation itself. Or, the buyer may walk away from the deal.

§ 2:2.3   Allocation of Risk

Representations allocate risk between parties to a contract. The party making a representation assumes the risk that if the representation is untrue, the other party will have a claim against it or some other remedy under the contract. The party being asked to make the representation may not have any better information on the subject matter of the representation than the party requesting it. But it may be forced to make the representation anyway, based on the principle that the representation recipient is entitled to some remedy if the fact being represented turns out to be false. In the example of a previous environmental spill, *neither* party may be aware of its existence, but from the buyer's standpoint the risk of there being such a problem should be borne by the seller. Having the seller make the appropriate representation is the method by which this risk is allocated. If it turns out that there is a spill that results in damages to the buyer, the existence of the representation gives it the ability to assert a claim against the seller.

§ 2:2.4   Categories of Representations

[A]   Representations as to the Contract Itself

Representations fall into three basic categories. The first category includes representations that relate to the contract itself. The purpose of these representations (referred to here as "enforceability representations") is to provide assurance that the party making them has the contractual capacity and authority to enter into the agreement, and that the contract is legally enforceable and doesn't result in a violation of law. The party asking for enforceability representations wants to ensure that the other party doesn't have any technical defenses available to it if the contract ever becomes the subject of litigation. These are standard representations and are rarely negotiated to any significant extent. Enforceability representations are discussed in greater detail in section 9:2.

[B]   Subject Matter Representations

The second category of representations is those that relate to the subject matter of the contract. These representations are made to ensure that a party is getting what it bargained for, and are tailored to the specific context of the contract in which they are contained. Here are some examples:

- A trademark license contains representations by the licensor that the trademark is properly registered and doesn't infringe other trademarks.

- An asset sale agreement includes representations by the seller that the property to be transferred is not subject to any lien.

- A real estate lease contains representations by the lessor that it has not leased the same property to anyone else.

- A contract to rust-proof sheet metal contains representations by the contractor as to the quality of the materials used and the capacity of the provider's plant to handle the contracted supply.

[C]   Representations about the Parties

Many contracts require the parties to make representations about themselves that go beyond the enforceability representations and subject matter-related representations discussed above. These are required where particular facts about a party are relevant to its ability to perform its contractual obligations. The most frequent of these are representations that relate to the financial condition of the party. These are required where a party's credit—that is, its ability to perform financial obligations—is being relied upon. These representations are described in greater detail in section 9:3.1. Other examples of this type of representation are the following:

- An employee is required to represent in an employment contract that the employment history on her résumé is accurate.

- An insurance company purchasing debt securities under a private placement agreement must represent as to the source of funds used to make the investment, in order to ensure that there is no "prohibited transaction" under the body of laws regulating pension plans.

- A purchaser of radio stations is required to represent that it is not subject to any investigations or proceedings before the Federal Communications Commission.

[D] Exceptions

As representations are negotiated, information that is inconsistent with the statements made in the representations will emerge. This information must be disclosed in the contract in order to make the representations true. This may be done by excluding, or carving out, the inconsistent facts in the text of the representation. The following is an example:

> The Purchased Assets are not subject to any liens or encumbrances, except for the mortgage in favor of Big City Bank dated June 30, 1995.

Alternatively, the information can be put into schedules to the agreement. This method is useful where the exceptions are numerous or the disclosure is lengthy or otherwise unwieldy to include in the representation itself. If this approach is used, the representation above would read as follows:

> The Purchased Assets are not subject to any liens or encumbrances, <u>except as set forth on Schedule 2.1</u>.

§ 2:2.5 *Representation "Bring-downs"*

Representations are statements of fact as of a particular point in time; that point in time can be the date that the contract is entered into, the date that the closing of the transactions under the contract occurs, or any other date provided for in the contract. Representations that are made again on a later date are referred to as being "brought down."

The bring-down of representations is usually required at times when a significant event occurs under the contract. For example, an acquisition agreement may provide for the transfer of a portion of the assets at a future date, after a necessary consent is obtained. The purchaser will want the seller to bring down its representations at the time of the delayed transfer; this ensures that there has been no change in facts since the date that the representations were originally made.

A common occurrence of the bring-down of representations is in connection with contracts that are signed before closing. The representations are made at signing to induce the parties to enter into the contract. They are brought down at closing, to induce the parties to close by assuring them that the facts covered by the representations haven't changed since the signing date.

Another common occurrence of representation bring-downs is in credit agreements that provide for multiple borrowings. The borrower is required to bring down its representations to the lender as a condition precedent to each loan. If an agreement like this requires bring-downs at future dates, be aware that changing facts may make the bring-down impossible. Consider a representation in a credit agreement that all the borrower's subsidiaries are listed in a schedule. If new subsidiaries are created or acquired after the closing date, the representation can't be brought down, because the schedule doesn't list the new subsidiaries. As a result, additional loans can't be made.

If the lender wants to prevent the existence of new subsidiaries, this would be the correct result. If, however, the creation or acquisition of subsidiaries is contemplated, the potential bring-down problem must be addressed. This can be done in a number of ways. First (and most common) is to limit the representation to facts in existence on a specific date:

> Schedule A describes all of the Company's subsidiaries <u>as of the Closing Date</u>.

Second, if there is a covenant restricting the creation or acquisition of new subsidiaries, the following approach is appropriate:

> All of the Company's subsidiaries are described in Schedule A or have been created or acquired in accordance with Section 5.15.

Third, the schedule can be updated, with or without lender approval rights:

> All of the Company's subsidiaries are described in Schedule A, as such Schedule may be updated from time to time [with the Lender's consent (such consent not to be unreasonably withheld)].

§ 2:2.6 *Survival of Representations*

Although these concepts are often confused, there is a difference between a provision stating that representations "survive the closing" and a provision stating that the representations are brought down at some future time. A survival clause means that the recipient of a representation continues to have the benefit of that representation after the closing. In other words, if a month after the closing date a recipient of a representation discovers that the representation was false at the time when it was made, the recipient will have a remedy under the contract. Some people incorrectly assume that a survival clause means that the representations are made or brought down on a continuing basis. This is inconsistent with the concept of representations as a snapshot and would have the effect of converting representations into covenants.

The alternative to a survival clause is a provision that the representations merge, or terminate, at closing. This type of provision is typical in residential real estate contracts. In these contracts, the representations made by the seller must be true at closing as a condition to the buyer's performance, but once title passes, cease to have any effect. The net result of such a merger provision is that the buyer acquires the real estate "as is–where is"—it assumes the risk of problems that are discovered after closing, even those that were the subject of a representation by the seller.

§ 2:3 Covenants

Unlike representations—statements of fact as of a specific point in time—covenants are ongoing promises by one party to take or not to take certain actions. Covenants can generally be divided into three categories: affirmative covenants—promises to take specified actions; negative covenants—promises not to take specified actions; and financial covenants—promises to maintain certain levels of financial performance or not to take specific actions unless certain levels of financial condition or performance exist at the time.[3] Negative covenants are also referred to as restrictive covenants, because they restrict or prohibit certain actions. (See section 9:3.3.) Broadly speaking, covenants are designed to ensure that a party receives the benefits that it bargained for in the operative provisions of the contract.

§ 2:3.1   A Simple Case

In the example of a six-year lease of manufacturing equipment, the main objectives of the lessor are to ensure that the lessee pays the rent when due and returns the equipment at the termination of the lease. These will be the subject of the lease's operative provisions. But the lessor will also want the lessee to maintain the leased assets, to maximize the value of the equipment when it is returned to the lessor. This is accomplished through the use of covenants that dictate what the lessee must do, and cannot do, with respect to the leased equipment.

A typical equipment lease will include covenants requiring the lessee to do, or not to do, the following (among others):

- keep the equipment insured
- maintain the equipment in accordance with the manufacturer's specifications
- operate the equipment in accordance with applicable laws
- not permit the creation of any liens on the equipment
- not sell or otherwise transfer the equipment
- permit the lessor to inspect the equipment
- use the equipment only for specified purposes

Each of these covenants is designed to help the lessor protect its residual interest in the leased equipment.

---

3.   In many cases, these different types of covenants are used without being labeled as such.

§ 2:3.2 *Credit-related Covenants*

The lessor, in addition to its concern regarding the value of the equipment, will want to ensure that the lessee will be able to make the rent payments over the term of the lease. The lessor will have received financial information as to the lessee and required the lessee to make representations as to its financial condition. This provides the lessor with some comfort that the lessee can handle its lease payments at the outset of the lease, but doesn't protect at all against the diminution over time of the lessee's credit, its ability to meet its financial obligations.

Credit-related covenants restrict a party's ability to engage in activities that may result in a worsening of its financial condition. These activities include the following:

- *Incurrence of debt.* More debt means more interest and principal payments, which create a greater drain on a company's cash flow. The lessor will also be concerned that if the lessee goes into bankruptcy a higher debt load will result in a smaller distribution to it.

- *Creation of liens.* Secured debt reduces the assets available to be used to satisfy the lessee's unsecured claims and general obligations in the event of insolvency.

- *Sale of assets.* Loss of income-producing assets could adversely affect the lessee's cash flow.

- *Payment of dividends.* Every dollar paid as a dividend to shareholders reduces cash available for payment of rent.

- *Making of investments.* From a creditor's standpoint, cash spent on investments would be better spent on paying amounts due to the creditor.

Financial covenants, which require the covenanting party to periodically meet certain financial benchmarks, are also used to address credit concerns. These benchmarks are set at levels that are designed to create an "early warning signal" in the event the covenanting party is having financial difficulties.[4]

---

4. Sections 9:3.2 and 9:3.3, contain a detailed discussion of credit-related covenants.

§ 2:3.3　　Exceptions

The general pattern for the negotiation of negative covenants is that Party A proposes a covenant that will restrict Party B's activities. This draft covenant is relatively absolute as Party A's preference would be to prohibit Party B entirely from engaging in the specified conduct. Party B then has the burden of proposing changes to the covenant that it believes are necessary to give it the flexibility to operate its business without the need to request consents from Party A.

The difference between crafting exceptions to representations and to covenants is like the difference between writing a newspaper article and writing science fiction: one deals with actual facts, while the other addresses potential facts. Ensuring that representations are correct requires only diligent fact gathering. Uncovering and disclosing all information that is called for by the representations is essentially a forensic exercise. On the other hand, the lawyer who must negotiate a covenant that restricts his client's ability to incur debt for the next six years, for example, has a much more challenging task.[5] First, the lawyer and his client must collectively consider all of the possible needs for debt over the term of the contract. Then, they must convince the other party of the need to build flexibility into the covenant to permit such debt. Last, they must draft the exceptions broadly enough to achieve their objective, taking into account that plans often change.

§ 2:3.4　　Types of Exceptions

There are two basic types of covenant exceptions: carveouts and baskets.

A carveout gets its name because it has the function of removing, or carving out, part of the restriction created by the covenant. If the paradigm of a typical negative covenant is "thou shalt not do A through Z," the paradigm of a carveout is "but thou shalt be permitted to do 'Y'." Here is an example of the use of a carveout:

5.　　However, drafting representations that need to be brought down in the future requires some of the same skills as are described here for covenants.

> The Borrower shall not sell any of its assets, <u>except for the sale of obsolete equipment in the ordinary course of business</u>.

A basket, on the other hand, is an exception that creates the right to deviate from the covenant's restrictions by some specified amount (often expressed in dollars). The purpose of a basket is to give the restricted party a limited ability to deviate from a covenant's restrictions. The above exception could be converted into a basket thus:

> The Borrower shall not sell any of its assets, except for the sale of obsolete equipment in the ordinary course of business <u>in an aggregate amount not to exceed $1,000,000</u>.

Here, the restricted party's ability to sell obsolete equipment is not open-ended. After the first such sale for $200,000, the party may only sell an additional $800,000 of obsolete equipment.

§ 2:3.5   *Remedies for Breach of a Covenant*

A contract usually provides for specific remedies in the event of a breach of a covenant (see section 2:5). A party that is entitled to performance of a covenant may also seek a judicial order of specific performance forcing the covenanting party to perform.

§ 2:4   Conditions Precedent

The provisions specifying the requirements that must be satisfied before a party is obligated to perform under a contract or before the contract is enforceable are known as *conditions precedent*. The quintessential examples of conditions precedent are found in purchase agreements: the seller is not required to transfer the assets unless the buyer pays the purchase price, and the buyer is not obligated to pay the purchase price unless the seller transfers the assets. Conditions are often colloquially referred to as "outs," because a failure by one party to satisfy its conditions allows the other party to get out of the contract or terminate certain of its obligations. Conditions precedent vary widely, depending on the type of contract, although as is discussed in more detail below there are many that are fairly standard. In agreements that lead to a closing, the conditions precedent section dictates what documents must be delivered and what other actions must be taken at the closing.[6]

§ 2:4.1   *Timing Issues*

A *simultaneous closing* occurs when an agreement is executed and delivered at the same time that all of the conditions precedent to the effectiveness of the agreement are satisfied. When an agreement is executed and delivered, but the conditions precedent aren't satisfied until later, a *delayed closing* is the result.

The main distinction between these two is that the conditions precedent relating to a delayed closing must be much more carefully negotiated than those that relate to a simultaneous closing. In a delayed closing, any element of uncertainty, discretion, subjectivity or ambiguity included in a condition precedent can give one party a basis to claim that a condition isn't satisfied and walk away from the transaction. Consider a stock purchase agreement containing the following condition to the purchaser's obligation to purchase:

> The Seller shall have delivered to the Purchaser the Target's financial statements for the quarter ending September 30, 2001, and such financial statements shall be satisfactory to the Purchaser in all respects.

This condition gives the purchaser the unilateral right not to close by asserting that it is not satisfied with the September numbers. Suppose that the purchaser wants out of the deal because the economy has suffered a downturn since the date that this stock purchase agreement was entered into, but there is no condition that gives the purchaser the right to get out of the transaction for that particular reason. The broadness of the condition precedent above relating to the financial statements could be used by the purchaser as its excuse not to close, even if the target's numbers aren't disappointing.

What if, instead, the same condition were contained in an agreement that was being entered into by the parties at the same time that the closing was taking place? The seller's lawyer should not care about the subjective nature of this condition. If the purchaser is not satisfied

---

6.   Contracts that do not contain conditions precedent are effective upon execution and delivery by the parties.

with target's financial condition (or anything else, for that matter, including the economy) at the time of the closing, it has the unfettered right to walk away from the deal, because it hasn't signed the agreement yet.

Why include conditions precedent at all if there is going to be a simultaneous closing? It is not a necessity, but it does serve two useful functions: while the agreement is being negotiated, it creates a roadmap as to what the parties expect at the closing, and it creates a permanent record of what occurred at the closing.

§ 2:4.2 Conditions as "Outs"

Conditions are often hotly negotiated because they potentially give one or both parties the ability to get out of the transaction. Each party will want to minimize the number of conditions that it must satisfy, and at the same time will want to impose conditions on the other party that satisfy its own business and legal concerns about the deal.

The conditions precedent section of a stock purchase agreement, for example, will start with the following language:

> The Purchaser's obligation to purchase the Shares shall be subject to the prior satisfaction of the following conditions precedent:

This will be followed by a list of all of the things that the purchaser requires in order to close, foremost among which will be the delivery of the shares being purchased. Others will be business oriented: for example, delivery of financial projections of the target company, and satisfactory interviews with the target's suppliers. Some will relate to legal issues, such as evidence of the target's corporate existence and delivery of legal opinions.

The obligation of the purchaser to purchase the stock will be subject to the prior satisfaction of each of the specified conditions. The seller's failure to satisfy even one of the conditions will normally give the purchaser the legal right to walk away from the transaction. Agreements often require both parties to satisfy a set of conditions, so that either party is excused from performance in the event the other party fails to satisfy the conditions applicable to it. In other cases, only one party is required to satisfy conditions precedent in order to force the other party's performance, the most notable among these being debt financing agreements, where the lender's performance is merely the provision of money. It is all a matter of negotiation and custom.

Does the failure to satisfy a condition precedent always result in a termination of the contract? It often does not—rather than terminating the contract, the party having the right to terminate may use it as a source of leverage to commence a new negotiation and extract concessions from the other party. For example, if the condition that isn't satisfied is a requirement that a business being acquired have a minimum amount of cash flow during the three months prior to the closing, the buyer may insist that the purchase price be reduced in order for it to waive the condition and proceed with the acquisition.

Often a condition will be waived and the agreement rewritten to require that it be completed on a post-closing basis. This is often referred to as a *post-closing condition*—an inaccurate name, as a technical matter, because such a requirement is no longer a condition to performance. Instead, it has been converted into a covenant that one party must perform or else suffer the consequences for breach.

§ 2:4.3   *Common Conditions*

Different contracts call for different types of conditions with some conditions precedent being traditional for certain types of transactions. Other conditions will be required to address specific issues or concerns in the particular circumstances of one transaction. A party with a high degree of bargaining leverage may force its counterparty to jump through hoops by requiring the satisfaction of many conditions before it will close.

Some conditions that are seen more often than others include:

- *No breach.* Performance is not required if the other party has breached its covenants or representations.

- *Bringdown of representations.* Representations first made at signing may be required to be brought down at closing. See section 2:2.5.

- *Certified organizational documents.* Entities will often be required to deliver copies of their certificates of incorporation, by-laws or other organizational documents, certified as accurate by an official in the jurisdiction of organization or by an officer of the entity.

- *Evidence of corporate or other action.* Corporations may be required to provide evidence of board action authorizing the execution, delivery and performance of the agreement. Noncorporate entities will be required to deliver similar proof of proper authorization.

- *Incumbency certificate.* This is a certificate signed by an officer of an entity attesting to the genuineness of the signatures of the officers that are signing the contract.

- *Governmental approvals.* If the transaction contemplated by the agreement requires a governmental approval, neither party will want to be obligated to close unless the approval is obtained.

- *Third party consents.* Similarly, both parties will want all material consents from third parties to be in hand before closing.

- *Legal opinions.* These are letters from counsel to one party addressed to the other party, stating legal conclusions relevant to the transaction.

§ 2:4.4   *When Are Conditions Satisfied?*

Many contracts provide for the satisfaction of conditions at a single time: the closing. For example, a private placement of equity securities will provide for issuance of the securities when all of the conditions precedent have been satisfied. Other contracts requiring performance on more than one occasion may have separate sets of conditions for each performance event. An example of this is a revolving credit agreement that permits multiple borrowings. These agreements will have a full set of closing conditions with respect to the initial borrowing or closing, and in addition a separate, usually shorter, set of conditions that must be satisfied by the borrower at the time of each borrowing. Many contracts provide that if all the conditions precedent to a party's performance have not been satisfied or waived by a specified date (called a *drop-dead date*), that party can terminate the contract. Without such a mechanism, the party that must satisfy the conditions would be able to keep the contract alive indefinitely, waiting until the most advantageous time to close.

§ 2:5   Remedial Provisions

A bare bones contract could omit any discussion of what happens if the parties fail to perform in accordance with the terms of the contract. As every lawyer learned in law school, the aggrieved party could ask a court to fashion a remedy for breach based on statutory and case law. However, sophisticated commercial parties are generally reluctant to rely on a judge or a jury to do this, and for this reason many contracts have remedial provisions.

Remedial provisions have two elements: a description of the events that give rise to the right to a remedy, and the remedies themselves. As with the other building block provisions, these vary greatly based on the type of agreement in which they are contained, and are often tailored to the specifics of a transaction.

§ 2:5.1   Triggering Events

One of the primary purposes of remedy provisions is to address the failure of the parties to perform the operative provisions of a contract in accordance with their terms. The operative provisions represent the fundamental business deal between the parties; each party will want to have the ability to enforce the other side's performance by having the contractual right to enforce remedies in the event of non-performance. For example, take a commercial real estate management agreement under which one party agrees to manage a property owned by the other party in exchange for a management fee. The property owner will want to have the right to terminate the contract if the management company is not performing its duties satisfactorily, and the management company will want to be able to walk away if its fees aren't being paid.

In addition, remedies are almost always provided in the event there is a breach of a representation. Representations facilitate the fact gathering and disclosure process, but this purpose would be significantly blunted if there were no remedy for false representations. Likewise, the inclusion of covenants in an agreement is considerably more useful if the contract spells out exactly what will happen if a covenant is breached. This way, the aggrieved party is not forced to seek judicial enforcement of the covenant by specific performance or a damage award.

A contract may also provide that events other than breaches by the parties trigger remedies under the contract. These are often things that are outside of the parties' control and therefore are not appropriate for making the subject of affirmative or negative covenants. Some examples of such remedial events are:

- Change of control of a party, for example, due to a tender offer or a proxy contest

- Change in a party's credit rating

- Judgments or orders being entered against a party

- Involuntary bankruptcy petitions being filed against a party

- Default or acceleration being declared under other agreements

The distinction between a covenant, the breach of which creates a remedial right, and a separate remedial event, is often a narrow one. The only difference between a covenant to maintain insurance and a remedial event occurring if insurance is not maintained is that a breach of the covenant may give rise to a claim for specific performance whereas the remedial event does not. Both would typically, however, give rise to the same remedies under a contract: the first as a result of the breach of a covenant and the second as a result of the occurrence of a remedial event. When a party is reluctant to covenant to something that it doesn't have the power to control, the solution is to frame these points as remedial events rather than as covenants.

§ 2:5.2   *Types of Remedies*

The remedies that are made available under a contract vary based on the type of agreement, the nature of the event giving rise to the remedy and the objectives of the parties. In some agreements the remedy provisions are highly negotiated; in others they are very standard and may not be subject to very much discussion. Some of the more typical provisions are discussed below.

[A]   Termination

Termination of the contract is one of the most common remedies, and results in neither party's being required to continue performance under the contract (although in some cases the right of termination may be exercised together with other rights, such as the right to receive indemnification payments or liquidated damages). For this reason, termination is not a useful remedy where significant obligations under the contract have already been satisfied. Consider the situation where a purchaser of securities discovers after the closing that the seller breached its representations in the contract. At this point, the remedy of terminating the contract would be useless to the purchaser. On the other hand, if the purchaser discovered the breach of representations *before* the sale occurred, a right of termination would be very useful and entirely appropriate.

Sometimes a contract will permit a party to terminate certain obligations without terminating the entire contract. An example is a revolving credit agreement, under which a lender is required to make loans to the borrower from time to time. If the borrower defaults, the lender will be given the right to terminate its ongoing commitment to make additional loans, but exercise of this right by itself will not terminate other rights and obligations under the agreement.

[B]   Acceleration

The remedy of acceleration is found primarily in debt financing agreements. The exercise by a lender of this right results in the indebtedness under the agreement being *accelerated*, i.e., becoming immediately due and payable by the borrower despite a later stated maturity date. A borrower rarely has the cash to repay the amount of a loan that becomes due as a result of acceleration. In addition, the existence of an acceleration often causes a number of other negative side effects: accountants will be unwilling to issue clean opinions on the borrower's financial statements; defaults may be triggered under other agreements of the borrower as a result of cross-default provisions; other debt of the borrower may be accelerated as a result of cross-acceleration provisions; if the borrower is a public company, it will have to publicly disclose that its debt has been accelerated. As a result, acceleration often has catastrophic consequences. Usually, the mere threat of acceleration is sufficient to cause the defaulting party to make significant concessions in exchange for the lender agreeing not to accelerate.

[C]   Indemnification

An agreement may provide that a party breaching its representations or covenants will be required to indemnify the other party for all costs, damages and losses incurred as a result of the breach. Indemnification would be an appropriate remedy for a purchaser of a manufacturing plant who discovers after the sale that the seller breached its representation that there was no hazardous waste contamination of the property. The seller would be required to reimburse the purchaser for remediation and related costs.

Liability under indemnification provisions is often limited by baskets, caps and termination provisions. If indemnification is not required for claims that are less than some specified dollar amount, that is referred to as a *basket*. A *cap* is a limitation on the maximum amount of payments that may be required under an indemnification provision. If the negotiated cap is ten million dollars, then the indemnitee may receive no more than that amount in total indemnification payments, even if its damages are greater. Indemnity clauses may also be subject to termination after a certain point in time. There are two variations on this: a cut-off of indemnification if the *event* giving rise to the indemnification claim arises after the cut-off date, and a cut-off if the *claim* is made after a certain date.

[D]   Liquidated Damages

Liquidated damages clauses provide for one party to make a specified payment to the other party upon the occurrences of certain events. Examples include the following:

* An equipment lease requiring the defaulting lessee to pay a lump sum calculated by estimating the decrease in rent that the lessor will receive upon re-leasing the property

* A severance payment under an employment agreement to an employee who is terminated other than for good cause

- An increase in the interest rate payable on debt securities issued under Rule 144A if the debt securities aren't registered
  under the Securities Act of 1933 by a specified date

Case law suggests that liquidated damages may be characterized as
an unenforceable penalty unless the actual amount of damages in the
event of a breach would be difficult to compute and the amount of
liquidated damages represents a good faith attempt to estimate the actual damages that may be suffered. Accordingly, liquidated damages
provisions often recite that these elements are present—although a
court is likely to look through any such conclusory statement to the
underlying substance.

A common example of a liquidated damages provision is the *make-
whole provision* found in certain financing agreements. Where a lender provides loans at a fixed (as opposed to floating) rate of interest,
the financing agreement will often require an additional payment
from the issuer if it prepays the loans prior to their stated maturity.
Without this provision, a borrower would refinance every time interest rates decreased, and fixed-rate lenders would lose the benefit of
their bargain—the right to receive a fixed rate of interest over a specified period of time. This payment is calculated by reference to the loss
that the lender will suffer by being forced to reinvest at a lower yield
than it was receiving on the prepaid loan.

§ 2:5.3   Softening Remedies

The concept of materiality is often used to prevent a remedial
provision from having too harsh an effect. For example, a stock purchase agreement may provide the purchaser with a right of termination in the event that the seller breaches any of its representations or
covenants *in any material respect.* The inclusion of the last phrase limits the breaches giving rise to the purchaser's right to terminate the
agreement to those that are material. Assume that the seller had made
a representation as to the amount of debt on the balance sheet of the
company to be acquired. If the purchaser discovers that the total debt
is $10,000,500 instead of the represented level of $10,000,000, the representation will be breached but not in a material respect. As a result,
the purchaser will not be able to terminate the agreement. Of course,
the question of what breaches are or are not material can become the
subject of debate.

Grace periods are also used to protect against hair trigger remedial provisions: instead of being immediately available upon the occurrence of a breach of covenant or other event, a remedy will be available only after a specified period of time (the grace or cure period) has elapsed following the event. If the act or condition at issue is cured during the grace period, the remedy is never triggered. In some cases, the grace period doesn't begin until the breaching party receives notice of the breach.

§ 2:6   Definitions

The image of a lawyer carefully defining his terms has become almost a cliché. However, precision with words is one of the most powerful weapons in the lawyer's arsenal. In no area of the private practice of law is the precise use of words more important than in the drafting of contracts, where imprecision can lead to multimillion dollar disputes, litigation and liability. The process of defining important terms increases the likelihood not only that there has been a true meeting of the minds but that it was properly reflected in the agreement. In addition to this valuable function, the use of defined terms also engenders consistency and reduces unnecessary repetition.

§ 2:6.1   *Where Do Definitions Appear?*

Definitions are included in agreements in one of two ways. Either terms are defined in a separate section or they are placed in the text itself, as in the following sentence:

> The Seller shall not enter into agreements to sell any parcel of owned real property having a fair market value of $1 million or more ("Material Owned Property").

Shorter agreements are more likely to place the definitions within the body of the text rather than in a separate definitions section. The disadvantage of this method is that the reader must flip through the agreement to find the location of a definition, although underlining the defined term (as is done in the above example) or placing the term in italics or boldface will help the reader find the buried definitions. A contract of any length that takes this approach should at least

29

have a table indicating the sections or page numbers where terms are defined, in order to make the reader's job easier.

When there are a number of related contracts using many of the same defined terms, the definitions will sometimes be contained in a single exhibit that can be attached to, and incorporated by reference into, each of the contracts. This avoids the risk that changes to a definition in one agreement won't be made to the same definition in one of the related agreements. Leveraged lease and project finance transactions often use this approach.

§ 2:6.2   *The Purpose of Definitions*

Definitions isolate a term or concept that is used repeatedly in the agreement, and ensure that it will be given the same meaning each time. Consider a real estate lease with both a representation and covenant dealing with the issue of encumbrances on the leased property. The landlord is required to represent as follows:

> On the Closing Date, there are no liens, mortgages, encumbrances, easements or encroachments on the Leased Property.

Further on in the contract, the landlord makes this covenant:

> Landlord shall not create, incur or permit to exist any security interest, lien, pledge or encumbrance on the Leased Property.

There are inconsistencies between these two provisions that are probably not intentional, but which could give rise to interpretation issues. The representation refers to easements and encroachments, whereas the covenant does not. If there were no easements or encroachments on the property at the time of closing (when the representation was made) but were subsequently created, is there no violation of the covenant because it fails to include these terms? Alternatively, can it be argued that the term "encumbrance" appearing in the covenant is intended to be broad enough to pick up things like easements and encroachments? If so, why were these words included in the representation?

The obvious solution is to create a defined term for encumbrances that would be used in both provisions. Of course, there is no reason why the representation and the covenant couldn't each have its own reference to encumbrances, particularly if the draftsperson took care to use the same wording in both provisions. But this approach creates a risk that changes in one section will not be carried forward into the other. It is both safer and more efficient to define a recurring concept, in order to avoid these complications.

§ 2:6.3   *What to Call Things*

There are no hard and fast rules as to what defined terms to use. An agreement that defined encumbrances as "Apples" would be perfectly enforceable, but it would not be an easy agreement to work with. A reader seeing the second or third reference to "Encumbrances," on the other hand, is unlikely to have to go back to the definition in order to make sense out of what she is reading. The overriding goal should be enhancing the user-friendliness of the agreement.

Terms that frequently appear in certain kinds of agreements are often called the same thing. In credit agreements, these include, for example, Indebtedness, Maturity Date, Guarantors and Majority Lenders. In an asset purchase agreement some examples would be Assumed Liabilities, Disclosure Schedule, Seller and HSR Act. The benefit of using a defined term that has a generally understood meaning is that an experienced reader will comprehend what is being referred to without having to flip to the definitions section each time.

What should something be called if it doesn't have some traditional defined name? There are several practical guidelines here. Choose a term that gives the reader a signal as to what it means. For example, in a real estate lease that deals with improvements that may be made on different parts of the property, a term defining improvements made on the ground floor after 2003 could be referred to as "Category Three Improvements" or as "Post-2003 Ground Floor Improvements." Although wordier, the latter defined term is more likely to help the reader orient himself, particularly if it is significant that the specified improvements are post-2003 and on the ground floor.

Going too far in the direction of specificity when creating defined names can become a problem, however, as extreme length in a defined name can become unwieldy. For example, "Adjusted Initial Closing Date Consolidated Total Capitalization to Indebtedness and Preferred Stock Ratio" is just too long. "Initial Capitalization Ratio" would be better and is probably equally likely to give the reader the orientation that she needs.

31

§ 2:6.4   *Nesting Definitions*

A common problem in complex agreements is that of *nesting definitions*. This occurs where a definition includes references to one or more defined terms, which in turn themselves refer to other defined terms, and so forth. The net result is that a reader doing a careful review, as he tracks through each definition in the chain, may easily forget where he started. Often, there is no simple fix to this problem. Sometimes a defined term that appears in one of these definition daisy chains appears nowhere in the document other than in another defined term in that chain. If this is the case, the substance of that defined term should be incorporated into the defined term where it is used, so as to avoid at least one extra link in the chain.

§ 2:6.5   *Avoid Substantive Requirements in Definitions*

Occasionally covenants, representations or mechanical requirements creep into definitions as a result of sloppy drafting. Here is an example from a shareholders' agreement:

> "Purchase Agreement" means the Stock Purchase Agreement dated October 6, 2000 between Buyer and Seller, as amended, modified or supplemented from time to time, <u>provided, that no such amendment may be entered into without each Shareholder's consent</u>.

Let's assume it is now time to amend the purchase agreement, and the shareholders' agreement is reviewed to determine whether consent of the shareholders is required. That the requirement is buried in the definition, and not included as a covenant, creates a greater likelihood that this requirement will be overlooked, because it is not where the reader would expect to see it. (Of course a diligent reader will check all definitions and catch the issue.) The guiding principle, once again, is to create a document that will be as easy to work with as possible.

Chapter 3

The Lawyer's Functions

§ 3:1   The Contract Formation Process: A Breeding Ground for Issues

The documentation of a business deal is where the worlds of business and law most clearly intersect. The business person often views lawyers as a necessary evil—in his view, he is capable of working out the terms of the business deal himself, and the lawyers are just there to wordsmith and make it legal. The lawyer, on the other hand, may view her role as preeminent—yes, the business people may have agreed to the nine or ten economic points that are the basis of the deal, but they have failed to consider the myriad other issues that flow from those key points, much less how to resolve these issues.

Something between these two extreme viewpoints is actually closer to the truth. Obviously, there would be no deal to document without clients. On the other hand, if business people were to document their transactions by writing down only the points *they* consider to be the business deal, a stream of unanticipated issues and problems that the documents didn't address would likely have to be resolved over time. Even between parties whose relationship is good, working out mutually agreeable solutions to these problems on an ongoing basis would be a constant and increasing source of stress. If compromises couldn't be worked out, the result might be litigation and the end of the business relationship.

There is another important advantage to resolving issues in advance as a part of the contract formation process. It is a time when both parties want a deal and therefore are more likely to reach a compromise. For example, during the negotiation of a trademark license agreement, the licensee may agree to a provision that a more rigorous set of quality testing requirements will apply to any overseas production. This is a concession that the licensee may be willing to make as one element of the overall negotiation process. On the other hand, if this provision weren't included in the contract, and the licensor requested more stringent overseas testing a year after the contract was signed, the licensee would be unlikely to agree. This will be the case even if the change is not that significant from the licensee's point of view, because of a fundamental tenet of human nature and business conduct: no one wants to give up something for nothing. The compromise that the parties might have easily agreed to if the issue were broached during the initial negotiation will be much more difficult to achieve after the contract has been entered into when all leverage is gone.

The time to anticipate and resolve potential issues is before the parties have bound themselves to the transaction, when deal momentum and mutual interest in completion greases the skids. Among the lawyer's most important functions are to help orchestrate this process, to identify issues, to propose solutions, to help identify workable compromises and to put it all into words that clearly express the parties' intent.

§ 3:2   Identifying Issues

A skillful lawyer is adept at sniffing out, sizing up and solving issues. Let's take a simple example. A client calls up his lawyer with the following instructions: "We've just agreed to acquire a used Model 780 pipe threader from Sellco for $3 million. Draw up the papers, but don't spend a lot of time on this."

The good lawyer will resist the suggestion that he shouldn't take up her or her client's time, and will ask the following questions:

- Is it a *particular* Model 780 (if Sellco has more than one), and, if so, how can I get the serial number to identify it in the contract?

- Have you examined the equipment and found it satisfactory? If not, what are the repairs or replacements that need to be made and which party is responsible for making them?

- Who is responsible for moving the equipment from Sellco's plant to yours? If Sellco, what is the method of transportation and delivery? When does the responsibility to insure the equipment shift from Sellco to you? Who is responsible for making the insurance arrangements?

- What rights do you want to have to inspect and approve the equipment after it has been installed in your plant? What if it is not working properly at that time?

- When is the sale expected to take place? What are each party's considerations as to the earliest and latest permissible delivery dates? Should either party be able to walk away from the contract if the other side doesn't perform by a specified date?

- Is the purchase price paid entirely in cash? Is Sellco requiring any portion of it as a deposit when the agreement of sale is signed? If a portion of the purchase price is a promissory note, what are the terms: interest rate, maturity date, amortization, interest payment dates, rights of setoff?

- When does the cash consideration get paid? What form of payment is expected—check or wire transfer? What is the source of the payment? Are you borrowing to pay the purchase price?

- Are there any special undertakings with respect to the equipment that you expect to get from Sellco? Is Sellco willing to warrant its performance for any period of time? Are there existing warranties from the manufacturer, and if so do you expect to be able to enforce them directly?

These are all issues that the client should care about. They may not be as fundamental to the deal as the purchase price, but they should all be of interest to the person buying the equipment. However, if the client in this example is not involved in buying and selling used equipment as a regular part of his job, he may not have considered all the necessary angles to make the transaction a success.

Many business people will take the view that any issues raised by a lawyer are legal issues and are therefore not worth spending their time on. The above example illustrates that this is most definitely not the case. (Note also that this example involves the simplest of fact patterns. Imagine how that list of questions would grow if the proposed transaction involved an acquisition of multiple businesses located in several countries for consideration consisting of a combination of cash and securities, and which is financed with senior secured bank financing and a public high-yield debt offering.) A good business lawyer, through training and experience, is skillful at spotting issues that have economic and practical significance for her client. It is one of the lawyer's most important functions.

§ 3:3   The Lawyer as the Client's Guide

It is often necessary for a lawyer to guide his client through the contract negotiation and drafting process. This, of course, depends on the circumstances. A lawyer in a leveraged lease transaction representing a banker who has spent her last ten years doing these transactions will not be able to identify many issues that the client hasn't seen before. On the other hand, a lawyer representing a client who is participating in her first leveraged lease transaction will have to educate the client as to the terms, risks and contractual intricacies of the transaction.

Agreements that involve significant ongoing obligations after the closing create the greatest challenge in this regard, as illustrated by the kinds of provisions that are found in many financing agreements: affirmative covenants, negative covenants, financial covenants, financial reporting requirements, representations that need to be brought down, and obligations regarding the maintenance of collateral. The lawyer must make sure that the client understands and has a reasonable expectation of being able to comply with these requirements.

Carefully negotiating a complicated set of provisions may be a long, laborious process. Often the negotiation of one agreement is taking place as a part of a larger transaction in which the client is being pulled in many different directions. Occasionally, a client will take the view that as long as he gets the deal closed, he can worry about the rest of the "legal mumbo-jumbo" later. Unfortunately, the legal mumbo-jumbo is likely to contain provisions that, if ignored, could create significant problems for the client and its business later.

In other words, it is the lawyer's job in the contract formation process to make the client understand and care about many things that the client may prefer to ignore. It is a task requiring not only technical knowledge of the issues but the necessary interpersonal skills to engage the client in this process. In order to perform this task well, the lawyer must also develop the skill to explain complicated concepts and issues in a clear and understandable way. A significant element of this is gauging the client's knowledge and interest level and tailoring the explanation accordingly.

§ 3:4   The Drafting Process

§ 3:4.1   *Getting Started*

At the outset, the lawyer responsible for drafting the contract will get some indication from his client as to what the terms of the transaction are to be. It may be a phone call of the type described above, it may be something in writing such as a letter between the parties, or it may be a term sheet. In any case, the lawyer will probably seek additional information from the client that will help him produce a credible first draft. At this stage the lawyer should explore whether the client has any documents that may be relevant. The client is unlikely to know what is relevant, so pointed questions must be asked. Are there any letters or other written communications between the parties relating to the transaction? Are there any written materials relating to the subject matter of the transaction? If the transaction is an acquisition, is there an offering book with respect to the target? Are there any relevant financial statements or reports? Are there any expert reports relating to the subject matter of the transaction, such as reports of accountants, appraisers or environmental experts? Such materials may or may not be helpful to the lawyer's task, but the lawyer must ensure that he has an opportunity to make that determination himself.

Then the lawyer prepares the first draft of the contract. During the drafting process additional issues and factual questions will arise. Some may be so important or wide-ranging that an answer must be obtained from the client before the drafting process continues any further. These may include fundamental structuring points that will broadly affect how the contract is to be drafted, or issues that may affect the viability of the deal. This type of concern will warrant immediate communication with the client.

Other issues will be of less importance. In the interests of efficiency (and not exhausting the client's patience and goodwill) a method of raising these issues other than repeated phone calls to the client should be employed. There are three approaches:

- Put the issues or question in the draft itself, bracketed and made bold to ensure that they are seen by the reader and to make them easier to find and delete as the contract is revised.

- Prepare a separate list of issues and questions to be delivered to the client with the first draft of the contract.

- Raise all of the issues and questions when the draft is first discussed with the client.

Under most circumstances, the best approach is to combine either the first or second method with the third. Have the client read the draft and the lawyer's written questions and issues (whether embedded in the document itself or in a separate list) together. Then, when it is time to go through the draft together, the lawyer should elicit discussion and response from the client as to each of these points.

The above process should also be followed in the situation where a junior lawyer is preparing a draft for a senior lawyer. By doing this, the junior lawyer will develop important issue-spotting skills, and she will demonstrate to the senior lawyer that she is actively thinking about the assignment rather than just going through the motions. Many of these will be valid points that ultimately will be addressed in the draft or raised with the client.

§ 3:4.2   *Drafting the Contract*

Which lawyer drafts the contract is often dictated by custom: financing agreements are drafted by lenders' counsel; acquisition agreements are drafted by purchaser's counsel; underwriting agreements are drafted by underwriter's counsel; employment contracts are drafted by employers' counsel; security agreements are drafted by secured party's counsel. The underlying principle is that the party with the most leverage or with the most to lose from an inadequately drafted contract will do the drafting.

What is the importance of being the draftsperson? The draftsperson can ensure that the issues he wants to be addressed are not only covered, but covered in the manner that best serves his client's purposes. The party that is reacting to the draft presented by the other side is functionally in a defensive posture: it is reacting to the other side's proposals rather than proactively asserting its own agenda.

The difference between these two positions can be illustrated in an example. What if, contrary to tradition, a purchaser of a business allows the seller's lawyer to prepare the purchase agreement? The seller's lawyer will prepare a very slim draft, omitting as many of the provisions that protect the purchaser as he feels he can get away with. (The seller's goal is to receive its consideration with as few strings attached as possible, whereas a purchaser wants representations regarding the purchased assets and indemnities for the breach of the representations, among other things.) The purchaser and its counsel will react by providing an extensive barrage of comments intended to turn the draft into a more middle-of-the road document. However, the purchaser in this case is in the posture of requesting numerous changes, rather than imposing its terms on the other side. From a purely mechanical standpoint, no changes to a draft document are made without the approval and cooperation of the party that has the draft on its or its lawyers' word processing system.

Another benefit of having drafting responsibility is being able to control the pace of the transaction. The ability to control when a draft agreement is delivered to the other participants in a deal can be an important strategic device, particularly for a party anxious to have the deal progress quickly.

§ 3:4.3   *Use of Precedent*

In contract drafting, plagiarism is a virtue. A lawyer drafting a contract should always try to start with a form designed for the kind of transaction involved, or from a contract previously used in a similar transaction. There are numerous reasons for not wanting to "reinvent the wheel": starting a contract from scratch is more time-consuming than marking up a good form; precedents contain provisions that address issues in ways that are generally accepted in the legal and business communities; and boilerplate provisions that have been used and accepted in previous transactions are less likely to require careful review and negotiation.

It is crucial to find a precedent that closely matches the transaction at hand. Ideally, you will have several good precedents. The closer the match is, the less redrafting and engineering will be required of the draftsperson. A lawyer using a stock purchase agreement as a precedent for an asset purchase, for example, will have to add all the provisions that identify the assets to be transferred and the mechanics of such transfer, since these provisions will not be in a stock purchase precedent. Another example is the use of a single-lender credit agreement precedent for a credit facility involving a syndicate of lenders. The draftsperson will be required to make some significant changes (e.g., adding all of the agency and voting provisions that are needed in syndicated credit agreements) as well as numerous clean-up changes (e.g., changing each reference in the agreement to "lender" to the appropriate plural reference). The extra effort and time expended in finding the most closely applicable precedent at the beginning of the drafting process will be well-rewarded.

If instead of a model form, the precedent is an agreement from a previous transaction, particular care must be taken to distinguish between standard provisions and the provisions that were specifically negotiated. Of course, to the extent these negotiated provisions are favorable to the draftsperson's position, it will not be harmful to include them in the first draft. But it can be very damaging to unknowingly give something up in the first draft by including a concession made in a previous transaction. The inexperienced lawyer may have a difficult time distinguishing between boilerplate and negotiated provisions. One way to address this concern is to obtain the first draft of the precedent (by getting the first word processing version or searching the files) and comparing it to the final version. This will not only prevent the unintended use of negotiated provisions but will also give the junior lawyer a road map of some issues that may come up (and their possible solutions).

If the reader of the first draft (whether it is a senior lawyer, the client or the other side) is familiar with the precedent used to create the draft, it may be useful to provide a copy that shows what changes have been made.[1] This will enable the reader to review the draft more efficiently by focusing on the changes to the precedent.

The effective use of precedents goes beyond finding the right agreement to start from. It also comes into play when the draftsperson needs to add provisions that don't appear in the precedent he is using. For example, a party to the transaction may be a quasi-governmental entity and the lawyer may want to add a waiver of sovereign immunity. He has two choices: draft from scratch or find a good form. If a good provision is found, it is an easy process adding it to the draft, although the draftsperson must make sure that all defined terms used in the inserted provision match those in the agreement, and that otherwise the style and format of the insert blend into the agreement.

On the other hand, in many cases it may be easier to draft from scratch (particularly as the draftsperson gains experience). Some lawyers seem to think there is magic to using precedent—that for every new concept or provision that must be inserted in a contract, there is precedent that works exactly right. This is often not the case, and a skillful draftsperson may be able to draft a better provision in less time than one found in a precedent after a lengthy search. This is particularly true where the concept to be written is not a frequently recurring one. It bears repeating that the purposes for the use of precedents are to streamline the drafting process and to rely on time-tested language covering recurring facts or circumstances.

For the junior lawyer who has not yet developed a feel for what is normally included in a particular type of agreement, it is a good practice to refer to one or two other precedents as the first draft is being prepared. This will provide guidance as to which provisions are customary and which are deal-specific.

---

1. This is a function of most word processing programs; it is generically referred to as "blacklining."

§ 3:4.4   *Marking up a Precedent*

This section addresses a mundane, mechanical matter: how best to mark up changes to a draft for word processing. A draftsperson who revises a contract by word-processing the revisions herself will not need any of the techniques discussed in this section. But those who do it the old-fashioned way—that is, by marking up a precedent by hand for input by a secretary or word processor—should heed the following guidelines. And in any event, the points that follow are important when the lawyer is called upon to provide comments to an agreement someone else has drafted by preparing a markup. See section 3:4.6.

All of these guidelines are presented with one goal in mind: efficiency. It is always more efficient to prepare a clear markup that is easily understood by the word processor the first time, rather than needing to make multiple revisions. Avoiding multiple revisions yields saved time for the lawyer.

The following pages show comparisons between difficult-to-read markups and easy-to-read markups. **Example A** shows the right and wrong way to make insertions. Note that it is much easier to see the insertions and where they are supposed to go in the second example. Drawing the insertion lines in between the lines of the text can force the reader to follow the lines as if trying to find his or her way out of a maze. **Example B** illustrates how best to reflect a number of small changes in close proximity. Sometimes crossing out the phrase or sentence and rewriting it is much cleaner, as is demonstrated here. **Example C** illustrates a very important point: for inserts of any significant length, it is far easier (both for the person doing the markup and the word processor) to do so by inserting a rider. This is particularly true if the draftsperson expands or modifies the inserted language as she goes along.

Example A

Wrong way

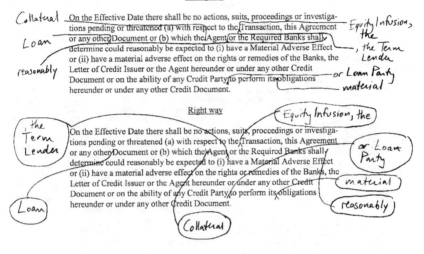

On the Effective Date there shall be no actions, suits, proceedings or investigations pending or threatened (a) with respect to the Transaction, this Agreement or any other Document or (b) which the Agent or the Required Banks shall determine could reasonably be expected to (i) have a Material Adverse Effect or (ii) have a material adverse effect on the rights or remedies of the Banks, the Letter of Credit Issuer or the Agent hereunder or under any other Credit Document or on the ability of any Credit Party to perform its obligations hereunder or under any other Credit Document.

Collateral
Loan
reasonably

Equity Infusion,
the
, the Term Lender
or Loan Party
material

Right way

On the Effective Date there shall be no actions, suits, proceedings or investigations pending or threatened (a) with respect to the Transaction, this Agreement or any other Document or (b) which the Agent or the Required Banks shall determine could reasonably be expected to (i) have a Material Adverse Effect or (ii) have a material adverse effect on the rights or remedies of the Banks, the Letter of Credit Issuer or the Agent hereunder or under any other Credit Document or on the ability of any Credit Party to perform its obligations hereunder or under any other Credit Document.

Equity Infusion, the
, the Term Lender
or Loan Party
material
reasonably
Loan
Collateral

Example B

Wrong way

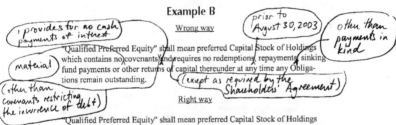

"Qualified Preferred Equity" shall mean preferred Capital Stock of Holdings which contains no covenants and requires no redemptions, repayments, sinking fund payments or other returns of capital thereunder at any time any Obligations remain outstanding.

, provides for no cash payments of interest
material
(other than covenants restricting the incurrence of debt)
prior to August 30, 2003
other than payments in kind
(except as required by the Shareholders' Agreement)

Right way

"Qualified Preferred Equity" shall mean preferred Capital Stock of Holdings which contains no ~~covenants and requires no redemptions, repayments,~~ sinking fund payments or other returns of capital thereunder at any time any Obligations remain outstanding.

material covenants (other than covenants restricting the incurrence of debt), provides for no cash payments of interest and (except as required by the Shareholders' Agreement) requires no redemptions prior to August 30, 2003, repayments other than payments in kind

43

Example C

Wrong way

[handwritten: , processes]

[handwritten: or (ii) a material adverse effect on the ability of any Credit Party to perform its obligations hereunder. To the best of the Operating Companies' knowledge, no third party is infringing or upon the Intellectual Property in any material respect.]

Except as disclosed on Schedule 6.18, all registrations for intellectual property rights owned by the Operating Companies are in full force and effect and are valid and enforceable. The conduct of the business of each Operating Company as currently conducted does not infringe upon, violate, misappropriate or dilute any intellectual property of any third party which infringement is likely to have a Material Adverse Effect. Except as set forth in Schedule 6.18, there is no pending or, to the best of each Operating Company's knowledge, threatened claim or litigation contesting any Credit Party's right to own or use any Intellectual Property or the validity or enforceability thereof.

[handwritten left margin: , including, but not limited to, all products or services made, offered or sold by each such Operating Company]

[handwritten: or under any other Credit Document]

Right way

[handwritten: Rider B]

Except as disclosed on Schedule 6.18, all registrations for intellectual property rights owned by the Operating Companies are in full force and effect and are valid and enforceable. The conduct of the business of each Operating Company as currently conducted does not infringe upon, violate, misappropriate or dilute any intellectual property of any third party which infringement is likely to have a Material Adverse Effect. *[handwritten: (i)]* Except as set forth in Schedule 6.18, there is no pending or, to the best of each Operating Company's knowledge, threatened claim or litigation contesting any Credit Party's right to own or use any Intellectual Property or the validity or enforceability thereof.

[handwritten: Rider A]

Rider A

, including, but not limited to, all products, processes or services made, offered or sold by each such Operating Company,

Rider B

or (ii) a material adverse effect on the ability of any Credit Party to perform its obligations hereunder or under any other Credit Document. To the best of the Operating Companies' knowledge, no third party is infringing upon the Intellectual Property in any material respect.

---

§ 3:4.5 *Final Steps in Producing a First Draft*

When a first draft is completed, it will be sent to the client for its review and comments. At this point, the draft will be cleansed of any internal commentary that was meant only for the eyes of the lawyers, and any questions or issues for the client will be incorporated into the document or on an attached list, as discussed above.

When the lawyer and the client go through this first draft together, the lawyer will want to ensure that the client's expectations as to how long this process will take are realistic—often a client will underestimate how long this session will last, particularly in the case of a long or complicated contract. In addition to the questions and issues directed to the client in the contract or in a separate list, the lawyer may want to focus the client's attention on particular issues that the lawyer considers likely to be of interest or importance to the client. The extent the lawyer will want to do this will be a function of the experience level of the individual client. A client who is a novice may need more of a guided tour of the contract. Even if such a client has carefully read the draft, she may need help recognizing the significance of certain provisions or the way certain provisions in the contract interact with each other.

The lawyer will then revise the draft to incorporate the input obtained from the client. Ordinarily, these changes should be made in a new version and blacklined so the next review by the client can be limited to the language which has changed. If time permits and the client wishes, the process of review, comment and revision can be repeated. Sometimes, the lawyers may be instructed to send the draft to the opposing party and counsel prior to the client's review and input. If the lawyer believes this approach may be disadvantageous to the client (because, for example, the draft opens some doors that the client may not want to open), she should discuss this concern with her client prior to circulating the draft. Eventually, the draft is ready to be sent to the other side. Under normal circumstances it will be sent to the business people on the other side of the transaction and their lawyers at the same time.

In multiparty transactions, strategic issues come into play in deciding who gets to see the contract and when. Often there is a desire for two parties to be able to agree to a contract and then present it as a *fait accompli* to other interested parties. This is based on the concern that sharing multiple drafts of a contract while it is being negotiated will be perceived by other parties as an invitation to comment. For example, a syndicated credit agreement is usually fully negotiated by the borrower, the agent bank and their respective counsel before it is sent to the other banks in the syndicate. The lender in an acquisition financing will have an interest in seeing the acquisition agreement but will usually not be given the opportunity until late in the process. In this situation, a bank and its counsel presented with a final (even signed) acquisition agreement will be reluctant to raise anything but the most important substantive points.

When the first draft is sent out to the other side, unless the drafting lawyer's client has given final approval of the draft, it is usually sent under a cover memo stating that the draft "is subject to the client's continuing review and comment." This is absolutely essential in the case described above where the lawyer is instructed to circulate the draft without any client review. Failure to provide this warning does not stop the client from making additional comments, but makes it far less awkward for the client or its counsel to do so.

If the agreement was based on a precedent familiar to opposing counsel, it is usually appropriate to offer a blacklined version as well as a clean copy. If there is such a precedent and counsel wants to compare it to the new draft, your failure to volunteer a blackline just makes the process more difficult for your counterpart. Such tactics are not conducive to a constructive negotiating process.

§ 3:4.6   *The Role of the Non-Drafting Lawyer*

So you and your client have just received an agreement to review and comment on. What to do?

First, you and your client must read it. Some people start reading a contract on page one and continue to the end. Others jump around, perhaps starting with the operative provisions, then the covenants, then the representations, and so on. A particularly helpful technique is to remove the definitions section and staple it separately, referring to it as necessary. This is usually much more helpful than slogging through the definitions, which are often the first section of the agreement, without any context.

This initial read leads to a discussion of the draft with the client. More often than not, that discussion involves a page-turning session in which both lawyers and clients raise and discuss their respective points. Occasionally, the client will want a markup of her lawyer's preliminary comments before this discussion takes place. If that is the case, the lawyer will prepare a formal markup of the document with her own questions or comments. This markup should be prepared following the same principles as for a word processing markup. (All riders should be typed, however.) This markup can be used to raise questions or issues with the client. One advantage of getting this markup in the client's hands in advance of the page-turning meeting is that it enables the client to better understand the context of her lawyer's comments.

After the client and the lawyer go over their comments, the next step is to pass those comments along to the other side. There are two approaches to this. There can be a meeting of all parties and their lawyers (or only lawyers), where all the comments can be raised and discussed. Alternatively, a markup can be prepared and sent to the other side in anticipation of such a meeting. The second approach is almost always preferable. At a meeting where comments are being raised for the first time, resolution of the issues is less likely because the other side will not want to concede on any single point without understanding the complete package of requested changes. Delivering a markup first gives the other side an opportunity to review, consider and discuss the comments prior to a meeting. As a result, the meeting is likely to be more constructive.

If the initial meeting included clients, the lawyers will want to follow up with another session that covers the so-called legal or drafting points: the typos, the grammatical and stylistic points, the substantive points that are truly legal in nature, and points that the lawyers should be able to resolve without the clients' input. A discussion of these points with clients in the room or on the phone often results in grumpy clients.

The markup that is sent out in advance of a meeting will be prepared by the lawyer and reflect both the lawyer's and the client's comments. The same principles discussed with respect to a word processing markup apply: once again, the theme should be user-friendliness. It should be easy to follow—the other side may need to struggle with the *substance* of your points, but causing them to struggle to *understand* them will certainly not help. Some thoughts in this regard:

(1) Whenever possible, provide suggested language rather than just a general comment. This is particularly true where the issue is a complex one or involves any degree of subtlety. It goes back to the basic premise that the act of drafting allows the

draftsperson to direct the resolution of the provision in a particular way. Of course, there is no assurance that your counterpart will accept your language, but in many cases she will either use it verbatim or use it as a basis for the change. In any event, you avoid the confusion as to the change you are requesting that which can be created if only a general comment is provided. In addition, by preparing language you will be forced to think through additional issues that would have gone unnoticed if a more general comment had been made. Even on uncontroversial points, by providing your own language you improve the chances that the change won't be drafted in some unfavorable (or incorrect) way. Further, this engenders cooperative spirit—the draftsperson won't feel that everyone is sitting back while he does all the work.

(2) The use of typewritten riders is extremely important here for several reasons. First, they are *always* easier to read than handwritten inserts. Second, you can revise and edit a rider much more easily than a handwritten insert. Last, providing riders makes it very convenient for the other lawyer to adopt your language in the revision process.

(3) Be neat. Do the markup in pencil, so that any changes to the markup itself can be made neatly. Don't write insertions too close to the margin, otherwise words will get cut off in the copying or faxing process. Make sure that the copies of the markup are legible and that all riders are attached.

(4) Don't hesitate to use your markup to *explain* a point as well as to convey it. For example, if you strike out a sentence because it covers a point already made elsewhere in the agreement, *say* that in the margin. Or, if you've provided a rider to address an issue that may not be readily apparent from the language itself, add a bracketed note at the end of the rider explaining the purpose for the language. The more you help the other side to understand your comments, the less time will be wasted *explaining* them, so that more time can be spent *discussing* them.

Most contracts are not finalized after one revision. The steps described above will be repeated each time a new draft is produced.

§ 3:5   The Lawyer as Facilitator

Under normal circumstances, it is the lawyer's job not only to draft and help his client negotiate the contract, but also to facilitate and co-ordinate the various requirements that must be satisfied for the contract to be effective. The qualities that are necessary for a lawyer to handle these matters successfully are organization, foresight, diligence and an attention to detail. In many cases, these are primarily responsibilities of the junior lawyer.

§ 3:5.1   Representations and Warranties

It is the ultimate responsibility of the client to ensure that the representations made about it and its business are correct. However, the lawyer is often closely involved in the process of getting the representations right.

[A]   Legal Issues

Certain representations and warranties are essentially statements of legal conclusions. Among these are the following representations,[2] with a description of the actions the lawyer may be asked to take to ensure their accuracy:

Representation	Action
The Company is duly organized, validly existing and in good standing.	Order and review a good standing certificate for the client from the state of the Company's organization.
The Company has the corporate power and authority to execute, deliver and perform the agreement.	Order a certified certificate of incorporation from the state of the Company's organization and review it and the Company's by-laws.
The Company has taken all necessary corporate action to authorize its execution, delivery and performance of the agreement.	Review the applicable board of directors' minutes or resolutions.

---

2. See section 9:2 for a more detailed discussion of these representations.

Representation	Action
The execution, delivery and performance by the Company of the agreement doesn't conflict with its certificate of incorporation, by-laws, material agreements, laws, rules, orders, judgments or decrees.	Review the certificate of incorporation and by-laws. Review the material contracts, if feasible. (This will depend on the circumstances. Sometimes the client will have inside counsel who can provide the proper level of comfort on this. In other cases, the client may not want to incur the expense of a full-scale review.) Obtain copies of and review any available orders, decrees or judgments that may be applicable. Consider and research legal impediments to the agreement that may exist. Consult (with the client's authorization) local counsel or legal specialists if the law of other jurisdictions or some special area of the law may be relevant.

[B]   Ensuring Proper Review by the Client

Even in the case of representations that don't relate to legal issues, the lawyer should think carefully about any potential issues. In the process of working generally for the client or working on the particular transaction, the lawyer may have obtained knowledge of a fact or circumstance that may need to be disclosed under a representation.

By the time that the contract is ready to be signed, the client should have carefully read and considered the representations. In the first instance, this means that the right individuals at the client have done so—that is, those people that are most likely to know what the relevant facts are. (In many cases, this will be the in-house general counsel, if there is one.) If the lawyer has any doubt that the client has properly focused on these provisions, the lawyer should sit down with the right person and walk through the representations with her.

[C]   Preparing Disclosure Schedules

Many representations need to be qualified by exceptions. For example, a representation that a company is in good standing in every state in which it does business will not be true if there is a state where the company is *not* in good standing because, for example, there is unpaid franchise tax that is being disputed. As discussed above, the lawyer can help his client uncover these exceptions. In most cases, it is also the lawyer's function to organize these exceptions and incorporate them into disclosure schedules.

Why use schedules instead of just putting the exceptions directly into the text of the representation? The latter method works fine if there are only one or two exceptions, but beyond that it's mechanically easier to use a schedule. Further, in most agreements with extensive representations, the parties expect the exceptions to be in the schedules. It is almost always best to put things where the reader will expect to see them.

Another reason for putting factual disclosures in schedules is that more often than not it is the non-drafting party who is responsible for the schedules (for example, the borrower under a credit agreement or the seller under an acquisition agreement). So the schedules are normally prepared as a separate document on the non-drafting party's (or its lawyer's) word processing system, to be attached to the agreement at the closing.

The facts that need to be incorporated into the schedules almost always have to come from the client. The lawyer, however, has several important roles in connection with the schedules:

▶ *Help the client understand the scope of the required disclosure.* The representation that gives rise to the disclosure will be written in legal language that the client may need assistance to understand. For example, the scope of a representation that there is no litigation "that could reasonably be expected to have a material adverse effect" may not be immediately clear to a person who is not well versed in contract language and who therefore might be inclined to disclose more or less than is actually necessary.

▶ *Act as a filter for the raw data provided by the client.* The client may provide information that is more or less detailed than it needs to be or that requires some massaging before it is appropriate to disclose. For example, what if in response to a representation requiring disclosure of all capitalized leases the client produces a printout showing all of its leases, both capitalized leases and operating leases, and indicating the monthly required payments on each? It would not result in a false representation to attach this list as the schedule, but it would be better to pare it down to be responsive only to what the representation requires. If all the extraneous information is included, the other party may be able to argue that the representation is breached if the information regarding operating leases or monthly payments is incorrect, even if those items were not required. A lawyer should not automatically accept information provided to him for inclusion in schedules; he should review it and convert the raw data into appropriate disclosure.

▶ *Be the keeper and processor of the schedules.* The task of organizing and processing the schedules is a detail-oriented and time-consuming one. The lawyer should always volunteer to take on this assignment. When the client wants to maintain control of this process, the lawyer should keep a close eye on the schedules as they are produced, to ensure that they are in the proper format, that they are responsive to the applicable contract provisions and that they don't give rise to significant substantive points that need to be addressed in some other fashion.[3]

It is best for all of the schedules to be prepared as a single word processing file. Any other approach makes it difficult to distribute revised drafts of the schedules. Even where parts of the relevant factual information are on another participant's word processing system, it is ultimately more efficient to consolidate all such information in one location.

Delivery of the first draft of schedules late in the process often leads to significant angst and delay, particularly when items being disclosed

---

3. An example of the latter would be disclosure showing that all of the assets to be sold in an asset sale transaction are subject to liens securing the seller's bank borrowings. This is not a mere disclosure item; the seller will have to arrange to have the liens released at closing.

identify risks or issues that the parties must then address. Remember that one of the primary purposes of representations (and therefore of disclosure schedules) is to smoke out negative facts. Once these facts come to light, they may give rise to substantive negotiations, which may in turn require that contract provisions be added or modified. It is easy to see how this process may become much more difficult if it occurs at the last minute due to a late delivery of schedules. To avoid this problem, it is often helpful to start circulating drafts of the schedules even before they are finalized. This way, the parties can review what is available at an earlier time, with additional information being included in subsequent drafts.

§ 3:5.2 *Covenants*

A lawyer will assist her client in understanding and getting comfortable with the covenants in the contract. This is often more challenging with covenants than it is with representations. The task of getting a representation to work is a purely forensic one, involving the determination and disclosure of the true state of facts at the time the representation is made. Getting covenants to work involves getting your client to look into the future in order to build in necessary flexibility.

The first step in this process is to be sure that the client understands what the covenant will or won't permit it to do. Do not assume that the client understands the scope of a covenant: it is not unusual for a business person to make incorrect assumptions regarding the covenant that could result in some necessary issue not being addressed. The best approach is to engage in a dialogue with the client when reviewing the agreement together. As the lawyer comes upon covenants that are likely to produce issues, he should point them out to the client and suggest some possible points that may need to be addressed. Such a dialogue might unfold like this:

Lawyer: This is a covenant that restricts the joint venture from incurring indebtedness . . .

Client: That's okay because there won't be any bank debt at the joint venture.

Lawyer: Well, let's look at the definition of "indebtedness"—it's very broad. For example, it includes letters of credit . . .

Client: Well, we will need room to have letters of credit issued, to back up some of the joint venture's insurance obligations.

Lawyer: How much room do you need for that?

Client: Looking at our current needs, I would say about $1 million at any one time.

Lawyer: But if the Atlanta project we were talking about earlier gets off the ground, won't your insurance needs increase and require more letter of credit support?

Client: You're right, we'd better ask for $2 million.

The lawyer has helped the client understand the true nature of the restriction by getting him to focus on the defined term instead of relying on his general sense of what "indebtedness" means. The lawyer has also brought his understanding of the client's business to bear in helping to identify a future item that needed to be addressed.

Of course, while there will be many covenants that require a fair degree of focus on the part of both the lawyer and the client, there will also be many that require little attention. A skill that a good contract lawyer must develop is to be able to home in on the covenants that are likely to cause his client problems.

§ 3:5.3   *Closing Conditions*

The lawyer has two primary functions relating to conditions precedent: negotiating them and making sure that they are satisfied. In many cases, the clients will feel that the signing of an agreement concludes the deal, whereas in many cases there is still a mountain of paper to be produced and finalized before the transaction is closed. A key element of the negotiation of the conditions precedent is avoidance of conditions that will be difficult to satisfy. A requested condition may also be objected to on the basis that it is onerous, or expensive, or not customary, but the cardinal sin is to have the contract require something that can't be delivered; this results in the other party being given an option to close or not.

[A]   Subjective Closing Conditions

A risk of non-closure arises each time that a condition is drafted to permit the other party to make a subjective determination as to whether a condition is satisfied. Examples of these are:

> Seller shall deliver a bill of sale, in form and substance satisfactory to Purchaser.

> Purchaser and Seller shall enter into a mutually satisfactory services agreement.

> No material adverse change shall have occurred with respect to Lessee's financial condition, as determined by Lessor in its sole discretion.

> Shareholder shall have completed its due diligence review of the business, assets, contracts and financial condition of Company, and shall be satisfied in all respects with the results thereof.

Let's examine how each of these could be reworked in order to make them more certain.

> Seller shall deliver a bill of sale, in form and substance <u>reasonably</u> satisfactory to Purchaser.

By the inclusion of a reasonableness standard, purchaser cannot avoid closing merely by objecting to the bill of sale; it must have a *reasonable* objection. Of course, the parties could disagree on whether a particular objection is reasonable, but as a practical matter, with a simple document such as a bill of sale, there are unlikely to be many controversial issues.

Another approach to the same problem is imposing a standard which is more objective:

> Seller shall deliver a bill of sale, <u>in form and substance customary for transactions of this type.</u>

> Seller shall deliver a bill of sale <u>substantially in the form used by Seller in transactions of this type</u>.

These approaches attempt to moderate the subjectivity of the condition by referring to market practice or to a party's own prior practice.

Here the goal is to employ an external standard instead of a party's discretion in determining whether a condition has been satisfied.

A redraft of the second example:

> Purchaser and Seller shall enter into a services agreement <u>substantially in the form attached as Exhibit 2</u>.

As in the bill of sale example, this condition as originally written allowed purchaser to walk away if the services agreement was not to its liking. On the other hand, it gave the same right to seller, but for the purposes of this analysis we will assume seller's goal is to lock purchaser in as much as possible, not to have an escape hatch itself. The change above achieves that objective for seller by having the parties agree in advance to the form of services agreement. Once the form of agreement is negotiated and attached as an exhibit, purchaser may not later take the position that the terms of the agreement are not acceptable to it. Of course, the circumstances sometimes make this approach impractical, particularly when an agreement must be entered into quickly before there is time to negotiate all of the ancillary documents. In such a case, one of the approaches described above must be relied on in order to avoid a completely subjective condition.

The third example above, with two alternative redrafts:

> No material adverse change shall have occurred with respect to Lessee's financial condition, as determined by Lessor <u>in its sole discretion</u>.

> No material adverse change shall have occurred with respect to Lessee's financial condition, as determined by Lessor <u>in its reasonable discretion.</u>

> No material adverse change shall have occurred with respect to Lessee's financial condition.

The first of these gives lessor the greatest leeway, allowing it to unilaterally determine if a material adverse change has occurred. If lessor fails to close on this basis and is sued for breach by lessee on the grounds that no material adverse change existed, the judge would conclude that the agreement gave lessor complete discretion.

In the second example, lessor must be reasonable in its determination. If lessor asserted that a material adverse change occurred because lessee's annual sales had declined .05%, that would be unreasonable. A decline of 15% would be a much more difficult call. A judge presented with the issue of whether lessor's assertion that a 15% drop constituted a material adverse change would have to determine whether it was reasonable for lessor to reach this conclusion. The judge would need to examine whether a reasonable lessor would consider this fact significant in deciding whether to enter into a similar lease transaction.

In the third example, whether a material adverse change has occurred is not determined by the parties at all. It is a completely objective standard. (Unfortunately it still contains a large amount of wiggle room, because material adverse change is a flexible concept.) If the parties found themselves in court because lessor failed to close, the question for the judge would not be whether a reasonable lessor would consider it material, but whether it was *in fact* material.

The above focuses on how to make conditions less subjective. However, for the party whose satisfaction is required, the more subjective the conditions are, the better. But where both parties' performance is subject to conditions, it is difficult for a lawyer to argue that the conditions to the other party's performance should be airtight, while those required for his client's performance should be riddled with subjective escape hatches.

[B]   Due Diligence Conditions

Let's take another look at the last of the initial four examples above:

> Shareholder shall have completed its due diligence review of the business, assets, contracts and financial condition of Company, and shall be satisfied in all respects with the results thereof.

The issue here is obvious: shareholder can assert that anything it finds in its review is unsatisfactory, and walk away from the transaction. Due diligence conditions are by their nature subjective. They are included when one party hasn't completed its basic review and analysis of the business and financial condition of the other party—and typically that first party is not going to want to be forced to close if it uncovers something that is sufficiently negative. On the other hand, an open-ended due diligence condition creates an option: the party can close the deal, or not, as it chooses.

One way of handling this is the insertion of a reasonableness standard, in the same manner as discussed above. In other words, the determination that some information discovered in the due diligence process is unsatisfactory has to be made on a reasonable basis. This is certainly helpful, although the approach is often resisted by a party who doesn't want to find itself in a dispute over what is reasonable.

Another approach is to wait to sign the agreement until the due diligence process has been satisfactorily completed. Unfortunately, this issue usually comes up where the party objecting to the due diligence condition has some business need to have the contract signed quickly. A common example is a bidder for an acquisition that must deliver a financing commitment with its bid. Often the lender providing the commitment letter will insist on a full due diligence out because it has not had time to do the level of homework that would support a sound credit decision.

There are cases, however, where the due diligence process is partly completed at the time an agreement is signed. In these cases, the due diligence condition can be modified to reflect that certain areas of diligence have been completed on a satisfactory basis:

> Shareholder shall have completed its due diligence review of the business, assets, contracts and financial condition of Company, and shall be satisfied in all respects with the results thereof, provided, however, that Shareholder has reviewed and is satisfied with all of Company's public debt indentures, its employee benefit plans and its employment agreements.

What if, after signing the agreement that contains the above condition, shareholder discovers that one of the debt indentures was amended in an adverse manner, or that there are other employee benefit plans or employment agreements that had not been available to it at the time of signing? This is the reason that a limited due diligence condition of the type above is usually accompanied by the following additional condition:

> Nothing shall have come to the attention of Shareholder in its continuing review of the business, assets, contracts and financial condition of the Company that is material and adverse to the Company and that is additional to, or different from, the information available to Shareholder on the date hereof.

[C] Third Party Deliveries

Another category of conditions precedent that may create a significant risk of non-closure are those that require a delivery or an action by a person other than the parties to the contract. Some examples of this type of condition (in increasing order of difficulty) are:

> Borrower shall have delivered certificates of insurance issued by its insurance company or insurance broker setting forth a summary of casualty insurance on its property.

> Mortgagor shall have received an appraisal from B&B Appraisal Company stating that the fair market value of the Property is not less than $10,000,000.

> Employee shall have received consent from her current employer to the termination of her existing employment agreement.

The first example is a relatively benign requirement because certificates of this type are routinely given by insurance companies and insurance brokers. All that is required here is that the certificate is delivered, not that the insurance coverage levels have to meet any particular standards. As a result, the lawyer's primary task here is to see to it that the condition is actually satisfied by the time of closing. The lawyer needs to coordinate with the client to make sure that the insurance company or broker is contacted sufficiently early so that this delivery is not a last-minute crisis.

The second condition is more troublesome. There are two issues: what if B&B Appraisal Company goes out of business or for any other reason does not deliver the appraisal? What if the appraisal comes in at less than $10,000,000? As to the first of these issues, the appropriate fix is to refer to "B&B Appraisal Company or such other appraiser as the parties reasonably agree to." The second issue is less easily resolved. Perhaps the mortgagor may be willing to accept a lower appraised value if other elements of the deal are adjusted. For example, the appraisal requirement could be reduced to $7,500,000, but the interest rate on the mortgage loan would increase in the event the appraisal comes in at less than $10,000,000. On the other hand, if a $10,000,000 valuation is an absolute necessity to the mortgagee's willingness to do the deal, the only alternatives are to sign the agreement and accept the risk of non-closure due to a low appraisal, or to delay the signing until the appraisal is completed.

The last condition is an example of a third party consent requirement. This type of condition presents the greatest risk to the party that must satisfy it. Why would the prospective employee's existing employer consent to the employee's jumping ship? The natural reaction of the employer in such a circumstance would be to say no, or to ask "what's in it for me?" Of course, there may be mitigating factors. The employer may be happy to get rid of this person, or there may be a strong personal relationship with management of the existing employer that will smooth the way.

The best way to ensure that a condition involving a third party action or consent can be satisfied is to rewrite it using one of the following standards:

> Employee shall have used its [reasonable] [diligent] [best] efforts to obtain consent from her current employer to the termination of her existing employment agreement.

With this approach, the condition does not require the existing employer's consent to be delivered, it merely requires that the employee make some level of effort to obtain the consent. Regardless of which standard is employed, the condition will be satisfied so long as the employee makes the required effort, whether or not it is successful. (See section 5:2.4.)

[D]   Legal Opinions

The requirement of legal opinions at closing is a topic that bears special mention. A legal opinion is a written statement of legal conclusions relating to the agreement, delivered by one party's lawyer to the other party. At first blush, a condition precedent that a legal opinion be delivered seems different from a requirement that a third party consent be delivered. After all, the lawyer whose opinion is required to be delivered is involved in the deal and has an incentive to see the transaction close. This is true, but sometimes an individual lawyer cannot be certain that the opinion required by opposing counsel will be an opinion that she, or her firm, will be willing or able to deliver.

Most law firms have a review process that must be completed before opinions bearing the firm's name may be delivered. Sometimes the opposing lawyers may disagree on the appropriate scope of the opinion. In other cases, a requested opinion can't be given because the necessary legal conclusion can't be reached. For these reasons, a closing condition requiring the delivery of an opinion "in form and substance satisfactory" to the other party and its counsel may be incapable of being fulfilled. Therefore, whenever possible, it is advisable for the form of necessary opinion to be negotiated in advance and attached as an exhibit. In addition, completing all of the necessary due diligence prior to the time that the agreement is signed and the form of opinion is attached as an exhibit will help avoid last-minute problems. If, for example, a review of the client's contracts shows the need for a consent that may be difficult or impossible to obtain, the lawyer required to give an opinion on this issue will be embarrassed if that important fact is uncovered at the closing, rather than prior to the signing of the agreement.

One of the worst places for a lawyer to find himself is at a closing where the very last issue, the one that stands between the clients and the consummation of their business deal, relates to a legal opinion. The clients will not understand the opinion issue, will not want to understand it, and will not understand why the lawyers can't just work it out among themselves like rational business people. In order to avoid this very awkward situation, it is preferable that the lawyers attend to the negotiation of the legal opinions at an early stage of the transaction.

[E]   Satisfying the Closing Conditions

After the closing conditions are negotiated, it is each lawyer's job to ensure the completion of the conditions that must be satisfied in order for his client to be entitled to performance from the other party, and also to confirm that the other party's conditions are satisfied. The mindset of some clients is that once the agreement is signed, the deal is done and the closing is just a legal technicality. A lawyer will be appreciated best by his clients at this stage of the transaction by organizing a closing that is smooth and uninteresting. This is achieved by foresight, organization and attention to detail. The first step in this process should be the creation of a "closing checklist," a document that lists all of the transaction documents and closing conditions, who is responsible for them and their current status. This checklist creates a roadmap to the closing and is typically shared by all of the lawyers working on the deal. The process of assigning responsibility for each closing item is extremely important; without this, participants in the transaction may each assume that another is taking care of something, with the result that that item falls through the cracks.

The lawyers on both sides of the transaction should confer regularly about the status of the closing conditions, using the closing checklist as a guide. At the closing the checklist is an invaluable tool. It serves as a guide to where on the closing table each closing document is located and is literally used to "check off" each closing document as it is finalized.

Certain closing conditions are very standard. In many transactions involving entities as opposed to natural persons, documents relating to the entity's existence and power are required. For example, agreements to which a corporation is a party may require the following closing documents:

- Certificate of incorporation, certified by the secretary of state of the jurisdiction where the corporation is incorporated

- By-laws, certified as accurate by the corporate secretary

- Good standing certificate issued by the secretary of state of the state of incorporation, and certificates from other states indicating that the corporation is qualified to do business in such states

- Resolutions of the corporation's board of directors authorizing the transaction, certified by the corporate secretary

- Certificate of the corporate secretary certifying the signatures and incumbency of the officers who are signing the transaction documents

It is almost always the responsibility of the lawyer (usually the junior lawyer) to prepare and/or gather these and similar documents. Although a review of these items doesn't often yield surprises, it can happen, and any issues are best dealt with early. For example, what if a company's certificate of incorporation requires a special shareholder vote for the company to enter into the particular transaction? Or, what if the by-laws require the signatures of specified officers to enter into certain contracts? Such issues may be easy to address if discovered early enough.

As discussed above, subjective conditions and conditions that require the participation of third parties are two potential closing condition pitfalls. The lawyer should make it a priority to get these conditions satisfied as early as possible prior to the closing. For example, if there is a condition that the other party has to receive a satisfactory environmental report, the lawyer should make sure that the report is being prepared, that once it is prepared it is looked at promptly, and that the party reviewing the report is satisfied with it. Never passively wait until the scheduled closing date to learn that a process like this hasn't been completed.

[F]   Closing Certificates

A certificate is a document signed by an individual, either in his individual capacity or as an officer of one of the parties to the contract, in which statements of fact are made.

A certificate that is often required as a closing condition is a certificate executed by a senior officer of one of the parties that states that all of the representations made by the party in the contract are true and correct. What is the benefit of receiving this certificate? After all, if a representation is untrue, there will be remedies available under the contract anyway, so what additional protection does delivery of the certificate add? The rationale is that requiring an individual (even in his capacity as an officer of an entity) to sign a formal-looking document will result in that individual making a more diligent inquiry into the truth of the matters certified to, than he would in the context of signing a larger document solely on behalf of the entity.

Chapter 4

Principles of Effective Drafting

§ 4:1   Introduction

Contract drafting is different from all other types of writing, including other types of legal writing. In high school and college (and in most law school and college writing classes) we learned a style of writing that organizes and presents facts, states positions, and makes arguments. The primary purpose of this type of writing is to convey information or a point of view to the reader. Stephen King characterizes such writing as a means of telepathy: a device allowing one person (the reader) to get into the mind of another (the writer).[1]

A contract is different. It represents the efforts of one person (the draftsperson) to accurately convey the agreement of two or more other persons (the parties to the contract). The primary audience for this writing is the parties and their counsel. The agreement may have additional readers, such as regulators, creditors and others interested in the contractual relationships and obligations of the parties. In the worst case, the ultimate audience will be a judge or a jury.

---

1.   STEPHEN KING, ON WRITING, Pocket Books 2001.

Let's examine the differences between the two basic forms of legal writing. Here is a sentence from a brief by counsel to a plaintiff in a personal injury action:

> These thoughtless actions of the defendant, taken without regard to either the basic standards of human decency or the minimal standards of care described in the cases cited above, resulted proximately and immediately in severe harm to the plaintiff.

The writer is expressing positions both as to questions of fact and of law: the actions of defendant were as described in the previous portion of the brief; these actions violated the applicable standard of care; the plaintiff suffered injury as a direct result; and the injury was serious. Defendant's brief will take contrary positions on some or all of these points. The primary goal of these writings is to persuade the reader—the judge—that the position being conveyed is the correct one. Persuasion is more art than science. It requires that the writing is tailored to the reader, and may employ rhetorical devices and the creative use of language.

Now let's take a well drafted contract provision:

> This agreement will terminate at 12:00 noon on June 30, 2002, unless before such time Buyer shall have delivered to Seller a letter of credit in the form of Exhibit A attached hereto.

Note that there are no rhetorical flourishes, no adjectives, no imprecise terms. Every word serves a precise purpose. Assuming that it accurately reflects the understanding of the parties, it is successful because it is drafted in a way that is clear and unambiguous.

Writing a contract involves two processes: determining what the parties have agreed to, and reducing that agreement to words. Each of these presents its own set of difficulties. The dynamics of negotiations often yield uncertainty rather than certainty: the hesitancy to make concessions, the tendency to slough over disagreements or contentious points, the emotional reaction to being told "no," the intrusion of personal abrasion, all stand in the way of consensus. The substantive complexity of the points under discussion, intersecting with the complexity of human psychology, can make the negotiation of contracts challenging. It is the lawyer's first task to extract the actual agreement of the parties. This is not a passive endeavor: the lawyer must insert herself into the process, explore inconsistencies, challenge positions, battle ambiguities, and raise uncomfortable issues, in order to best extract a meaningful and comprehensive agreement.

§ 4:2 Precision

The lawyer then faces the challenge of putting words on paper that precisely reflect the agreements of the parties. (This is not to suggest that negotiation and drafting are separate and distinct. They are inextricably entwined. For one thing, the mere act of putting a concept into words often leads to further discussion and refinement.) The difficulty is crafting language accurately describing what the parties have agreed that will be interpreted by all subsequent readers (including the contract parties) to have the exact same meaning.

A well-written contract provision is one that provides no traction for either party or their counsel to argue that something else was intended. In order to fully understand this point, it is helpful to imagine the position of a litigator asked to review a contract. The litigator will look for every weakness in the contract language that can be raised for his client's benefit. A responsible litigator will not take positions that have no basis, but *will* identify every issue for which there is a credible argument.

Consider the weaknesses a litigator could exploit in the following provision from a real property management contract:

> Owner, by notice to Manager, may terminate this agreement, if Owner asserts a breach by Manager of the terms and conditions hereof, to the extent Manager is given a reasonable time to cure such breach.

Owner and manager have had a series of increasingly heated conversations over several months regarding a problem in the property's plumbing system that has damaged some furnishings. Owner refers to a section of their contract that requires manager to make all necessary repairs promptly. Manager hires a contractor to repair the plumbing, but the contractor has some other priorities and the repair work is not completed. To manager's surprise, owner sends manager a written notice terminating the management contract. Each party calls its lawyer. Each lawyer separately advises its client that the following arguments may credibly be asserted by owner and would probably survive a motion for summary judgment:

67

- The phone conversations in which owner asserted that manager failed to comply with the contractual requirement to promptly make the repairs constituted the required notice of termination.

- Manager is not entitled under the contract to the defense that it promptly hired a responsible third party to make the repairs and that the delay was attributable to the third party and not within manager's control.

- The period of time commencing on the date that owner first complained about the failure of manager to make the repairs and ending on the date that owner sent the notice of termination constitutes a reasonable cure period.

Although manager justifiably feels misused by owner, his lawyer advises him that a judge or jury could very well determine that the contract supports the action taken by owner. The result would have been different had the provision been drafted with more care:

> If (a) Manager breaches any of its obligations hereunder, (b) Owner delivers a written notice to Manager stating that it is a "Notice of Termination" which identifies such breach, and (c) Manager fails to cure such breach within 30 days after the date of such notice, this Agreement shall terminate, <u>provided, however,</u> that if the cure of such breach reasonably requires the action or cooperation of a third party, no termination shall occur so long as Manager is using its diligent efforts to cause such third party to act or cooperate.

This improved language demonstrates two important lessons. First, it is always possible to make contract language more precise and thus more resistant to the attempts of a party to assert aggressive or spurious interpretations. Second, it is often difficult to craft language so precise that some "gray area" doesn't exist: under the improved language owner can still argue that manager has not employed its diligent efforts to make the third-party contractor perform.

Precision must always be a goal of the contract draftsperson. A precise provision doesn't lend itself to competing interpretations. One principle of contract interpretation to be kept in mind in this context is that an ambiguous provision will be construed against the draftsperson. Common sources of imprecision include:

§ 4:2.1   Use of Antecedents

Do not use a pronoun unless it is clear who or what is being referred to. An example of the failure to follow this rule:

> If by December 31, 2001, Contractor fails to deliver the Certificate of Occupancy to Owner, it shall promptly give written notice to Lessee of such failure.

Who has the obligation to give the notice to Lessee? It is not clear because the pronoun "it" as used in the quoted provision is imprecise. It could be a reference to either owner or contractor. It may be that the context provides some clues about which party is being referred to, but why not write the sentence clearly in the first place:

> If by December 31, 2001, Contractor fails to deliver the Certificate of Occupancy to Owner, <u>Owner</u> shall promptly give written notice to Lessee of such failure.

Stylists may be concerned that the use of the word "Owner" twice in such close proximity is inartful and awkward. Inartful, perhaps, but remember that art is not the goal; precision is.

§ 4:2.2   Time References

A contract provision calling for one party to perform an action or to make a payment must be clear as to when such payment or performance is required. Failure to provide properly for the timing component may create confusion:

> Vendor shall provide Vendee with copies of its annual audited financial statements.

When is this delivery required? There may be a longstanding course of conduct between the two parties that these annual statements are delivered 90 days after the end of vendor's fiscal year. The failure to specify this in the contract, however, allows vendor to argue for more time than the parties may have intended.

If an action must be taken by a certain time, the provision would be drafted as follows:

> Borrower shall deliver a borrowing base certificate <u>no later than the fifteenth day of each month.</u>

Conversely, if the action is to be taken after a certain time, the following approach is used:

> Seller may sell the Topeka Warehouse <u>at any time after April 1, 2003.</u>

What if an action is required to be taken between two dates? The way to draft this is by defining the relevant period:

> Lessee may provide a notice of renewal <u>during the period beginning on October 31, 2001 and ending on December 31, 2001.</u>

In some cases, the parties may want to be even more precise and specify the *hour* that performance is required on a specified day. This is often the case where the provision calls for the payment of money. If payment is to be made by wire transfer, for example, payment will be required during the hours that wire transfers can be effected. If this level of precision is used, it is important to specify the applicable time zone, e.g., Eastern Standard Time. Contracts drafted by New York lawyers, with characteristic hubris, often refer to "New York City time."

Sometimes this level of precision is not possible or does not reflect the deal between the parties. Often contracts will use phrases such as "promptly" or "as promptly as practicable" instead of a specific deadline or time period. These are more subjective standards that can give rise to differing interpretations. Another formulation is: "promptly, but in any event not later than the fifteenth day of the month." This puts an outer limit on how late performance may be and still be considered prompt.

Another important concept in the precise drafting of timing requirements is the distinction between business days and non-business days. A business day is usually defined to mean a day that banks are open for business in a particular area or jurisdiction. This is an important distinction in provisions requiring payment. A contract that requires a payment to be made on the first day of each fiscal quarter but does not address what happens if such day falls on a non-business day will be impossible to perform if a payment falls due on a Saturday or a Sunday. For that reason, there is usually a provision to the effect that any payment that is due on a day other than a business day will instead be due on the next business day.

§ 4:2.3 Legalese

Lawyers are often accused of writing in "legalese" instead of plain English. It is true that too much legal writing is obfuscatory, wordy, dense and stilted. Many lawyers seem to believe that sounding like a lawyer is as important as the subject matter being communicated. A frequent result is that the effectiveness of the communication suffers.

In the context of complex commercial contracts, however, much that might be criticized as legalese by the uninitiated observer is instead completely appropriate. Effective writing consists of clear communication of the subject matter to its intended audience. The audience for commercial contracts is sophisticated business people and their lawyers. The notion that commercial contracts should be written in plain English so as to be understood by people who would never be expected to read them is an unreasonable extension of the plain English movement, which is aimed at helping consumers and other unsophisticated parties.

The following sentence from an acquisition agreement is clear and precise. It contains no unnecessary words and expresses its points in a way that readers of acquisition agreements will readily understand.

> Seller shall use, and shall cause each of its subsidiaries to use, commercially reasonable efforts to obtain from each of their licensees (except licensees under licenses with annual base royalty payments of less than $200,000), a consent to assignment substantially in the form of Exhibit S (or in such other form as Buyer may reasonably approve), no later than 10 days prior to the Scheduled Closing Date.

No one would ever suggest that a report whose audience consists of medical doctors should avoid medical terminology that could not be understood by the layperson. By the same token, a contract that embodies a complex commercial transaction will contain specialized diction and vocabulary familiar to its audience. Any attempt to avoid this would make the contract much longer, certainly, but of less utility to its readers.

All of the terms listed below (as well as hundreds—perhaps thousands—of others), and all of the terms defined in this book's glossary are terms that are not self-evident to the uninitiated and could therefore be incorrectly referred to as legalese. On the contrary, these are terms with specialized and precise meanings that function to streamline contracts and make them more useful to their intended audience.

validity	judgment creditor	leasehold interest
to the best of its knowledge	indenture trustee	financial statements
successors and assigns	paying agent	inverse order of maturity
governing law	gross negligence	purchase price adjustment
event of default	joint and several	pro rata
duly authorized	remedies	liquidation preference
all or substantially all	statute of limitations	chattel paper
contingent liability	beneficiary	anti-assignment clause
indebtedness	trustee	provision
fully paid and nonassessable	fiduciary duty	tax indemnity
consideration	fiscal year	partnership interest
choice of law	audit opinion	special purpose entity
submission to jurisdiction	subsidiary	capital contribution
counterparts	solvency	change of control
duly organized	board resolutions	arbitration
reasonably	pro forma balance sheet	good standing certificate
execution and delivery	environmental remediation	ordinary course of business
best efforts	legal opinions	perfection

directly or indirectly	specific performance	capitalization
unconditionally	minute books	marketable title
enforceability opinion	capital expenditures	

The next example, on the other hand, illustrates truly bad legalese. This sentence is filled with unnecessary words, phrases and rhetorical throat-clearing devices and is marked by a generally bombastic tone.

> It is hereby agreed among the parties hereto that upon the occurrence of each and every failure by Borrower to comply and perform in all respects with the covenants, restrictions and limitations set forth in Article 6, Lender shall have and be entitled to exercise, and shall be deemed to have, and be entitled to exercise, the right and privilege to cause the termination and extinguishment of the Loan Commitments, provided, however, that delivery of prior notice of said termination and extinguishment be made to Borrower.

This can be rewritten more clearly, simply and precisely as follows:

> If Borrower shall breach any covenant in Article 6, Lender may terminate the Loan Commitments upon notice to Borrower.

§ 4:2.4 *Conveyance Provisions*

One type of provision requiring a high degree of precision is a provision conveying or granting an interest in property. Applicable property law requirements must be followed. For example, a security interest isn't created under Article 9 of the Uniform Commercial Code unless the agreement provides for a present grant of the security interest.

§ 4:3 Simplicity

Each point in a contract should be expressed as simply as possible. The benefits of simplicity are many. Simple provisions are easier to read and understand. Simple provisions in a draft agreement are easier to negotiate and rewrite. Simple provisions are less likely to be imprecise or unclear, and are therefore less susceptible of competing interpretations.

Unfortunately, there are a variety of factors that can make simplicity difficult to achieve:

- The fast pace of transactions—the advent of fax machines, word processing systems and email have resulted in the pace of transactions being much faster than was the case fifteen or twenty years ago. As a result of this, lawyers may not have the time to edit and simplify excessively complicated provisions.

- The increased complexity of transactions—as deals become more and more complex, it becomes harder to keep the agreements governing them simple.

- Creative solutions—the tendency of transaction participants to come up with solutions that are creative and complex. These "solutions" to one problem often create a set of additional problems that must be addressed.

On the other hand, the majority of overly complicated contract provisions could easily be simplified by the use of proper drafting and editing techniques.

§ 4:3.1   *Keep Sentences Short*

Often an unduly complicated sentence can be simplified by dividing it into several sentences. This old chestnut from every writing class and writing book is equally true in the context of contract drafting. Here is an example of an unfriendly sentence:

> In the event Lessee fails to obtain insurance as required in this section, Lessor may obtain such insurance without any obligation to give Lessee notice thereof, which insurance may provide the minimum levels of coverage described above or such increased coverages as Lessor reasonably deems appropriate, and the premium payments in respect of which shall be for Lessee's account.

Notice that the following rewrite, which breaks the above language into three sentences, is much easier to follow:

> In the event Lessee fails to obtain insurance as required in this section, Lessor may obtain such insurance without any obliga-

tion to give Lessee notice thereof. Such insurance may provide the minimum levels of coverage described above or such increased coverages as Lessor reasonably deems appropriate. The premium payments in respect of such insurance shall be for Lessee's account.

Sometimes an overly convoluted sentence needs to be broken up, even at the expense of creating more words:

Seller shall not disclose Confidential Information to any Person, except its professional advisors to the extent necessary in connection with their work on the Transaction, and the Seller's lenders, and such disclosure is acknowledged by any such recipient to be subject to the confidentiality restrictions of this section 10.3.

The last clause of the above sentence does not quite fit. It needs to be broken out as a separate sentence, even though the two resulting sentences, taken together, are longer than the original sentence:

Seller shall not disclose Confidential Information to any Person, except its professional advisors to the extent necessary in connection with their work on the Transaction, and the Seller's lenders. Seller shall obtain an acknowledgment from each such party to whom disclosure of Confidential Information is made that such Confidential Information is subject to the confidentiality requirements of this Section 10.3.

§ 4:3.2 Use the Active Voice

This is another old workhorse from writing texts, but as worthy in drafting contracts as in any other form of writing. The passive voice results in a sentence that is wordier and less direct than it should be. Not only does the active voice keep a sentence simpler, it tends to make the sentence clearer:

If the Seller wishes to defer the closing date, notice thereof shall be given to Buyer no later than two business days prior to the scheduled closing date.

Is this sentence as clear as it could be? Not until it is rewritten in the active voice, which also removes any ambiguity about who gives the extension notice:

If the Seller wishes to defer the closing date, it shall give notice thereof to Buyer no later than two business days prior to the scheduled closing date.

§ 4:3.3   *Delete Unnecessary Words*

This rule is even more important in contract drafting than in other forms of writing. A wordy fiction writer may bore his reader; a wordy contract draftsperson, on the other hand, may create confusion, fuzziness or ambiguity that could lead to legal disputes.

A well-drafted contract is like a wristwatch or any other well-engineered piece of machinery. Every part has its role in relation to every other part, and the parts fit together to achieve a certain result in the most efficient manner possible. The designer of a wristwatch would not introduce an unnecessary part. At best, it would just take up space and add to the cost of the watch. At worst, it would interfere with the operation of the other parts and result in the watch not keeping proper time. Likewise, the use of unnecessary words in a contract provision may lead to unwanted breakdowns in interpretation. Here is an example of a provision that includes unnecessary words:

> ~~Licensor hereby agrees and acknowledges that~~ Licensee may exercise the Option in accordance with its terms ~~and conditions~~, upon Licensee's delivery of ~~advance~~ written notice ~~promptly~~ delivered to Licensor no later than 10 days prior to the expiration of such Option.

The words "Licensor hereby agrees and acknowledges that" add nothing to the above sentence. Licensor, by signing the agreement, has agreed to *all* of its provisions, and therefore stating it again in this provision is redundant. Further, could the use of these words here result in an argument being made that some other provision that omits these words is one licensor has not really agreed to? Best not to find out.

What about the reference to the option's "terms and conditions"? While this phrase is often used, it is twice as long as it needs to be. A reference to "terms" includes all of the terms (including conditions) and is therefore sufficient.

The words "advance" and "promptly" that modify the written notice requirement are potentially troublesome. The sentence clearly requires that the written notice be delivered at least ten days prior to the option's expiration. What could the "advance" and "promptly" concepts add to this? An argument could be made that these words *must* have been intended to mean *something*, perhaps that a separate notice must be given before the 10-day period preceding the option expiration date. Eliminate the possibility of this type of spurious argument by omitting unnecessary words.

§ 4:3.4   Accretive Drafting

Accretive drafting, the process of making successive revisions to a contract, will often result in a provision becoming awkward and overly complex. The changes made to the provision at each step seem reasonable, but the cumulative effect is a hodgepodge. This problem is compounded by the tendency of a busy draftsperson to tack new concepts to the end of a provision and not harmonize the old and new parts with an overall rewrite. Let's look at four successive versions of a covenant in a note purchase agreement, blacklined to show the changes made in each version.

> Issuer shall not pay any dividends or make any distributions in respect of Capital Stock, or repurchase, redeem or otherwise acquire for value any Capital Stock.

> Issuer shall not pay any dividends or make any distributions in respect of Capital Stock (except for dividends paid in additional Capital Stock), or repurchase, redeem or otherwise acquire for value any Capital Stock.

> Issuer shall not pay any dividends or make any distributions in respect of Capital Stock (except for dividends paid in additional Capital Stock), or repurchase, redeem or otherwise acquire for value any Capital Stock, provided, however, that Issuer may repurchase Capital Stock from members of management in an amount not to exceed $1 million in any year.

> Issuer shall not pay any dividends or make any distributions in respect of Capital Stock (except for dividends paid in additional Capital Stock), or repurchase, redeem or otherwise acquire for value any Capital Stock, provided, however, that Issuer may repurchase Capital Stock from members of management in an amount not to exceed $1 million in any year, and provided, further, that such repurchases shall not be permitted at any time an Event of Default has occurred and is continuing.

This is not a terrible provision, but it can be simplified by putting the two exceptions together in serial form and changing the second proviso to a condition, as follows:

> Issuer shall not pay any dividends or make any distributions in respect of Capital Stock or repurchase, redeem or otherwise acquire for value any Capital Stock, except for (i) dividends paid in additional Capital Stock, and (ii) so long as no Event of Default has occurred and is continuing, repurchases of Capital Stock from members of management in an amount not to exceed $1 million in any year.

§ 4:4   Consistency: Learn to Love the Hobgoblin

According to Ralph Waldo Emerson, a foolish consistency is the hobgoblin of little minds. However, when it comes to drafting contracts, there is no such thing as too much attention to consistency. Why is consistency so important? Inconsistent contract provisions can be a breeding ground for ambiguity and differing interpretations.

Consider the following two sentences from the same asset purchase agreement, the first providing for the payment of the purchase price at closing, the second for a post-closing purchase price adjustment payment:

> On the closing date, the Seller shall pay the Purchase Price to Buyer's Account in immediately available funds.

> The Seller shall pay the Purchase Price Adjustment on the fifth Business Day following the delivery of the Closing Date Balance Sheet.

Under the second sentence, can the seller pay the Purchase Price Adjustment by check, because there is no reference to "immediately available funds"? It is unlikely that the parties intended the payment mechanics to be different for these two events. However, the treatment of similar requirements in an inconsistent manner allows the seller to take the position that the second payment may be made by check. The buyer's protests that there was no mutual understanding that payment could be made in this manner will be unavailing: the plain words of the contract govern.

Inconsistent use of individual words can also create a potential booby trap. Consider these two sentence from the same guarantee:

> Guarantor guarantees the full payment and performance when due of all <u>liabilities</u> owing by Debtor to Creditor, whether now existing or hereafter arising.

> Guarantor shall not be obligated to make any payments hereunder in respect of <u>indebtedness</u> of Debtor to Creditor at any time that Debtor's Net Worth is at least $20 million.

A credible argument could be made that the word "liabilities" has a broader meaning than the word "indebtedness" and that therefore the second sentence suspends less than all of guarantor's guarantee obligations.

Draftsmen must also be wary of inconsistency in the use of word strings:

> Seller shall indemnify Buyer for all <u>damages, liabilities and expenses</u> to the extent arising from Seller's breach.

> Buyer shall indemnify Seller for all <u>damages and liabilities</u> to the extent arising from Buyer's breach.

The omission of the word "expenses" in the second provision could be quite significant. If Seller is sued by a third party as a result of Buyer's breach, any damage award against it would be covered by Buyer's indemnity, but not its legal expenses.

Another area where consistency should be the goal is in the numbering of a contract's articles, sections and subsections. Any system chosen for this task is fine, but the draftsperson should take care to follow the same system throughout. Thus, if a subsection in Article 1 is "Section 1(a)(5)," a subsection in Article 3 should not be numbered as "Section 2.b.4" or "Section 2(B)(4)." Will the failure to follow the same numbering system throughout the agreement really create any problems? Probably not, but an attention to this kind of detail demonstrates that the draftsperson cares about her work product and its readers.

Many transactions involve a number of related agreements that are executed and delivered at the same time. To the greatest extent possible, the draftsperson should avoid inconsistencies among related agreements of this kind. For example, it will avoid confusion if the parties are referred to consistently. If a party is referred to as "Borrower" in one agreement, "Debtor" in another and "Assignor" in yet another, confusion may be the result.

Another source of inconsistency in the context of related agreements is in their boilerplate provisions. Take an acquisition transaction where the seller agrees to provide transition services to the buyer and to grant an easement in respect of the property to be sold. The draftsperson chooses to cover these matters in separate agreements. It is not at all unlikely that the boilerplate provisions, such as the governing law, notice, assignment and consent to jurisdiction provisions, will be different in form (and perhaps in substance) in each of the precedents. The draftsperson should work at making these provisions consistent.

§ 4:5   Clarity

The ultimate goal of contract drafting is clarity. Clarity is not a separate technique but flows directly from the application of the other principles advocated in this chapter. If a contract is written with precision, simplicity and consistency, it will be clear. If it is clear, it will accurately reflect the agreement of the parties in a way that will be understood in the same way by all readers.

A rule of thumb to determine whether a contract has been clearly written: If a contract cannot be understood reasonably well by a reasonably intelligent judge who spends a reasonable amount of time reviewing it, the draftsperson has failed.

It is easy to get swept up in the vortex of a transaction, to succumb to the tunnel vision that legal specialization produces, and to revel in the ability to draft thickets of overly complicated contract language. One should not, however, lose sight of the primary goal of drafting: to create an agreement that is precise, simple, consistent and clear—in other words, an agreement that is user-friendly.

Chapter 5

Drafting Techniques

§ 5:1   Introduction

The previous chapter explored the general principles of good drafting. These precepts are broad and abstract. This chapter digs a little deeper, by examining a number of the most commonly-used concepts, techniques and phrases that are unique to contracts. Facility in using the matters covered in this chapter will not by itself make you a good draftsperson. On the other hand, these items represent some of the basic tools of the trade—you can't draft contacts effectively without them.

§ 5:2   Softening the Edges

One of the main themes covered in the preceding chapter was the need for precision in the drafting of contracts. There are many circumstances, however, where one or both parties will want to limit contract language that would otherwise be inflexible or absolute. In some cases, this can be achieved by means that result in no loss of precision: for example, the creation of a basket that permits a party to engage in a restricted activity, up to a certain dollar amount or value.

The addition of flexibility cannot always be achieved with such precision, however. The drafting tools explored in this section are all somewhat subjective standards which necessarily introduce a "gray area" into the provisions in which they are used.

§ 5:2.1   *Materiality/Material Adverse Effect*

The concept of materiality is used to modify provisions that would otherwise be too absolute. Consider the following covenant from the first draft of a credit agreement:

Borrower will not violate any laws, rules or regulations.

This covenant prompts the following negotiation between a borrower and a lender:

Borrower: Under this covenant as written, we would be in breach if one of our employees were given a speeding ticket while driving a company vehicle on company business. Come on, that makes no sense, does it?

Lender: Okay, we'll carve out that situation.

Borrower: Don't be ridiculous, that's just one example. What if we violate a regulation where our maximum exposure is a $1,000 fine? Surely you don't think we should be in default if that happens?

Lender: Fine, we'll carve out violations giving rise to a fine or penalty not exceeding $1,000 in each case.

Borrower: Look, its impossible to conjure up all the possible scenarios where there is some violation of law that shouldn't trouble you. We understand that you want a remedy if we have violated the law in a manner that impairs your position in a significant way. By the same token, we don't want to worry about being in default due to some de minimis infraction, and by the way, you don't want that result either. You don't want to be pestered with numerous requests for waivers of inconsequential events.

Lender: Alright, you win, we'll put in a materiality standard.

The above discussion illustrates that softening concepts like materiality are used when more precise techniques of creating flexibility are not effective. These create flexibility at the cost of introducing a certain level of uncertainty to the interpretation of the provisions in which they are used. Here are a number of examples in which materiality qualifications are appropriately used:

> The Company shall not default in its obligations under any material contract.

> Party A shall provide Party B with copies of all material notices received by it under the Receivables Purchase Agreement.

> Set forth on Schedule I is a list of all material litigation to which the Lessee is a party.

In many cases, however, materiality qualifications like this don't do the trick. Let's go back to the negotiation of the covenant requiring compliance with laws. The lender grudgingly changes the covenant in the next draft as follows:

> Borrower will not violate any material laws, rules or regulations.

This approach is still unsatisfactory to the borrower. She argues: "What if we violate the tax code (which is clearly a material law) in a minor way resulting in no significant loss or penalty? This would trigger a breach under the covenant as rewritten!" Unable to refute this logic, the lender offers this version:

> Borrower will not violate any laws, rules or regulations in any material respect.

The borrower is not satisfied with this approach, either. What does it mean, she asks, for a law to be violated "in a material respect"? In the case of the speeding employee, could it be argued that a ticket for doing 35 in a 40-mph zone is an immaterial violation, whereas one for doing 65 would be material? Shouldn't the materiality standard focus on the effect on the borrower instead of the quality of the infraction? Finally, the parties agree to this wording:

> Borrower will not violate any laws, rules or regulations in a manner <u>that could reasonably be expected to have a material adverse effect on Borrower's business or financial condition.</u>

"Material adverse effect" is a standard that is often employed in the softening of contract provisions. It is often used in more than one provision in a contract, and as a result may be separately defined:

> "Material adverse effect" means any material adverse effect on the Borrower's business, assets, liabilities, prospects or condition (financial or otherwise).

In order to fall within the ambit of this definition, the matter in question must be both *material* and *adverse* to the party. Materiality is a subjective concept; a change that would be reasonably likely to affect the other party's evaluation of the transaction will generally be viewed as material. The change must also be *adverse*. Obviously, if it's a change for the better, it isn't covered.

The definition refers to the areas where the material adverse effect has occurred: the party's business, assets, liabilities, financial condition and prospects. Let's look at examples of each of these. The loss of a customer that represented 40% of the borrower's earnings would have a material adverse effect on its *business*. An uninsured casualty loss in respect of the borrower's primary manufacturing plant would have a material adverse effect on its *assets*. The entering of a judgment against the borrower for damages in an amount equal to its total annual sales would have a material adverse effect on its *liabilities*. A loss of sales resulting in a diminution in cash flow that impairs the borrower's ability to pay its operating expenses would have a material adverse effect on its *financial condition*. Lastly, the development of proprietary technology by a competitor that allows it to produce goods at a more favorable price may have a material adverse effect on the borrower's *prospects*, because it may be forced to reduce its profit margins.

Inclusion of the word "prospects" as a component of the definition of material adverse effect is almost always a point of contention. The party to whom the material adverse effect standard is applicable will argue that the use of prospects gives the other party too much room to speculate about the future impact of an event. The other party will argue that its counterparty's future condition and performance is important to it, and the party should not be required to wait until a reasonably foreseeable bad result has occurred before having any remedies.

Closely related to material adverse effect is material adverse change, referred to colloquially as "MAC." It is used most often to measure the present condition of a party against its condition at a previous time. This representation provides an example:

> Since December 31, 1999 there has been no material adverse change in the business, assets, liabilities, financial condition or prospects of the Company.

In determining whether it can make this representation, the company will not evaluate the materiality and adversity of individual events that have occurred since December 31, 1999. Instead, it will compare two "snapshots" of itself: one on December 31, 1999 and one on the date that the representation is made. Let's assume that the company lost one-third of its net worth in March 2000 due to an uninsured tort judgment, but brought its net worth back up to the original level over the next four quarters through increased profits. On March 31, 2001 the company could make the representation, because on a net basis its position had not worsened.

"Material adverse change" and "material adverse effect" are often used interchangeably. The following usage creates a potential pitfall, however:

> Since the Closing Date, no event, act or condition has occurred that could reasonably be expected to have a material adverse effect on the Company.

The company discussed above whose net worth dipped and then recovered would not be able to make this representation as written. The reduction in net worth was an event that had a material adverse effect at the time that it occurred. The increase in sales that subsequently counteracted it is irrelevant. The representation written in this fashion identifies individual events, not overall changes from one point in time to another.

§ 5:2.2   *Reasonableness*

The reasonableness standard is the device most frequently used to soften the hard edges of contract provisions. It turns an absolute requirement into one that is subject to the test of what a "reasonable person" might do or require. An example:

> The Company shall reimburse the Agent for all of its <u>reasonable</u> out-of-pocket expenses arising in connection with its activities hereunder.

Without the term "reasonable" in this sentence, there would be no limit on reimbursable out-of-pocket expenses: officers of the Agent could travel to meetings on a chartered jet, for instance. By virtue of the reasonableness standard, the provision must be interpreted in the context of what would be reasonable under the circumstances (such as the use of commercial flights as opposed to chartered jets).

Another common appearance of the reasonableness standard is where one party has the ability to exercise its discretion in making a decision or reaching a conclusion under a contract provision. The party who has the right to make the decision will want to be able to make it in its "sole discretion" or its "sole judgment." If the provision is written this way, whatever it decides may not be disputed by the other party. The party who isn't making the decision will push for a "reasonable discretion" or "reasonable judgment" standard, which would give it the right to object to the decision of the other party on the basis that the decision was not reasonable.

§ 5:2.3 *Consent Not to be Unreasonably Withheld*

This is a specific use of the reasonableness standard in a contract provision that requires the consent of one of the parties to some specified action. Look at the underlined language in this sentence:

> Party A may not consummate any Prohibited Transaction <u>without the consent of Party B</u>.

As a technical matter, the underlined language is unnecessary, because Party A always has the ability to ask Party B to consent to something that is prohibited by their contract. Party A, however, may anticipate taking actions for which consent will be required, and may want to soften Party B's absolute right to deny its consent. The way it does this is to use the "consent not unreasonably withheld" concept:

> Party A may not consummate any Prohibited Transaction <u>without the consent of Party B, which shall not be unreasonably withheld</u>.

Under this provision, Party B may not withhold its consent to a proposed transaction without a reasonable basis for doing so. If there is a concern that the party whose consent is needed may drag its heels in responding to request for a consent, the phrase can be written as:

without the consent of Party B, which shall not be unreasonably withheld <u>or delayed</u>

§ 5:2.4   *Best/Diligent/Reasonable Efforts*

Sometimes a party may be uncertain whether it will be able to satisfactorily perform one of its contractual obligations. This issue usually arises in the context of a requirement that some third party's action or cooperation be obtained. For example:

> The mortgagor shall, no later than November 15, 2002, cause
> each of its insurance policies to be modified to contain the en-
> dorsements described on Exhibit 5.

The mortgagor anticipates stiff resistance from its insurers to the required language. It knows that it doesn't have the leverage to force the
insurance companies to make the changes. Under the language written above, the mortgagor would be in breach if any one of its insurers
refuses to provide the requested endorsement. It argues, therefore,
that it should not be in breach of the covenant as long as it has diligently pursued getting the changes made:

> Mortgagor <u>will use its diligent efforts to cause</u> each of its insur-
> ance policies to be modified to contain the endorsements de-
> scribed on Exhibit 5.

The mortgagor's obligation under this provision is not to obtain the
policy changes, but to exert diligent efforts to do so. From the mortgagee's standpoint, this is obviously a much weaker and more subjective requirement. If, as a business matter, the mortgagee feels it must
have these endorsements, it will either insist on the original absolute
requirement or make the policy endorsements a condition to closing.
   This concept can employ a number of different standards: good
faith efforts, reasonable efforts, diligent efforts, and best efforts.
"Good faith effort" is probably the weakest of these standards, requiring only a genuine attempt to meet the stated goal. A "reasonable effort" is the level of effort a reasonable person would expend in the circumstances. Arguably, "diligent efforts" requires a greater degree of
effort than "reasonable efforts." "Best efforts" is the most stringent
standard. Many practitioners take the view that an obligation to use
best efforts includes the obligation to use all possible financial resources to achieve the desired goal. If the mortgagor in the above ex-

ample were required to use best efforts to obtain the policy endorsements, it would be required to pay any fee or premium demanded by the insurer. For this reason, a "best efforts" standard is often resisted. Sometimes, the following approach is utilized in order to impose the more stringent "best efforts" standard without creating open-ended financial risk:

> Mortgagor will use its best efforts (<u>without being required to pay any additional fees, premiums or other amounts</u>) to cause each of its insurance policies to be modified to contain the endorsements described on Exhibit 5.

§ 5:2.5   *To the Best of Its Knowledge*

Compare the following two variations of the same representation in an acquisition agreement:

> Seller is not in violation of any Environmental Law.

> <u>To the best of its knowledge,</u> Seller is not in violation of any Environmental Law.

The first representation is a statement as to a *fact*. The second representation is a statement about the representing party's *awareness of a fact*.

What if, after the closing, the buyer discovers a pre-existing violation of environmental law relating to the purchased property that results in significant economic harm to it? Its posture as against the seller would be markedly different under these two provisions. Under the first provision, the existence of the pre-existing violation makes the representation untrue, providing the buyer with a claim against the seller for breach. Under the second provision, however, the buyer's claim for breach of representation will only succeed if the buyer can demonstrate that the seller *knew* of the violation at the time that the representation was made. Obviously, it is much more difficult to prove a party's state of awareness of a fact than it is to prove the fact itself.

The seller may make the following argument to support its need for this knowledge qualification: "Our business consists of assets that were obtained in numerous acquisitions over the last few years, so we may not know about all previous events that may continue to give rise to potential environmental violations. How can you ask us to make a rep that we don't know is true?"

This argument usually falls on deaf ears. One of the primary purposes of representations is to allocate risk between the parties. In the above example, the buyer will respond: "We don't care whether you know the statement is true or not. What we want is recourse against you if the statement turns out to be wrong. Your failure to do adequate environmental due diligence when you bought properties in the past should be your problem, not ours."

§ 5:2.6 *Substantially in the Form Of*

Sometimes a contract will refer to another agreement that is expected or required to be similar to another agreement or to an exhibit to the contract. For example, a condition to closing may require a party to execute and deliver another agreement, the form of which has been negotiated and which is attached as an exhibit. Or, there may be a requirement that if Party A enters into an agreement with a third party in the future, it must enter into the same agreement with Party B. In cases like this, the phrase "substantially in the form of" is an important one. Without it, performance of the condition or covenant may be thwarted due to immaterial inconsistencies between the two documents. Such inconsistencies may be necessary, for example, to properly identify the parties, to correct typographical errors, and the like. Read the following condition precedent from a lease both with and without the underlined word to understand its substantive effect:

> As a condition to the effectiveness of this Lease, the Lessee shall execute and deliver a solvency certificate <u>substantially</u> in the form of the solvency certificate delivered by the Lessee to XYZ Realty Co. on September 20, 1996.

§ 5:2.7 *To the Extent Permitted by Law*

A contract should never require a party to violate the law. There are two approaches to address the possibility that a party will have to violate the law by complying with a contract provision. First, the law at issue can be researched and the provision modified to ensure that compliance would not result in a violation. A broader approach is to modify the provision with the phrase "to the extent permitted by law." This also has the advantage of addressing potential conflicts with new or changed laws. Here is an example:

Company shall, <u>to the extent permitted by law</u>, close facilities and reduce employee headcount by January 31, 2003 so as to reduce its aggregate expenses on an annualized pro forma basis by at least $2 million.

§ 5:2.8 *Promptly*

This term is employed to create a modest degree of flexibility in the time required for performance of a contractual requirement. It is used where some time may be needed for performance and where a precise number of days for performance may be difficult to specify. The "promptly" standard may also be imposed with an outside date for the specified performance. Examples:

The Borrower shall notify the Lender <u>promptly</u> of any notice of default received by it under the Mezzanine Notes.

Following the Lender's request, the Company shall <u>promptly, but in any event within 30 days</u>, provide the Lender with appraisals of the Specified Real Estate.

Often, the concept of promptness is a negotiated compromise from first drafts which requires some action to be taken *immediately*. This term should be used sparingly; very few things can be made to happen immediately.

§ 5:2.9 *In Form and Substance Satisfactory*

This phrase is used to give a party the right to be satisfied with a particular document. Compare the following two provisions:

The Contractor shall deliver a plumbing subcontract to the Owner.

The Contractor shall deliver a plumbing subcontract <u>in form and substance satisfactory</u> to the Owner.

Under the first provision the contractor has satisfied its obligation by delivering a plumbing subcontract to the owner, regardless of whether it is correctly drafted, or whether it is otherwise satisfactory to the owner. In the second provision, the contractor's obligation is not satisfied unless the owner is satisfied with both the form and substance of the document. If the contractor believes that this gives too much discretion to the owner, it would insist on the insertion of a reasonableness standard:

> The Contractor shall deliver a plumbing subcontract in form and substance <u>reasonably</u> satisfactory to the Owner.

Sometimes a distinction should be drawn between the *form* and the *substance* of a document. For example, a bank agreeing to issue a letter of credit on behalf of its customer may not have an interest in the terms or substance of the letter of credit but may have an interest in its form or appearance. In such a case, the relevant provision would read as follows:

> The Bank will, at the request of the Borrower, issue one or more letters of credit in a <u>form satisfactory</u> to the Bank.

§ 5:2.10   *Substantially All/Substantial Portion*

Two parties are negotiating a covenant restricting asset sales. The parties have agreed that only extremely significant asset sales will be restricted, but are not willing to agree to a precise dollar limitation. Therefore, they agree on this language:

> The Company may not sell or otherwise dispose of <u>all or substantially all of</u> its assets.

A slightly looser version would be as follows:

> The Company may not sell or otherwise dispose of <u>all or any substantial portion of</u> its assets.

A draftsperson employing these phrases should be aware of case law that suggests that these standards are not as loose as they may appear.[1]

---

1. *See, e.g.,* Gimbel v. Signal Cos., Inc., 316 A.2d 599, 606 (Del. Ch. 1974); Sharon Steel Corp. v. Chase Manhattan Bank, 691 F.2d 1039 (2d Cir. 1982), *cert. denied,* 460 U.S. 1012 (1983); Katz v. Bregman, 431 A.2d 1274 (Del. Ch. 1981).

§ 5:2.11   *In the Ordinary Course of Business*

This phrase is used in restrictive provisions to permit activities that are customary and typical for the restricted party. Take, for example, the following provision in a note purchase agreement involving a construction company:

> The Issuer may not incur any contingent liability in respect of surety bonds, except for those obtained in the ordinary course of business.

The issuer is routinely required to provide surety bonds in connection with its construction contracts. This language permits it to continue that practice. But the provision would not permit the issuance of a surety bond to secure the payment of a financial obligation (as opposed to the performance of its obligations under a construction contract), because at the time that the agreement was signed the issuer did not regularly use surety bonds for such purposes. The ordinary course of business standard is used to prevent flexibility granted to one of the parties from being used by it in an unusual or unanticipated way.

§ 5:2.12   *Consistent with Past Practice*

Unlike "in the ordinary course of business," which focuses on *whether* a specified action is customary for a party, this phrase puts more emphasis on *how* an action is taken. Here is an example:

> Guarantor shall not make capital contributions to its foreign subsidiaries, <u>except in a manner consistent with past practice</u>.

If the guarantor over the last five years had made capital contributions to its foreign subsidiaries only to the extent necessary to satisfy local minimum capitalization rules, this provision would prevent the guarantor from making capital contributions to its foreign subsidiaries to acquire machinery and equipment. If the applicable standard were "in the ordinary course of business" rather than "in accordance with past practice," the guarantor would have an easier time arguing that it was customary for it to make capital investments to its foreign subsidiaries, and therefore that it could do so even for new purposes.

§ 5:2.13   Not More Restrictive

This phrase and its variations are used in provisions that impose limitations on a party's ability to agree to restrictions under other agreements. This may come up, for example, where the contract permits one party to incur indebtedness in order to refinance existing obligations. Rather than try to outline the specific terms that an acceptable refinancing would include, the parties agree on the following language:

> Debtor may incur Indebtedness the proceeds of which are used to repay the Senior Notes, so long as the agreement governing such Indebtedness is not more restrictive to Debtor than the Senior Notes.

The difficulty with this approach is that it is not clear how it is applied. If one out of 15 covenants in the refinancing agreement is tighter while the other 14 are looser, has the requirement been satisfied? This concern can be addressed, to a certain extent, by modifying the phrase to read "not more restrictive, taken as a whole."

§ 5:2.14   Would vs. Could: Levels of Probability

Party A is reviewing a first draft of an agreement prepared by Party B that requires Party A to give "notice of the commencement of any action, suit or proceeding that could result in a material adverse effect on Party A." The following discussion ensues:

Party A: As you know, the nature and scope of our business results in us being the subject of several hundred lawsuits every year, 95% of which are either unmeritorious or settled for small amounts. However, virtually every one of these lawsuits asserts a multimillion dollar claim for damages. Any of these, if successful, could be material to us. We can't conclude at the outset of these cases that the plaintiff has absolutely *no* chance of success. Therefore, we would have to disclose all of these to you because, technically, they all "could" result in a material adverse effect.

Party B: Don't make such a fuss. We understand your concern. What would you like to do?

Party A: Why don't we say "would have a material adverse effect" instead?

Party B: That brings it much too far in the other direction. Under that standard, you would only have to disclose to us if there was a *certainty* of a material adverse effect. Just as a "could" standard casts too wide a net, a "would" standard doesn't cast a wide enough net.

Party A: How about "would reasonably be expected to"?

Party B: Done.

This negotiation illustrates the difference between the use of could/would/reasonably be expected to. (A word of warning: the fewer discussions among the lawyers on this particular topic a client hears, the better. Notwithstanding the important substantive result that is at stake, the typical client, perhaps not understanding the issue, may view it as a ridiculous (and costly) legal cul-de-sac.)

§ 5:3 Trumping Provisions

Contracts often contain inconsistent provisions. A general restriction in one provision may conflict with another that requires some specific action. Broad principles that generally apply to the entire contract may need to be overridden in specific circumstances. The careful draftsperson will always note these possible inconsistencies and employ trumping provisions to indicate which provision overrides the other. Otherwise, confusion and potential disputes are the result.

§ 5:3.1 *Provisos*

A proviso is a clause that begins with either "provided" or "provided, however." Often these words are underlined, which is done merely to make the proviso stand out from the rest of the sentence. The purpose of a proviso is to override the concept that immediately precedes it:

> Seller shall deliver sales reports to Buyer on the last business day of each week, <u>provided, however,</u> that such delivery may be made on the first day of the following week if the number of business days in the week covered by the report is less than five.

Here, the proviso creates an exception to the general rule that the report be delivered on the last business day of the week.

Provisos are sometimes incorrectly used as a substitute for the terms "to the extent that" or "if":

> Seller may enter into leases with respect to the Subject Assets, <u>provided, however,</u> that Seller's interest under such leases is transferable to Buyer.[2]

The proviso in the above sentence does not override the concept that the Seller can enter into leases; it creates a condition to the Seller's right to do so. A better rendition of this sentence would be:

> Seller may enter into leases with respect to the Subject Assets <u>if</u> Seller's interest therein is transferable to Buyer.

Here is another example of the incorrect use of a proviso, with a modification correcting the error:

> Employee shall be entitled to reimbursement for Covered Expenses <u>provided</u> that it produces reasonably satisfactory documentation thereof.

> Employee shall be entitled to Covered Expenses <u>to the extent that</u> it produces reasonably satisfactory documentation thereof.

§ 5:3.2   *Notwithstanding Anything to the Contrary*

The several variations of this phrase each acts as a signal that what follows will be inconsistent with (and trumps) other contractual provisions. One such variation, the phrase "notwithstanding the foregoing" has the same effect as the proviso, in that it trumps the immediately preceding concept. For example, the sentence:

> Borrower shall pay accrued interest on the last business day of each month, <u>provided, however</u>, that on up to three occasions during the term of this agreement, Borrower may, by prior notice to Lender, delay such payments by a period not to exceed in each case 5 business days.

---

2. The use of the word "provided" as a synonym for "if" or "on the condition that" is acceptable, but it should not be underlined. "<u>Provided, however</u>" may not be used this way.

could be expressed equally well as follows:

> Borrower shall pay accrued interest on the last business day of each month. <u>Notwithstanding the foregoing</u>, on up to three occasions during the term of this agreement, Borrower may, by prior notice to Lender, delay such payments by a period not to exceed in each case 5 business days.

Unlike the proviso, this phrase can be used to trump sentences other than the one in which it is contained. Consider a stock purchase agreement containing covenants that restricts the target's ability to engage in a variety of transactions. The parties agree that the target may engage in a specific joint venture transaction, different aspects of which would be blocked by several of the restrictive covenants. This potential conflict could be addressed by either (a) adding an exception for the joint venture to each of the relevant covenants, or (b) more simply, by adding the following at the end of the covenant section:

> <u>Notwithstanding anything in this Section 5 (Covenants) to the contrary</u>, Target shall be permitted to enter into the Portuguese Joint Venture.

This tool can also be used to trump inconsistent provisions appearing throughout an entire agreement. In the above example, the parties may be concerned that there may be other provisions in the contract that would restrict the target's ability to enter into the joint venture. They could therefore use the above language, modified to refer to "anything <u>in this agreement</u> to the contrary. . . ." Since this refers to the entire agreement, the placement of this language is irrelevant: it could be placed at the beginning, the middle or the end of the agreement.

§ 5:3.3 *Except as Otherwise Provided*

This phrase is used to indicate that the provision in which it is included is trumped by other provisions in the agreement. Often, a provision that includes this phrase directs the reader to the specific provision that overrides it:

> Except as provided in Section 4, the Shareholder may not transfer any of the Preferred Shares.

Another use of this phrase is to indicate that a general statement is subject to being overridden by other, more specific provisions, without specifically referring to such other provisions. An example would be an agreement which generally provides that all payments thereunder are to be made in dollars, but with several specific provisions requiring payment in euros. The general provision would read as follows:

> Except as otherwise provided herein, all payments made hereunder shall be made in U.S. dollars.

Thus, it is not necessary in this agreement to specify in each payment provision that payment is to be made in dollars. That is taken care of by the above general language; only the payment provisions requiring euros need to be specific.

§ 5:3.4 *Without Limiting the Generality of the Foregoing*

One rule of contract interpretation is that the specific overrides the general. A concern may arise that where the statement of a general principle is followed by a specific application of that principle, the general principle may be ignored. This may arise in the context of a provision like this one:

> Debtor shall maintain insurance at levels and with deductibles consistent with customary business practices in Debtor's industry. Debtor's insurance for casualty losses in respect of its Deerfield plant shall at no time be less than $5 million.

This provision raises the concern that, at least as it relates to casualty insurance, the second sentence trumps the first. The provision could be rewritten as follows:

> Debtor shall maintain insurance at levels and with deductibles consistent with customary business practices in Debtor's industry. Without limiting the generality of the foregoing, Debtor's insurance for casualty losses in respect of its Deerfield plant shall at no time be less than $5 million.

This change prevents Debtor from arguing that it has complied with the covenant by insuring the Deerfield plant for $5 million, even if industry standards would suggest a larger amount of coverage is required.

§ 5:3.5 Inconsistency Among Agreements

Sometimes a concern will arise that one or more agreements among the same parties may be inconsistent with each other. If it is clear where the conflict lies, one of the methods referred to above can be used. For example:

> Notwithstanding anything to the contrary in Section 5.4 of the Stockholders Agreement, the Company may not transfer any of its Shares to an Affiliate without prior written notice to XYZ Inc.

In other cases, the concern about conflicts may be more general. This calls for a more general trumping provision:

> To the extent there is an inconsistency between a provision in the Credit Agreement and a provision in any of the Transaction Agreements, the provision in the Credit Agreement controls.

These only work to the extent the parties to the agreement that is being overridden are parties to the agreement containing override language. A provision in a contract between Party A and Party B that purports to override a provision in a contract among Parties A, B and C is not enforceable against Party C.

§ 5:4 Accounting Terms/Terms of Measurement

It is easy for a lawyer faced with a numerical or accounting issue in a contract to disclaim: "I'm a lawyer, not a numbers person—have the accountants look at this." There are situations where this is appropriate. To the extent the resolution of an issue or the proper drafting of a contract requires complex calculation or an understanding of the effect of GAAP or other accounting rules, the lawyer should defer to accounting or financial experts.

On the other hand, a lawyer's claim of a complete lack of numbers skills is often a cop-out. Most contracts are, to one extent or another, about money. Complex commercial contracts involve complicated treatment of monetary and other numerical issues: how payments are computed, how financial condition is tested, how permitted economic activities are measured. The skillful business lawyer must master the basics of accounting and the ability to express quantitative ideas in words.[3]

§ 5:4.1   *Formulas*

Contracts often contain mathematical formulas expressed in words. The key issue here is clarity; the provision must clearly specify the mathematical functions and their order. Let's say the parties to a contract want to provide that one party will make a payment to the other equal to half of certain asset sale proceeds that aren't required to be paid to the recipient's banks. The provision could be written as follows:

> Party A shall pay to Party B 50% of (a) an amount equal to the excess of (i) the proceeds of the Allentown Sale received by Party A over (ii) the amount of such net proceeds that Party A is required to pay its lenders under Section 5.02 of the Credit Agreement.

This could be rewritten in algebraic style as follows:

> payment = .50 x (proceeds of Allentown Sale - proceeds used to pay the lenders)

Why is the phrase "an amount equal to" included? The purpose of the sentence is to create a device to compute the amount of a required

---

3. Several years ago, the author got a call at home at 9 P.M. on a Sunday night from the lawyer on the other side of a transaction and that lawyer's client. They had spent the entire day trying to draft anti-dilution provisions that were unusually complicated, as a result of the number of parties and potential future dilutive events that were contemplated by the contract. They had concluded that it was literally impossible to effectively translate these concepts into words and suggested attaching to the contract as an exhibit (and incorporating by reference) a copy of the spreadsheet software that actually did address all of the scenarios. Concerns over the enforceability of this approach (including statute of frauds considerations) led the parties to continue to pursue the translation of the concepts into words. They were ultimately successful.

payment, not to identify the actual money that will be paid. Money is fungible; Party B wants to be paid the required amount but doesn't care whether it receives the money actually paid in connection with the asset sale.

Here is an example of a formula that needs to clarified by the use of appropriate numbering:

> The amount of capital expenditures that Borrower may make in any fiscal year is an amount equal to 10% of Borrower's net income for such fiscal year plus the amount of all capital contributions received by Borrower in such fiscal year.

Does the 10% apply to only the Borrower's annual net income or also to the capital contributions that it has received? Without numbering, the provision is fatally unclear. Here is a revised version that makes it clear that only the net income is subject to the 10% multiplier:

> The amount of annual capital expenditures that Borrower may make in any fiscal year is an amount equal to (i) 10% of Borrower's net income for such fiscal year plus (ii) the amount of all capital contributions received by Borrower in such fiscal year.

A common element of formulas is the quantification of some amount by reference to the passage of a certain amount of time. Take, for example, a provision that provides for the payment of liquidated damages based on how long a seller delayed the closing of an acquisition:

> Seller will pay to Buyer as liquidated damages an amount equal to (a) Target's EBITDA for the fiscal year ending December 31, 1999, multiplied by (b) a fraction, the numerator of which is the number of days in the period beginning on the Expected Closing Date and ending on the actual closing date, and the denominator of which is 365.

This provision has the effect of prorating an annual number for a period of time that is less than a year. This formula could be expressed algebraically as follows:

$$\text{1999 EBITDA} \times \frac{\text{number of days in measured period}}{365}$$

§ 5:4.2   Floors and Ceilings

There are many circumstances in which a contract must set a floor or a ceiling—that is, a minimum or maximum amount. This device is used to create a maximum amount:

> On the tenth Business Day of each month Licensee will pay to Licensor an amount equal to the <u>lesser</u> of (a) $100,000 and (b) 30% of the gross sales of the Licensed Products during the prior month.

Under this provision, a maximum amount of $100,000 is required to be paid; if 30% of gross sales exceeds $100,000, only $100,000 is due. If the above provision is modified to change the word "lesser" to "greater," the effect of the provision is to set the amount of the *minimum* payment at $100,000.

This same approach can be used with respect to dates, where it is necessary to specify the latest or earliest date that a particular action may be taken:

> Seller shall complete the Post Closing Audit by the <u>earlier of</u> (i) March 31, 2000 and (ii) 30 days after the accountants have delivered the Preliminary Inventory Calculation.

§ 5:4.3   On a Consolidated Basis

"Consolidated" is an accounting term indicating that financial measurements are made to include both a parent company and its subsidiaries. If something is measured on a consolidated basis it is measured for an entity and its subsidiaries, taken as a whole, as if they were a single entity. One effect of this type of measurement is that intercompany transactions (such as intercompany receivables and payables) are eliminated. The financial statements of most companies with subsidiaries are prepared on a consolidated basis.

§ 5:4.4   On a Consolidating Basis

This phrase is used to describe financial statements that are broken out separately for an entity and each of its subsidiaries.

§ 5:4.5 *Company and Its Subsidiaries, Taken as a Whole*

This is a similar concept to "on a consolidated basis," but is used in non-accounting contexts. For example:

> Since December 31, 2000 there shall have occurred no material adverse effect on the financial condition of the Parent and its subsidiaries, taken as a whole.

Without the inclusion of "taken as a whole" there would be an implication that the material adverse standard should be applied individually to the parent and each subsidiary, looked at separately. The effect of this could be unfair. Consider an example involving a parent that has one hundred subsidiaries of equivalent value. A 20% reduction in one subsidiary's annual net income would be material to the subsidiary, but immaterial to the consolidated group.

§ 5:4.6 *Frozen GAAP*

Covenants frequently require financial computations to be made in accordance with generally accepted accounting principles (GAAP). An issue that must be addressed in this context is how to treat changes to GAAP that occur after the contract is entered into. It is often agreed that such changes to GAAP will be ignored for purposes of making the computations. This issue is typically addressed with language along the following lines:

> Changes in GAAP after the Effective Date shall not be given effect for purposes of the calculations made under Section 4.4.

The benefit of this approach is that the parties' intent as to the operation of the covenant won't be undermined by a change in accounting methods. The disadvantage is that because a change in GAAP *will* have to be followed in the preparation of a party's financial statements, there will be a discrepancy between the financial statements and the covenant calculations. In this case, the party providing financial statements will usually be required to prepare and deliver a reconciliation, showing how the financial computations would have appeared had the change in GAAP not occurred.

§ 5:4.7   ***Outstanding***

The use of the term "outstanding" can have a very important effect when used to describe the principal amount of indebtedness or other obligations. Compare the following two provisions:

> The Company may issue notes as consideration for acquisitions in an aggregate principal amount not to exceed $5,000,000.

> The Company may issue notes as consideration for acquisitions in an aggregate principal amount not to exceed $5,000,000 <u>outstanding at any time</u>.

Under the first example, if the Company issues a $5,000,000 note in connection with an acquisition, and then repays it, it will be unable to issue any further notes in connection with acquisitions. The introduction of the "outstanding" concept, on the other hand, results in the provision not restricting the amount of notes that have been issued over time, but instead the amount of notes that are outstanding at any particular point in time. If the Company issues a $5,000,000 note, and repays $1,000,000, it will have $4,000,000 of notes outstanding. Under this provision, it will then be permitted to issue another $1,000,000 of notes.

§ 5:4.8   ***Per Annum***

This phrase is used in connection with rates of interest or other amounts that are measured on an annual basis. So, for example, an interest rate of "5% per annum" in respect of a principal amount of $100,000 would mean that for an entire year the accrued interest would be $5,000, for six months, $2,500, and so forth.

§ 5:4.9   ***Absent Manifest Error***

This phrase is used where one party is permitted to make a calculation or determination that is binding on the other party unless the calculation or determination is incorrect:

> Investor's calculations of accrued and unpaid commitment fees shall be binding on Issuer, <u>absent manifest error</u>.

It is not entirely clear what the word "manifest" means in this phrase, but it suggests that the error must be demonstrably false. The use of this language places the burden of proving that a calculation or determination is false on the party not making the calculation or determination.

§ 5:4.10 In Arrears/In Advance

Payments that are made in respect of a specified period of time (for example, the payment of interest or the payment of a quarterly management fee) are paid either in arrears or in advance. Payment at the end of a specified period of amounts that have accrued during such period is payment in arrears. Payment in advance is made at the beginning of a period in respect of amounts that will accrue during such period.

Regardless of which approach is used, the draftsperson must address what happens if the contract is terminated between payment dates. In the case of a provision requiring quarterly interest payments in arrears, a termination of the contract on June 20 will leave the lender shortchanged for 20 days' of interest. Conversely, the party that receives quarterly management fees in advance will receive a windfall as to the fees already collected for the last 10 days of June. The drafting required to address each of these concerns is straightforward. The provision requiring payment quarterly in arrears should provide that accrued and unpaid interest should be paid on the date the agreement is terminated. Conversely, the agreement providing for the payment of management fees quarterly in advance may provide that if the agreement is terminated in the middle of a quarter, a proportionate amount of the last payment made must be rebated.

§ 5:5 Terms of Inclusion and Exclusion

Contract provisions often take the form of a general prohibition, subject to one or more exceptions, which in turn may have exceptions of their own. This tracks the way these issues are negotiated: one party suggests an absolute rule to be applicable to the other party, who in turn suggests numerous broad carveouts to the absolute rule, which may be accepted (subject to limitations) by the first party. Let's look at a hypothetical negotiation of a provision in a shareholders agreement relating to the ability of the minority shareholder ("Little Corp.") to transfer its shares. Counsel to the majority shareholder ("Big Corp.") has prepared a first draft of the shareholders agreement that reads: "Little Corp. may not transfer any Shares during the term of this agreement." The following discussion ensues:

Little Corp.: This provision is way too tight. We may need to move the shares around internally for tax or other planning purposes. The provision should freely permit transfers to affiliates.

Big Corp.: All right, you can transfer to affiliates, but not Medium Corp. The fact that you own 15% of Medium Corp. means it falls under the definition of "Affiliate," but since they compete with some of our business lines, we don't want to have them in this deal.

Little Corp.: We hear you, but if you're in default under the agreement we should be able to transfer our shares to anyone, including Medium Corp. And by the way, we think the definition of "Affiliate" is unclear as to whether Micro Co. would be included. That needs to be clarified in this provision.

Big Corp.: Agreed.

The resulting provision is as follows:

> Little Corp. may not transfer any Shares during the term of this Agreement, except for (i) transfers at any time to its Affiliates (including, without limitation, Micro Co.) other than Medium Corp., and (ii) so long as an Event of Default attributable to Big Corp. shall have occurred and be continuing, transfers to any Person (including, for the avoidance of doubt, Medium Corp.).

What follows below is a discussion of some of the terms of inclusion and exclusion that are necessary tools of the draftsperson's trade.

§ 5:5.1   *Make Exceptions Consistent*

Inconsistencies often arise as a provision is drafted and redrafted in the negotiation process. A common example of this is a representation or covenant subject to a list of exceptions. Particularly if the exceptions are added at different stages in the drafting process, they may not be expressed in a consistent or grammatical fashion. Here is an example:

> The Borrower may not incur or permit to exist liens on any of its assets, except:
>
> (i) mechanics' liens arising in the ordinary course of business;
>
> (ii) the Borrower may grant liens on equipment to secure indebtedness incurred to finance the purchase price of such equipment; and
>
> (iii) liens described in Schedule 1.04 shall be permitted.

The approach represented by each of these three exceptions is fine; the problem is that each of the approaches is inconsistent with the others and as a consequence the provision is more difficult to follow. The draftsperson should have either (a) made each exception conform with clause (i) (which has no verb phrase), (b) made each exception conform with clause (ii), by using "the Borrower may," or (c) made each exception conform to clause (iii), by using "shall be permitted." In the above example, the approach represented by clause (i) is preferable, because it eliminates unnecessary words.

§ 5:5.2   *Specific Exclusions to Avoid Doubt*

If it is unclear whether a particular matter is covered by a provision, it may be necessary to add clarifying language. For example, a draft employment agreement may contain the following provision:

> Employee will not engage in any outside activities that significantly reduce her attention to her responsibilities as Chief Executive Officer.

The employee is planning to write a book. She doesn't believe that this project will significantly reduce her attention to her job. Her lawyer, however, is concerned that a dispute may arise over this issue. To address this concern, the employer's lawyer proposes adding the following proviso:

> provided, however, that Employee may write a book about her experiences as a rising star in the plastics business

The employee is unhappy with this language, however. It suggests that her book *will* create a significant distraction. Her lawyer then proposes the following language, which both permits her book-writing project and acknowledges that it doesn't interfere with her job responsibilities:

> it being understood that Employee's writing a book about her experiences as a rising star in the plastics business will not constitute an outside activity significantly reducing her attention to her responsibilities as Chief Executive Officer

§ 5:5.3   Unnecessary Exceptions

Unnecessary exceptions may create ambiguities and confusion. If it is clear that the scope of a provision doesn't cover a particular event or circumstance, it is counterproductive to include an exception. Including the exception in this circumstance merely permits an argument to be made that the scope of the provision is really intended to be broader than it appears; otherwise why would the exception be necessary?

Let's look at an example. Here is a provision found in an equipment lease:

> Lessee will cause the Equipment to be kept in good operating condition, <u>except that Lessee shall not be required to comply with any safety regulations to the extent such noncompliance is being diligently contested by Lessee.</u>

The underlined language is unnecessary. Compliance with safety regulations is not required by the provision, but inclusion of this language creates the implication that compliance *is* required. It allows the lessor to argue that the covenant generally requires compliance with regulatory requirements; otherwise, why did the parties consider this exception necessary? This example illustrates the kind of mischief that can result from the use of unnecessary exceptions.

This issue also arises frequently in connection with the preparation of disclosure schedules. Consider a representation in a loan agreement that there are no environmental issues that could reasonably be expected to have a material adverse effect on the borrower, except those that are set forth on a schedule. It is a normal reaction for the borrower to include as much information as possible on that schedule, in order to minimize the risk of making a misrepresentation by omission. However, this representation requires only the scheduling of items that could reasonably be expected to have a material adverse effect. There are many reasons why the borrower would not want to characterize immaterial matters as material. For example, such a disclosure could be harmful to it in litigation relating to the matters disclosed. Therefore, the disclosure should be limited to material items.

§ 5:5.4 *Including Without Limitation*

A frequently-used device to clarify the scope of a provision is the use of the phrase "including without limitation" followed by one or more specific examples of items that the draftsperson intended to be included. For example, look at the following provision from an asset purchase agreement:

> Seller will obtain all consents or approvals necessary in connection with the transfer of the Purchased Assets to Buyer, <u>including without limitation</u> (a) the consent of XYZ Landlord Co. to the assignment of the Paramus Lease from Seller to Buyer and (b) the consent of the Food and Drug Administration to the transfer of the Pharmaceutical Licenses from Seller to Buyer.

The addition of the underlined language doesn't change the meaning of the provision, because it merely lists items that are already included by virtue of the broad introductory language. So why use this technique? For one thing, in the example the buyer may want the underlined language included to act as a reminder to the seller of exactly what consents are required. (Of course, if there are others that are not enumerated, the seller is responsible for those too.) Furthermore, this technique can be used to clarify uncertainty as to what a particular provision is supposed to cover. In the above example, there may have been discussions between buyer and seller as to which of them had the legal responsibility to obtain the consents. Specifically referring to them here resolves the question of allocation of responsibility.

What is the significance of the words "without limitation"? Arguably, the omission of these words creates the implication that the list that follows is a *complete* list of what the parties intend to cover. In the above example, this would mean that the two consents referred to were the only consents required. This is not a very convincing position, but to avoid any ambiguity, if the intent is to create a non-exhaustive list, use the words "without limitation." Some agreements provide explicitly that the use of the word "including" is to be interpreted as "including without limitation."

Never follow "including" or "including without limitation" with something that is *not* covered by the provision. An example of this would be the following:

> Company may not make any investments in its subsidiaries, <u>including the payment of cash dividends by a subsidiary to Company</u>.

The payment of dividends by a subsidiary to a parent is *not* an investment by the parent in the subsidiary. Without the underlined language, the payment of dividends would not be restricted. What is the result of the inclusion of this language? One argument would be that the payment of cash dividends *is* prohibited. If this view is correct, what about the payment of stock dividends? It could be argued either way. On the other hand, a position could reasonably be taken that the payment of dividends is not covered by the prohibition on investments, that the reference to it in the underlined language was done in error and should have no effect. What is the correct answer? There may not be one. Avoid making this mistake.

§ 5:5.5 *Disorganized Exceptions*

Sometimes a sentence will become subject to a number of exceptions and qualifications that do not work well together and are difficult to follow. Here is an example:

> Except for the issuance of additional options pursuant to the 1999 Option Plan, the Seller shall not increase the compensation of any employee (other than hourly workers) from the levels in effect on the Effective Date, <u>provided, however,</u> that increases in cash compensation may be made if the aggregate amounts paid in respect of such increases do not exceed $1 million.

This sentence will read much better if the basic point of the covenant—that the Seller may not increase compensation—is put at the beginning and all the exceptions are placed together in a series at the end:

The Seller shall not increase the compensation of any employee from the levels in effect on the Effective Date, except that (i) the Seller may issue additional options pursuant to the 1999 Option Plan, (ii) the Seller may increase the compensation of hourly workers, and (iii) the Seller may increase cash compensation in an aggregate amount not exceeding $1 million.

§ 5:6 Miscellaneous Drafting Issues

§ 5:6.1 *Incorporation by Reference*

There are occasions when it is necessary for one contract to incorporate all or some of the provisions of another contract. There are two ways to achieve this: repeating the other provisions verbatim, or "incorporating by reference." Here is an example of incorporation by reference:

The Company agrees to perform and be bound by all covenants in the Pittsburgh Lease Agreement that relate to it, and all such covenants are incorporated by reference as if set forth at length herein.

This language has the same legal effect as copying all of the covenants that appear in the lease that relate to the company, but is obviously easier from a drafting standpoint. This shortcut may make life more difficult in the future for someone reviewing this agreement, however, particularly if a copy of the Pittsburgh Lease Agreement is not readily available.

What if the draftsperson would like to incorporate provisions by reference that are close but not an exact fit for the purpose for which they are to be incorporated? For example, what if the goal is to have the company perform covenants that appear in another agreement that relate to a third party, as if they covered the company? In such a case, the provision would be written as follows:

The Company agrees to perform and be bound by all covenants in the Buffalo Lease Agreement as if such provisions applied to it, and all such covenants are incorporated by reference <u>mutatis mutandis</u>, as if set forth at length herein.

The term "mutatis mutandis" means that the provision that is being incorporated by reference is deemed to be modified as necessary to fit the purpose described. So, for example, if one of the covenants that is being incorporated by reference is a covenant to maintain corporate existence, such covenant would be construed to refer to partnership existence if the company is a partnership instead of a corporation. (Warning: the use of "mutatis mutandis" is likely to elicit sarcastic comments from clients and other non-lawyers.)

§ 5:6.2   *On an Arm's-length Basis*

This phrase is used to describe a transaction with terms that are equivalent to fully negotiated market terms. It is usually used in the context of transactions that might not be fully and fairly negotiated. For example, here is a provision restricting transactions with affiliates found in many types of agreements:

> The Company will not enter into any transaction with an affiliate, except on an arm's length basis.

This provision would prevent the company from entering into a sweetheart deal with an affiliate.

§ 5:6.3   *As Determined by the Board of Directors*

Sometimes Party A will be willing to permit Party B to take an action only if the action is specifically approved by Party B's board of directors, or if Party B's board of directors makes some specific determination regarding the action. The basis for this approach is that a board of directors is less likely than an individual officer to stretch the limits of a particular contract restriction. For example, look at the following provision:

> The Company may not amend the provisions of any of its securities unless the Company's board of directors shall have determined that any such amendment does not adversely affect the interests of the Noteholders.

This provides the noteholders with an extra level of protection against an adverse amendment being agreed to, as a result of the entire board of directors looking at the issue and making the relevant determination.

§ 5:6.4 Upon the Occurrence and During the Continuance of an Event of Default

Many agreements provide that remedies may be exercised if there is an event of default. One must be careful in the way that this is expressed. Take, for instance the following provision:

> Lender may accelerate the Loans if an Event of Default has occurred.

Let's say that the borrower has failed to deliver its annual financial statements to the lender by the date it is required to do so under the contract. As a result, an event of default has occurred. Five days later, the borrower delivers the financial statements. Can the lender accelerate the loans two weeks after that? Under the language above, arguably it can. This language states that the remedy of acceleration is available to the lender if an event of default *has occurred*, even if subsequently cured. To avoid this undesirable result, the language should be revised as follows:

> Lender may accelerate the Loans if an Event of Default has occurred <u>and is continuing</u>.

§ 5:6.5 Gross Negligence and Willful Misconduct

An issue that comes up frequently in indemnification provisions is whether the indemnitee should be indemnified for the results of its own misbehavior. A common approach is to exclude costs that result from the indemnitee's "gross negligence or willful misconduct." In other words, costs incurred by the indemnitee as a result of its own gross negligence or willful misconduct are not subject to indemnification.

An example of this is the following. A company has indemnified an investor for all damages incurred by the investor "arising in any manner as a result of the investor's making the investment, except for damages arising from the investor's gross negligence or willful misconduct." The investor and the company agree on a plan for the company to make an illegal payoff to a public official in order to win a government contract. The investor is fined for its participation in this scheme. It turns to the company for indemnification, on the basis that the payoff was financed by the company with financing provided by the investor. The company is not responsible for making the indemnification payment under the "gross negligence and willful misconduct" carveout, because the investor's damages were the result of its own misconduct.

What if, under the above facts, the exclusion was worded as follows: "arising in any manner as a result of the investor's making the investment, except for damages arising <u>solely</u> from the investor's gross negligence or willful misconduct"? The inclusion of the word "solely" is often a negotiated point in this provision, and the example shows why. If the indemnification provision had been written this way, the investor would have a persuasive argument that it is entitled to indemnification, since the bad act was one which both the investor and the company participated in.

As an alternative to the use of the term "solely," a middle ground on this issue can be achieved by the following insertion:

> arising in any manner as a result of investor's making the investment, except for damages arising <u>to the extent of</u> the investor's gross negligence or willful misconduct.

This requires the comparative fault of the parties to be analyzed in determining the level of indemnification to be provided.

An issue that arises with respect to this provision is whether the proper standard should be gross negligence or merely negligence. Under the gross negligence standard, the indemnitee's claim for indemnification can only be denied if its behavior is grossly negligent. Clearly, the indemnitee will push hard for this standard because it requires indemnification even where the damages are the result of its ordinary negligence.

§ 5:6.6   *From Time to Time*

This phrase is used to clarify that an action is required or permitted more than once:

> Party A may <u>from time to time</u> require Party B to provide it with a certificate of insurance showing Party A as loss payee.

Without the underlined language, Party A may only request this certificate once. With the underlined language included, Party A may ask for the certificate as many times as it likes.

§ 5:6.7 *As the Case May Be*

This phrase is used in a sentence that presents more than one alternative, and indicates that the reader should apply the correct alternative. An example:

> Each of the Subsidiaries has been duly organized and is validly existing as a corporation or a limited liability company, as the case may be.

§ 5:6.8 *Respectively*

This word is used in sentences that contain corresponding series, and is used to indicate that the items in the second series correspond in order to the items in the first series:

> Company A, Company B and Company C may make political contributions in any fiscal year in an amount not to exceed $1 million, $2 million and $1 million, respectively.

§ 5:6.9 *For a Party's Account*

This phrase indicates that a certain cost or payment is to be borne by the specified party. For example, if a provision states "All of the costs and expenses of syndication shall be for the Issuer's account," it means that the issuer is agreeing to pay all such costs and expenses or to reimburse any other party for any such costs or expenses.

Chapter 6

Review and Interpretation of Contracts

§ 6:1   Introduction

It is a mistake to think that a contract can be filed and forgotten about once it is executed and delivered and the related closing is completed. Lawyers are frequently required to review and interpret existing agreements. Three types of circumstances give rise to a need for such review. The first is as a part of the "due diligence" process, in which one or more contracts must be reviewed in connection with another transaction. The second is a lawyer being asked by her client to review a contract to determine whether a particular action is required or permitted. The last is really an offshoot of the first: a lawyer is asked to advise her client on structuring transactions or courses of action in a manner that complies with the client's existing contracts.

One of the more difficult aspects of reviewing contracts is that more often than one might expect there is a question as to what particular language means. Often contract provisions are difficult to interpret—they may be ambiguous, overly complicated, imprecise, or contain confusing errors. Sometimes a provision is perfectly clear but contains a subjective element, such as a materiality or reasonableness qualification. Clients, particularly those who are not very experienced with complex agreements, can be surprised and impatient when there is no black-and-white answer to a question under a contract. Often, the interpretation of a single contract provision will dictate whether the client can enter into a transaction or take some other action. In some cases, the lawyer is required to render a legal opinion as to an interpretation issue. For all of these reasons, the interpretation of contracts gives rise to some of a transaction lawyer's most significant challenges.

§ 6:2   Basic Principles

§ 6:2.1   *Look at the Right Agreement*

The first task of a lawyer in the review of a contract is to ensure that he has the correct contract, and the most current version. It is surprising how often there are missteps at this stage. If a client requests a review of its credit agreement, the lawyer should be sure that the credit agreement that is handed to him or is in his files is the one that the client is concerned about. Does the agreement involve the right parties? If the document in question involves only a holding company and the client wants to know what restrictions exist as to a subsidiary, the lawyer should determine whether a separate credit agreement for that subsidiary exists. The date of the agreement may be a tip-off that there is a mistake—there may be facts and circumstances that suggest a contract should be of recent vintage, but it dates back ten years, for example.

Even when it is clear that the correct agreement is in hand, the lawyer must be sure that he has all amendments, waivers and consents. Advice as to the operation of a particular provision may be 100% wrong if a modification to that provision has been overlooked. If the contract is in the lawyer's files, this issue should be addressed by the lawyer's own filing system (assuming he has received copies of all modifications). (See section 7:4 for some practical tips to maintain access to all modifications to a contract.)

If the agreement is instead provided by the client, the lawyer should inquire whether any modifications have occurred. This question must be asked carefully: sometimes a modification may have been effected through something that is not called an amendment, waiver or consent but may on its face appear to be mere business correspondence. In other cases, an amendment to several related contracts may have been done in a single amendment document.

If there is any doubt as to the existence or nonexistence of amendments of a contract to which a public company is a party, it is a good idea to examine the schedule of material agreements attached to the company's SEC filings. In addition, if there are other counsel involved in the situation, it may be appropriate to ask whether they have any modification documents. For example, a lawyer asked by his client to review its credit agreement in connection with a proposed amendment should confirm with the bank's counsel that he has the most recent and complete set of documents.

The lawyer should not follow the client blindly when instructed to review a specific contract. For instance, if the lawyer is asked to review a warrant agreement to determine whether there are any transfer restrictions, he should ask for copies of the warrants that were issued under the warrant agreement, as well as any shareholder agreements, because it is conceivable that restrictions might appear in either of those documents instead of (or as well as) in the warrant agreement itself.

§ 6:2.2   Scope of the Review

The lawyer should make sure that he fully understands the issues or transactions giving rise to the review, so that the review will be complete. For example, if a lawyer is told to summarize the noncompete provisions in an employment contract (but is not told that the client is planning to terminate the employee), the lawyer will miss the opportunity to advise the client of an issue arising under another provision of the contract giving the terminated employee the right to put his stock options to the company. Often a client believes its interests are best served by narrowing the scope of a lawyer's assignment in order to minimize fees. This backfires in many cases, due to clients' frequent failure to anticipate what all of the issues are or may be.

Often, a junior lawyer instructed to perform due diligence is not given any specific guidance as to precisely what he is looking for as he sifts through mountains of legal documents. His task may be quite different if the diligence is being done in connection with an asset sale transaction as opposed to a secured financing, for example. The lawyer in this position has two initial responsibilities: to learn as much as possible regarding the transaction in connection with which the due diligence is being performed, and to understand the specific issues that he is meant to be looking at.[1] The diligence process and some of the different focuses thereof are discussed in greater detail below in section 6:4.

§ 6:2.3   Look at the Right Provisions and Everything Else

Let's say you are asked to review an indenture to determine whether it restricts the ability of your client to repurchase preferred stock from its founder. If you have reviewed a few indentures, you may know that this issue is likely to be covered in the restricted payments covenant. Sure enough, you determine that the repurchase is

---

1. This is often easier said than done. The senior lawyer giving the assignment may assume that the junior lawyer has a greater knowledge or skill level than he actually does, or may be in a big hurry and therefore not take the time to explain the assignment fully. In any event, it is preferable to incur a senior lawyer's short-term annoyance by pressing for clear instructions, instead of his long-term dissatisfaction with an assignment not properly performed.

permitted under that covenant to the extent of room in the restricted payments basket, which is determined by a reference to a detailed formula. Stopping your review at this point, however, would be a mistake. The indenture also contains a covenant restricting transactions with affiliates which, as defined, would include the founder from whom the shares are being purchased. This covenant requires that the transaction be done on an arm's length basis and if the size of the transaction exceeds a specified dollar amount requires the delivery of a third party fairness opinion. This example illustrates a fundamental principle in the review of contracts: particular issues may be affected by more than one provision.

Does this mean that each time a contract is reviewed every word must be read? This question has no clear answer; it depends on the circumstances. A lawyer who has extensive experience with a particular type of contract will be able to do a more focused review than a novice, since she can predict with a high degree of certainty which provisions are likely to be relevant. Even an experienced lawyer, however, faced with a contract outside her scope of expertise, will probably read (or at least skim) the entire document to ensure that no relevant provision is overlooked.

This discussion brings into play a frequently-repeated concept: the importance of a contract's being user-friendly. A user-friendly contract is easier to review because things are located where the reader expects them to be. Covenants are not buried in the representation section. Defined terms are helpfully named. Obligations are not hidden in definitions. The agreement is organized and drafted clearly and logically. Headings are relevant and the table of contents is complete. Unfortunately, these rules are sometimes not followed and the task of reviewing that contract is made more difficult. Further, the lawyer who assumes that these rules have been followed in a contract that she is reviewing, does so at her own (and her client's) risk.

§ 6:2.4   Don't Forget the Definitions

A contract provision has not been completely reviewed unless the definition of each defined term contained in it has been reviewed. Flipping back and forth between a provision and the definitions section may seem tedious and distracting, but the failure to do so may lead to significant oversights.

§ 6:3   Review and Interpretation

§ 6:3.1   The Imperfection of Contracts

A client's fondest hope is that after a contract is executed and delivered the business transaction will progress as it is supposed to without any issues and, most particularly, without the need for further interaction with the lawyers. If this hope is dashed, the client will then expect the lawyer to quickly and concisely opine, with absolute certainty, that the contract says what the client wants it to say regarding the issue at hand.

Unfortunately for the client, neither of these desires is always satisfied. There are many reasons why contracts may not work perfectly:

- It is impossible to anticipate every eventuality. As a contract is being negotiated and drafted, the parties and their counsel will engage in an implicit cost-benefit analysis weighing the economic and time costs against the need to anticipate and draft for unlikely scenarios. Even if the parties are willing to cover every possible conceived situation, they may fail. One of the risks of business is the risk of unanticipated conditions and events.

- Transactions are being consummated at ever-increasing speed. The less time that the parties and lawyers have to review and reflect on contract drafts, the more likely it is that gaps and ambiguities will result.

- Word processing and e-mail technology has led to greater pressure to draft, circulate, review, comment on, redraft and recirculate documents in ever-faster cycles. As a result, many provisions are grafted onto a contract in an isolated fashion, increasing the likelihood that the ripple effects of such provisions on other parts of the contract or the transaction may not be adequately considered.

- In recent years, business people and lawyers have shown an increasing willingness to deviate from standard transaction structures and contract provisions. In many cases, the secondary effects of such innovations aren't readily apparent.

- Finally, lawyers are human and fallible. We make mistakes.

§ 6:3.2 *The Life of Contracts*

Different types of contracts give rise to differing levels of post-signing review and analysis. On one end of the spectrum, there are contracts that are fully performed by all parties at closing. An example is a typical residential real estate purchase contract—once the closing occurs, the contractual relationship is completed. There are no continuing obligations, and as a result, no need for the lawyers to review or discuss the contract post-closing. A typical corporate acquisition agreement has a longer shelf life. The seller will have made representations regarding the sold business and will have agreed to indemnify the buyer in the event such representations are untrue. Often the agreement will provide for a post-closing purchase price adjustment based on a determination of the target's working capital at or after closing. All of these provisions are likely to require continued review and interpretation by the lawyers.

Another type of contract that may involve regular involvement by the lawyers is an agreement that requires regular performance by one or more parties over its term. An example is a supply agreement pursuant to which a seller agrees to ship grain to a buyer. This agreement will have provisions with respect to quantities, methods of delivery, quality of product, risk of loss, pricing and payment. In the ordinary course, the parties will transact business under contracts like this without their lawyer's input, but as disputes or unusual circumstances arise, the lawyers will be called.

At the farthest end of the spectrum are credit agreements and other debt agreements that impose tight restrictions on a company's operations and activities over the life of the agreement. Unlike the supply agreement and other similar agreements, which as a general rule will regulate the parties' activities with respect to the subject matter of the contract only, debt agreements will to varying degrees restrict a wide range of a company's activities and operations. As a result, the lawyers' input is frequently required, particularly when the borrower wishes to consummate a significant transaction or is in financial difficulty. See section 9:3.

§ 6:3.3   *Timing Issues*

There is a simple guideline as to the best time for a lawyer to review potential issues under a contract: the earlier the better. Unfortunately, in most cases the lawyer will not control the timing, particularly if an issue only comes to his attention when his client decides it is appropriate. Often, that may be at the last moment, as a result of a variety of factors: the client may want to minimize legal fees; the client may not recognize the potential issue early enough; or the client may believe that she is capable of reviewing, interpreting and understanding the relevant contract provisions without the advice of counsel.

These factors may result in a scenario where the lawyer receives a frantic phone call from the client saying "We are about to sign an agreement that does X, Y and Z. That doesn't create any problems under our indenture, does it? By the way, if we don't sign this in the next two hours, we will lose a large security deposit." This is a tricky situation for the lawyer—he wants to be helpful and responsive, but at the same time he wants to provide correct advice. That advice cannot be properly given unless the lawyer has the opportunity to understand and review the contract that the client is about to sign, and to carefully analyze its effect under the indenture. Furthermore, there may be other issues that the lawyer may identify during the process that are beyond the four corners of the two agreements at hand—for example, the lawyer may be aware of other contracts that may be affected.

How can this conflict between the client's tight timetable and the lawyer's need for adequate time to do a proper job be reconciled? Unfortunately, there may not be a good answer to this question. First, the client should be pressed to determine if the urgency is legitimate: often, the deadline is artificial and/or self-imposed. If the lawyer is forced to provide advice without sufficient information and without sufficient time, he should make it clear that this is the case and that issues that may have been identified in a more thorough review may be missed. Failure to provide this caution to the client may result in blame being unfairly laid at the lawyer's doorstep if any issues later come to light.

Of course, the best medicine is preventative. What steps can the lawyer take to prevent this situation from occurring?

- At the time any contract is being drafted and negotiated, the client should be sensitized to the various circumstances where the provisions of the contract are likely to come into play.

- If the client is a company, the lawyer should endeavor to make the right company officers or employees aware of contract provisions that are relevant to their roles. For example, the proper people in the client's treasury department should be aware of any financial reporting requirements (in fact, they should be encouraged to provide input on these provisions during the negotiation process).

- The lawyer should be alert to any indications from the client that there are circumstances that may affect or be affected by a contract. The lawyer then should ask for information. A bit of pushiness and intrusiveness by the lawyer in such a case may provide a significant benefit to the client, by allowing the lawyer to address any issues at the early, rather than the final stages, of a new situation.

- Lawyers who are responsible for one area of a client's legal needs should be alert to developments that may be relevant to another area. For example, a financing lawyer who is asked whether a round of layoffs will be permitted under the client's debt documents, should mention the issue to the lawyer at his firm who handles the client's employee benefit matters.

§ 6:3.4   *Levels of Review*

The review of contract provisions in response to a client's question may take a minute or two, or it may require hours or even days of review and discussion. The depth and complexity will depend on several factors: the type of issue being raised, the number of agreements to be reviewed, the number of contract provisions that are implicated, the level of advice that is being requested, and whether the contract provisions' treatment of the issue is clear or ambiguous.

[A]   Types of Issues

The simplest situation is a narrow question for which the contract provides a clear answer. The client asks what it should do under a lease that requires a rent payment to be made on November 30, a Saturday. The section of the lease treating payment requirements provides that any rent payment that is stated to be due on a day that is not a business day shall be paid on the next preceding business day. Under the definition of business day, Saturdays are treated as non-business days. The advice, therefore, is straightforward: make the rent payment on Friday, November 29.

The question posed to the lawyer may be much more complicated. It may be open-ended or general: what are the lessor's remedies if we fail to make a payment required under the lease? An appropriate answer to a question like this will involve a more thorough review of the contract and a much more detailed response, since the lease will provide for several different remedies, each of which involves a different process and leads to a different result.

Sometimes the lawyer must advise the client how to structure a transaction or conduct its activities in a way that complies with a contract's restrictions. What if, for example, a client wants to acquire a company whose sole asset is a warehouse facility. First, the lawyer will identify the contract provisions that may have an impact on the client's ability to achieve this goal. Next, the lawyer will identify ways of structuring the transaction that will not run afoul of these provisions. For example, the client's credit agreement may prohibit transactions involving the acquisition of controlling equity interests in another person. The lawyer would advise the client that it may avoid the need to obtain the lender's consent by structuring the transaction as an acquisition of the warehouse, rather than an acquisition of the entity that owns the warehouse. Of course, the lawyer will also need to be certain that there are no other provisions that might affect the client's ability to structure the transaction in this fashion.

[B]   What Is at Stake?

Without suggesting that a lawyer should ever provide his client with inadequate or incomplete advice, the circumstances of each situation will dictate the level of intensity that is required in the review and analysis of a contract. Contrast the following two examples. In the first, the client has asked its lawyer about the proper operation of a provision in a receivables sale agreement that permits it to defer the delivery of financial information as a consequence of force majeure, defined to include acts of war. The client's Mexican subsidiary (which represents no more than 3% of the client's sales, profits or assets) has been unable to compile its year-end numbers because of technology glitches resulting from revolutionary attacks, and as a result the client will not be able to deliver the required financial information until a week after it is required under the agreement. Failure to comply with the financial information delivery requirements does not give rise to any specific remedies.

In the second example, the client has entered into an agreement to merge with another public company. The merger agreement is subject to a condition that allows the client to terminate the contract if it reasonably determines that there has occurred "one or more events, acts or conditions which, individually or in the aggregate, could reasonably be expected to have a material adverse effect on the financial condition, assets, liabilities or business" of the target. The target has announced that it is under investigation by the Justice Department for possible violations of the Foreign Corrupt Practices Act, and has announced that its quarterly net income is off 15% from the level reported for the same period in the previous fiscal year.

Both of these situations involve potentially tricky interpretation issues. In the first example, was the situation in Mexico an act of war? Was the client required to include the Mexican subsidiary's results, or could it have delivered all of the financial information other than that relating to the Mexican subsidiary? In the second example, does the mere existence of the investigation have any effect on the target's financial condition, assets, liabilities or business, and if so, how can its materiality be measured? Does it require an analysis and estimate of the potential liability for violating the federal statute? What are the possible remedies under the statute? Is the drop in net income by itself, or together with the potential liability for the possible statutory violation, material?

While each of these situations involve potentially difficult interpretation issues, the first situation is much easier to address because there is far less at stake. The risk to the client of being wrong is much smaller, because the contract does not provide any defined remedy. Of course, another party to the contract could assert a breach by the client, but the client's ability to cure the breach quickly blunts this concern.

The other situation is far different. Since both parties to the merger agreement are public companies, the deal had been publicly announced. A termination of this agreement by the client would also be publicly announced and would probably be the focus of negative media attention. Because the other party's stock price had fallen since the date the merger agreement was signed, any termination by the client under these circumstances would probably lead to litigation. This situation presents a much greater challenge to the lawyer asked for advice on the meaning and effect of the relevant contract provisions. The lawyer in the second example is likely to pursue more lines of inquiry and analysis than the lawyer in the first example. These would include: (a) consulting with other lawyers (including litigators and those familiar with the Foreign Corrupt Practices Act); (b) researching case law relating to material adverse change clauses; and (c) reviewing notes and drafts from the time that the contract was in negotiation for any relevant background on what was intended by the provision.

These examples illustrate that every situation involving the review and interpretation of a contract involves a cost-benefit analysis weighing the scope of the review against the significance of the issue being examined.

[C]   Degrees of Certainty

Both lawyers and their clients are happiest when a question under a contract has a clear answer. When the answer is not entirely certain, both the lawyer and client must make the best of the situation. The lawyer must do her best to provide the greatest amount of guidance to her client, taking into account any uncertainty in her conclusions, and to make sure that the client is aware of the existence and the extent of the uncertainty. The client ultimately will have to come to terms with not having a 100% clear answer.

There are different sources of uncertainty. Some are a result of contract terms that are inherently subjective. Terms such as "reasonable," "material" and "could reasonably be expected to" are always going to be subject to differing interpretations at the margins. Another source of uncertainty is contract provisions that are drafted unclearly or ambiguously, or that do not specifically address the situation at hand.

Different circumstances require different levels of certainty. In a case where the lawyer believes that there is no absolutely clear answer to a question under a contract, he can provide his best advice to the client and help the client formulate its response. If the lawyer believes that an interpretation is almost certainly correct, he should have no qualms about letting the client act in reliance on such interpretation, as long as the client is made aware of possible other interpretations and their consequences. Even when the lawyer believes that his conclusion as to the interpretation of a contract provision is more likely than not to be the correct one, the client must be given the opportunity to decide for itself, on a completely informed basis, to act or not to act based on this conclusion.

A different situation arises where the lawyer's conclusion must be provided in a formal written legal opinion to a third party. Contract interpretation issues often arise when a lawyer is required to opine that the execution, delivery and performance by his client of a contract does not violate, conflict with or result in a breach of one or more other contracts (a "no-conflict opinion"). A responsible lawyer will never render an unqualified no-conflict opinion (a "clean opinion") unless he is reasonably certain that his conclusion is correct.[2] This must be the case even if the lawyer believes that he and his firm bear no risk if the opinion turns out to be incorrect; a legal opinion constitutes a lawyer's best conclusions as to specified matters of law, not an insurance policy.

What if the lawyer being asked for a no-conflict opinion believes that the issue is not entirely free from doubt, and is therefore unable to render a clean opinion? He may deliver a "reasoned opinion," in which his analysis and conclusions are explicitly set forth. The strongest form of reasoned opinion states that a court, if faced with the issue, "should" reach a particular result based on the analysis described in the opinion. If the lawyer rendering the opinion is less certain, the opinion may state that a court would be "more likely than not" to reach the result.

In many cases, the inability of the lawyer to deliver a clean no-conflict opinion will result in the parties being unwilling to complete the transaction. Take, for example, a mortgage financing where there is an issue as to whether one of the mortgagor's contracts would permit the granting of a mortgage to the mortgagor. Mortgagor's counsel is willing to deliver a reasoned opinion on this issue, but in most cases the mortgagee would be unwilling to close on this basis. It would potentially be exposing itself to a claim by the counterparty to the other contract that by taking the mortgage the mortgagee tortiously interfered with the

---

2. This principle applies to *all* opinions, not just no-conflict opinions.

mortgagor's rights under the contract and induced its breach. Additionally, a contract may be unenforceable if it is entered into by parties aware that it conflicts with the provisions of another contract.[3]

As a result of these dynamics, the existence of conflicts should be identified as early as possible in the course of a transaction. The client that consults its lawyers after a transaction has been structured and the principal terms negotiated risks having to restructure its transaction as potential conflicts are uncovered.

§ 6:4   Due Diligence

Due diligence is a broad concept that generally describes the review of existing contracts and other legal documents in connection with another transaction. It can run the gamut from a complete review of the material contracts of a company in connection with a detailed description of the company and its business in a securities offering document, for example, to a far more limited review of certain contracts relating to a leasing transaction.

§ 6:4.1   *Scope of the Assignment*

Because due diligence is such an open-ended concept, it is insufficient for a senior lawyer to send a junior lawyer to conduct a due diligence review without giving specific guidance as to what the scope and goals of the process are.

Specifically, the following questions should be answered:

- What work product is expected to be produced? Should each contract reviewed be summarized, and, if so, in what level of detail? (It is helpful to refer to comparable summaries prepared in previous similar due diligence exercises.)

- What specific contracts or categories of contracts should be reviewed?

- What entities' contracts are to be covered? One important thing to keep in mind is that contracts of a parent company

---

3.   RESTATEMENT (SECOND) OF CONTRACTS § 194 (1981).

often contain restrictions on the activities of its subsidiaries (and, less frequently, the reverse may be the case).

- Is part of the assignment locating the contracts? If so, what is the strategy for that process? What are the possible sources?

- What is the purpose of the examination? Is it to gain a general understanding of the contracts being reviewed, or is it to determine the possible contractual restrictions on a proposed transaction? If so, what are all of the elements of the transaction?

In no event should any due diligence exercise be commenced without a clear understanding of the answers to these questions.

Following is an overview of certain areas of contract due diligence that come up in the context of certain types of transactions.[4]

§ 6:4.2 Due Diligence of Seller's Contracts in an Asset Acquisition

A due diligence review of the contracts of an entity that is selling assets should include a review of the following general issues and specific provisions:

Transfer Restrictions

- Provisions restricting the sale, lease, transfer, encumbering or other disposition of the assets to be sold.

- Due on sale clauses: typically found in real estate mortgages, these provide that indebtedness automatically becomes due upon the sale of the mortgaged asset.

---

4. This discussion focuses only on the review of contracts. Most due diligence reviews include as well such things as organizational documents (e.g., charters and by-laws), policy manuals, minutes of board of directors' meetings, litigation papers, SEC and other governmental filings and the like. Although a discussion of the review of such materials is beyond the scope of this chapter, many of the principles described are applicable. In addition, the scope of the due diligence will vary depending on the situation and the client's preferences.

- If the assets to be transferred include a contract or a contract right, anti-assignment provisions in the contract itself.[5]

- Clauses providing that a sale of assets triggers an event of default, event of termination or other remedial rights.

Existing Encumbrances

- Provisions creating liens, pledges, mortgages, security interests, easements or other restrictions on the assets to be transferred.

- Leases or license agreements covering the assets to be transferred.

- Provisions permitting the release of the assets from any applicable encumbrances or contract restrictions.

- Provisions permitting or requiring the filing of a financing statement regarding the assets to be transferred.

Mandatory Payment Provisions

- Provisions requiring payments upon the consummation of asset sales.

Change of Control Provisions

- Provisions in which remedial or other rights are triggered by a sale of "all or substantially all" or "a substantial portion" of an entity's assets.

---

5. Many anti-assignment provisions have been rendered unenforceable by Sections 9-406 and 9-408 of the Uniform Commercial Code. See section 10:2.10.

§ 6:4.3 Due Diligence of Purchaser's Contracts in an Asset Acquisition

Issues and provisions to look for in a due diligence review as to a party that is buying assets include:

Restrictions on Purchase

• Restrictions on the purchase or acquisition of assets.[6]

Restrictions on Capital Expenditures

• Restrictions on the making of capital expenditures, if the assets being acquired include fixed or capital assets.

Restrictions on Investment

• Sometimes "investments" is defined to include certain asset acquisitions, such as the purchase of the assets of an ongoing line of business, or the purchase of all or substantially all of the assets of another entity.

Lien Requirements

• Provisions requiring after-acquired property to be pledged to a creditor. This may be an issue if the acquired assets are supposed to secure acquisition financing.

• Negative pledge clauses, which prohibit the creation of liens on property. Again, an issue may arise if the assets to be acquired are to be pledged to secure the acquisition financing or other financing of the purchaser.

Receivables Agreements

• If the purchaser is a party to a factoring agreement, receivables transfer agreement or receivables securitization transaction, its effect on the acquisition of assets consisting of receivables, general intangibles or contract rights must be analyzed.

---

6. To the extent the assets constitute contracts, see note 5 as to the unenforceability of certain anti-assignment provisions.

Line of Business Restrictions

- If a business is being acquired and is different from the purchaser's existing business, covenants restricting the scope of the purchaser's business must be reviewed.

§ 6:4.4   *Due Diligence of a Target's Contracts[7] in a Stock Acquisition[8]*

In the acquisition of an entity through the purchase of all of its outstanding stock, a thorough review of the target entity's contracts is advisable to determine whether they (a) impede or prohibit the acquisition, (b) conflict with any of the purchaser's contracts, or (c) interfere with any proposed financing.

Change of Control Provisions

- These provisions may be triggered by (a) the transfer of shares (usually voting shares), (b) the existence of contractual agreements pursuant to which voting rights or control are transferred, and (c) the changing of the membership or composition of the board of directors or similar governing body of the target.

- Certain agreements (particularly real estate leases) provide that a change of control is deemed to be a transfer of an asset to the entity to which control is transferred. The effect of this is often to trigger a default or prepayment under the agreement.

Subsidiary Restrictions

- The purchaser's contracts may contain a number of provisions that apply to the purchaser's subsidiaries. Most of these will relate to the subsidiaries' business and activities (these are

---

7. A due diligence review of a target's contracts may go well beyond what is outlined here. For instance, the potential purchaser of a chemical company may request a review and summary of all of the target's supply contracts to determine the reliability of its raw materials sourcing.

8. References here to "stock" and "shares" are meant to encompass other equity interests including partnership interests and limited liability company interests.

discussed in greater detail in section 6:4.6). One frequently occurring covenant relates to subsidiaries' *contracts*. This provision is usually entitled "Payment Restrictions Affecting Subsidiaries" or something similar. It prohibits the existence of certain restrictions in the subsidiaries' contracts, on the basis that such restrictions impede the free flow of assets and cash from the subsidiary to its parent. The types of contractual restrictions in the contracts of the target and its subsidiaries that may conflict with this provision are the following:

• Restrictions on dividends.

• Restrictions on asset sales to its parent company.

• Restrictions on making loans to parent.

• Restrictions on making payments on indebtedness or other obligations of the parent.

Restrictions on Transactions with Affiliates

• Restrictions on the target's ability to conduct transactions with its affiliates may impede transactions between the purchaser and the target that are planned as a result of the acquisition, such as sales of assets, assumptions of liabilities, and the like.

Debt Provisions

• If the target has debt that is to be repaid or refinanced in connection with the acquisition, provisions relating to the target's ability to repay such debt and the mechanics thereof.

Existing Encumbrances

• Provisions creating liens, pledges, mortgages, security interests, easements or other restrictions on the target's assets.

• Leases or license agreements covering the target's assets.

• Provisions permitting the release of the target's assets from the applicable encumbrances or restrictions.

• Provisions permitting or requiring the filing of a financing statement under the Uniform Commercial Code regarding the target's assets.

Financing-related Provisions

- If the target is expected or required to borrow, guaranty debt and/or grant liens on its assets as a part of the acquisition financing, provisions restricting such actions must be reviewed.

§ 6:4.5   *Due Diligence of a Seller's Contracts in a Stock Acquisition*

A seller of stock may have contractual restrictions on its ability to sell the stock, or may have pledged the stock to a creditor.

Transfer Restrictions

- Provisions restricting the sale, lease, transfer, encumbering or other disposition of the stock to be sold. These could include drag along and tag along rights.

- Clauses providing that a sale of assets triggers an event of default, event of termination or other remedial provision.

Existing Encumbrances

- Provisions creating pledges, liens or other restrictions on the stock to be transferred.

- Provisions permitting the release of the stock from any such lien or other restriction.

- Provisions permitting or requiring the filing of a financing statement under the Uniform Commercial Code in respect of the stock to be transferred.

Mandatory Payment Provisions

- Provisions requiring payments upon the occurrence of asset sales.

Change of Control Provisions

- Provisions in which remedial or other rights are triggered by a sale of "all or substantially all" or "a substantial portion" of an entity's assets.[9]

---

9.   See note 3.

§ 6:4.6   Due Diligence of a Purchaser's Contracts in a Stock Acquisition

A purchaser of stock may have contractual restrictions on its ability to purchase the stock. Furthermore, if as a result of the acquisition the target becomes a subsidiary, there may be issues under provisions in the purchaser's contracts that apply to subsidiaries.

Restrictions on Purchase

- Restrictions on the purchase or acquisition of equity interests.

Restrictions on Investment

- Provisions restricting investments (a purchase of shares is usually defined as an investment).

Existence of Subsidiaries

- Provisions restricting the creation, acquisition or existence of subsidiaries, if the acquisition of stock results in the target and its subsidiaries becoming subsidiaries of the purchaser (as defined in each of the purchaser's contracts).

Restrictions on Subsidiaries

- If the acquisition of stock results in the target and its subsidiaries becoming subsidiaries of the purchaser (as defined in each of the purchaser's contracts), each provision that applies to the purchaser's subsidiaries must be analyzed to determine whether facts pertaining to the target and its subsidiaries would result in a breach of such provision. A list of examples (by no means exhaustive):

    - Restrictions on debt and liens that may not permit debt and liens of the target that are expected to continue in place after the acquisition.

    - Covenants that require subsidiaries to provide guaranties, to pledge assets, or to take similar actions.

    - Restrictions on asset sales that may block sales of assets by the target that are already contracted for or that are anticipated.

- Representations that apply to the purchaser's subsidiaries, covering matters as diverse as good standing, litigation, violations of law and contracts, employee benefit plans, absence of material adverse change, among others.

Payment Restrictions Affecting Subsidiaries

- There may be provisions in the purchaser's contracts that prohibit certain restrictive provisions in its subsidiaries' agreements. See the discussion above in section 6:4.4 under "Subsidiary Restrictions."

Lien Requirements

- Provisions requiring after-acquired property to be pledged to a creditor. This may be an issue if the acquired stock is supposed to secure acquisition financing.

- Prohibitions on the creation of liens on property. Again, an issue may arise if the stock to be acquired is to be pledged to secure the acquisition financing.

§ 6:4.7   *Due Diligence of the Contracts of an Issuer of Stock*

In a transaction involving an issuance of stock, whether in a public offering or a private placement, the issuer's contracts must be reviewed for provisions that relate to equity issuances.

Restrictions on Issuance of Securities

- Provisions prohibiting or restricting the issuance of equity securities.

Change of Control Provisions

- Provisions that trigger remedies if the identities of shareholders or directors change.

Mandatory Prepayments

- Provisions requiring payments to be made with the proceeds of the issuance of equity.

Preemptive Rights

- Provisions granting existing shareholders the right to purchase shares on the same terms as purchasers in any stock offering.

§ 6:4.8 *Due Diligence of the Contracts of a Borrower in an Unsecured Loan or Debt Issuance Transaction*

When a company is borrowing money on an unsecured basis, either under a bank credit facility or through a private placement or public offering of debt securities, the following contractual issues must be examined.

Debt Restrictions

- Provisions restricting an entity's ability to borrow or to incur indebtedness (particular care should be given to the definition of "debt" or "indebtedness," which often includes things not traditionally considered debt, such as letters of credit and guaranties).

- If the new debt is to be guaranteed by subsidiaries or other related entities, provisions restricting such entities' ability to guarantee another's obligations (sometimes there are separate restrictions on "contingent obligations" that may cover guarantees and, if applicable, reimbursement obligations in respect of letters of credit).

- Financial covenants that may be affected by the incurrence of indebtedness or the payment of principal and interest.

Prepayments

- Provisions restricting the ability of the entity to make payments or prepayments of the indebtedness to be incurred.

- Provisions requiring that the proceeds of certain events (such as the issuance of equity, the receipt of insurance or asset sale proceeds, the receipt of excess cash flow) be applied to pay specified obligations. If there are such provisions, the agreement governing the new debt cannot require similar prepayments with the same proceeds.

- A provision that requires the proceeds of indebtedness to be applied to the payment of an existing obligation may apply to the debt to be incurred. This may be inconsistent with the proposed uses of the money to be borrowed.

Liens

- Provisions providing for the granting of security interests or other liens—the unsecured lender will want to know about other obligations that are secured.

Payment Restrictions Affecting Subsidiaries

- If the agreement governing the new debt limits the borrower's subsidiaries from agreeing to or permitting payment restrictions (see the description of this under "Subsidiary Restrictions" in section 6:4.4 above), the subsidiaries' contracts must be reviewed to determine if any such restrictions exist.

§ 6:4.9 Due Diligence of the Contracts of a Borrower in a Secured Loan or Debt Issuance Transaction

In addition to the items enumerated above for unsecured loan and debt issuance transactions, the following issues must be addressed if the loan or debt obligations are to be secured by liens on the assets of the borrower/issuer:

Lien Covenants

- These are provisions that restrict a party's ability to grant security interests, mortgages and other liens on its assets.

Equal and Ratable Security Clauses

- These are provisions that require existing obligations to be "equally and ratably" secured to the same extent and with the same collateral that new obligations are secured. The granting of such security to preexisting debt would normally be prohibited by the terms of the new debt.

Anti-assignment Provisions

- If the security package includes contracts or contract rights, all contracts must be reviewed for provisions that prohibit the granting of a security interest in them. Prohibitions or restrictions against their assignment must also be looked for, as assignment will be required if the secured lender must foreclose on the collateral.[10]

---

10. Such prohibitions may be unenforceable under the Uniform Commercial Code. See section 10:2.10.

Chapter 7

Amendments, Waivers and Consents

§ 7:1   The Amendment Process

It is not unusual to make changes to a contract after it has been entered into: the contract may contain mistakes that need to be corrected; circumstances may arise that were not anticipated and therefore not addressed; or one party may want to change the deal.

In these situations, a new negotiation will occur which will dictate how and whether an amendment, waiver or consent is entered into. Under most circumstances, neither party is under any legal compulsion to amend the contract and the normal rules of leverage apply: a rational person will not agree to a concession unless she is compensated in some fashion. For example, a landlord will not agree to reduce the rent under a long-term lease, even though market rent levels have decreased, unless it receives some reciprocal concession from the tenant.[1]

---

1. Sometimes a contract will obligate the parties to negotiate amendments to address certain events or circumstances. This is an exception to the general rule that no party to a contract is under any legal compulsion to amend the contract. A provision like this usually requires the parties to "negotiate in good faith" toward a particular end. Note, however, that each party's obligation is satisfied by the act of good faith negotiation, and if such good faith negotiations have taken place the lack of final agreement will not constitute a breach.

An amendment, waiver or consent is a new contract as to which all of the legal requirements of contract creation and enforceability apply. Additionally, amendments, waivers and consents contain many of the same building block provisions found in other agreements. The amendment may have one or both parties bring down the representations made in the original contract, or new representations may be required. There may be conditions precedent to the effectiveness of the amendment similar to those in any other agreement. On the other hand, covenants appearing in amendments are most often new covenants that will become part of the amended contract, as opposed to covenants that exist only in the amendment itself. Likewise, it is quite unusual for an amendment to contain its own remedial provisions. Once an amendment, waiver or consent is effective, the underlying contract continues to be effective, as modified by the amendment, waiver or consent.

§ 7:2   Amendments, Waivers and Consents: Different Tools for Different Tasks

Technically, the difference between an amendment, a waiver and a consent is the following:

* An *amendment* is a change to a provision in an existing contract, or the deletion or addition of a provision. Example: an employment contract is amended (a) to increase the employee's base pay, (b) to provide for a new option package, and (c) to delete restrictions on the employee's outside activities.

* A *waiver* is a party's agreement not to enforce a contractual right. Example: an employer agrees not to enforce its right under an existing employment contract to prevent the employee from engaging in certain unrelated activities.

* A *consent* is an agreement by one party to permit something that is prohibited by the contract. Example: an employer consents to an employee's engaging in certain unrelated activities that are restricted under an employment contract.

You will notice that a single result may be achieved through the use of any of these techniques. Sometimes the form of a particular modification may be dictated by custom or course of conduct. In other cases, the form may be selected to create a certain impression: for example, a document called a consent may cast the desired modification in a better light than an agreement called an amendment or a waiver.

Waivers and consents do not modify the underlying contract but instead suspend enforcement of specified provisions. For this reason, a waiver is often used where a temporary solution to a problem under a contract is needed. An example of this is a limited partnership agreement that requires each limited partner to deliver annual financial statements to the general partner by March 31 of each year. If one year a limited partner can't make this delivery until April 30, the general partner might execute a waiver by which the delinquent limited partner's performance of this covenant is waived until April 30. Of course, the same result could be achieved by permanently amending the agreement to specify that the financial statements of that limited partner could be delivered on April 30 instead of March 31 of that year. The one-time nature of the occurrence, however, and the parties' interest in not making this exception part of the agreement itself, would militate toward the use of a waiver and not an amendment.

A standstill (also called a forbearance) is a waiver of a party's rights to take remedial action in respect of another party's breach, instead of a waiver of the breach itself. This may be less favorable to the breaching party than a complete waiver. A breach of a contract provision may have several ancillary legal effects: among these, it may trigger defaults under other agreements ("cross-defaults") or it may give rise to disclosure obligations. If a potential breach is addressed by amending the agreement to permit the offending action or circumstance or by waiving the breach itself, there will be no violation and such negative ancillary effects will be avoided. This will not be the case where a standstill is given and the underlying breach survives; a party's agreement not to exercise its remedies does not eliminate the fact that the breach has occurred and is continuing, and the continuing breach may have independent legal consequences.

§ 7:3   Amendment Techniques

Amendments that change existing provisions can be drafted either to amend specific language or to restate the entire provision. For example, take the following provision:

> The Lessee shall not enter into any sublease of the 32nd floor, except to entities approved by the Lessor (such approval not to be unreasonably withheld).

The parties want to amend this provision to permit subleases to the Lessee's affiliates without the need for the Lessor's consent. This can be drafted in two ways. The first is more surgical in nature:

> Section 10.14 is amended by adding the phrase "to affiliates of the Lessee and" after the word "except" appearing therein.

The second approach is to restate the provision in its entirety:

> Section 10.14 is amended in its entirety as follows:

> The Lessee shall not enter into any sublease of the 32nd floor, except to affiliates of the Lessee and to entities approved by the Lessor (such approval not to be unreasonably withheld).

The benefit of the first type of amendment described above is greater brevity. The disadvantage is that it is harder to read. There is no way for a reader to understand the first example without cross-reference to the original agreement. This is why it is often preferable to employ the second approach—it results in a longer amendment but it is much more user-friendly.

Deleting and adding provisions is a more straightforward task. Here is an example of the deletion of a provision:

> Section 3(b)(ii) is deleted in its entirety.

Here is an example of an amendment provision which adds a new sentence:

> Section 7 is amended by adding the following clause (d) at the end thereof: "(d) All determinations made by Seller in this Section 7 shall be made promptly and in a commercially reasonable manner."

In the context of modifying, deleting or adding provisions, the lawyer should always be attentive to cross-references. If, for example, the deletion of a section would require a number of subsequent provisions to be renumbered, it is a good idea to replace the deleted text with the words "Intentionally Omitted." This leaves all the subsequent numbering intact and eliminates the risk of a blown cross-reference.

Similarly, it is usually preferable to add a new item to a series of items of the end of the list. For example, if section 5 of an agreement restricts a party's actions but sets forth a list of exceptions to such restriction in clauses (a) through (f), then the best way to add a new exception is as follows:

> Section 5 is amended by (i) deleting the word "and" at the end of clause (e) thereof, (ii) deleting the "." at the end of clause (f) thereof and replacing it with "; and", and (iii) adding the following new clause (g) at the end thereof: "(g) actions required by applicable law".

Note that the changes being effected by clauses (i) and (ii) of the preceding example are not substantive, but are included to place the word "and" correctly before the last item in the series and to adjust the punctuation accordingly. (It is the author's view that these changes, while technically correct, are not substantively necessary and can be omitted in order to streamline the amendment.) By adding the new exception at the end of the series, the draftsperson eliminates the need for more relettering of the existing exceptions and reduces the risk of creating incorrect cross-references.

The form of the actual modification document is a matter of choice or custom. An amendment may have the appearance of a formal contract, with a heading, whereas clauses, section headings, and the like. Alternatively, the same goal could be accomplished by the delivery of a letter agreement from one of the contracting parties to the others (so long as all parties sign it). Typically, the latter format would be more common for simpler amendments.

A choice also needs to be made between an amendment and an amendment and restatement. An amendment and restatement is an amendment which amends the agreement by restating it in its entirety, with the amendments incorporated into the body of the new contract. This approach is used where there are many changes to be made, where modifications flow through the agreement in a pervasive way, or where there have been a number of amendments that are becoming increasingly unwieldy to monitor.

§ 7:4   Keeping Track

The lawyer reviewing an agreement must also review all previous amendments, waivers and consents. The failure to do so could result in a misreading of the agreement. The key to avoiding this problem is to develop a good system for keeping track of all such modifications.

One method is to annotate a working copy of an agreement to indicate amended provisions. Another technique is to create a "conformed copy," that is, a version in which all of the amendments have been actually run in the document as if it were a restatement. However, on important issues it is unwise to rely on this without referring directly to the amendments and the original agreement.

Where an agreement has been the subject of multiple amendments it may be more efficient to do the next amendment in the form of an amendment and restatement. After it becomes effective, the restated contract will act as the complete and operative document incorporating the original agreements and amendments. This is particularly helpful for contracts that must be reviewed regularly.

In any event, it is an extremely sensible and efficient practice to put each amendment to an agreement physically together with the agreement itself. If the agreement is kept in the files as a separate document, put the amendments in the same file. If the agreement is in a velobound set, insert the amendment immediately behind the agreement and have the set re-bound. If the original agreement is in a hard-bound volume, note the existence of the amendment on with the agreement itself. The goal of all of this is to facilitate a complete and accurate review of the contract in the future when circumstances require.

§ 7:5   Satisfying Amendment Requirements

Agreements usually have provisions governing how modifications may be effected. Usually these will state that all amendments, waivers and consents must be in writing. Irrespective of whether such a provision is enforceable, it is better not to make any modification to an agreement other than in a writing that satisfies all of the requirements of an enforceable contract. Sometimes these provisions will require that amendments must be executed by "the party to be charged," i.e., the party whose interests are being modified adversely by the amendment. Most often, the amendment provision will require amendments to be signed by all of the contract parties.

Multiparty agreements such as syndicated credit agreements may have amendment provisions specifying which parties' approval is required for different types of amendments. Typically, only changes to certain important economic terms require approval of all the lenders: extensions of maturities or payment dates, forgiveness of principal or interest, reduction of interest or fees, or release of material collateral or other credit support. Otherwise, amendments, waivers and consents under these types of agreements usually require an affirmative vote of lenders holding some stated percentage (usually more than 50% or 66 2/3%) of the commitments and loans. In some cases, different percentages may apply to different types of amendments. In loan agreements with multiple credit facilities, there may be class voting as to amendments which affect particular facilities—for example, an amendment changing the minimum amount of any revolving advance may require approval from a majority of the revolving lenders.

The voting provisions in any type of debt agreement play a significant role in dictating the dynamics of debt restructurings and workouts. An individual lender who has a small piece of the credit may have no negotiating leverage as to the resolution of an issue requiring a majority vote. On the other hand, each lender has huge negotiating leverage on an issue that requires a unanimous vote. This leverage is amplified by the universal reluctance of borrowers and lenders to pay out a lender who "holds out" against an amendment. Such payouts only encourage more holdouts in troubled situations.

Amendments under debt indentures are entered into in a different manner. The noteholders are not a party to the indenture that contains the operative provisions governing the notes. Instead, the indenture is entered into between the issuer and a trustee for the noteholders. An amendment to an indenture is called a "supplemental indenture" and is executed by the issuer and the trustee. However, in many situations, such as substantive amendments, the trustee may act only at the specific instruction of the noteholders. Therefore, a document called a consent solicitation is sent to noteholders. The consent solicitation describes the requested amendment, usually attaches the actual language of the amendment and requests each holder to indicate by a stated date whether it consents to the proposed amendments. Upon receipt of signed consents from the requisite number of noteholders and satisfaction of other conditions precedent to supplemental indentures specified by the amendment provisions in the indenture, the trustee will enter into the supplemental indenture with the issuer.

Like other debt documents, the amendment section of an indenture will make the usual distinction between amendments requiring the approval of all of the noteholders and those requiring less than unanimous approval. Additionally, indentures usually authorize the trustee to enter into amendments to cure mistakes, typographical errors and ambiguities without the noteholders' consent. Indentures sometimes also permit amendments without the noteholders' consent which impose additional requirements on the issuer or which are otherwise favorable to the noteholders.

§ 7:6   Amendments to Assigned Contracts

Section 9-405 of the Uniform Commercial Code creates a trap for the unwary in the context of amendments to a contract the rights under which have been assigned by one of the parties (see section 10:2.10). An assignee is not bound by amendments that are entered into when the assignee's rights to payment under the contract have been fully earned by performance. An assignee is also not bound by amendments if the rights to payment under the assigned contract have not been fully earned by performance and the other party has not been notified of the assignment. A party to a contract that is being amended will want to protect itself against the risk that the other party's rights under the contract have been assigned to a third party who may not be bound by the amendment. This is achieved by asking the other party for a representation that it hasn't assigned any of its rights under the contract. If the request for the representation results in disclosure of the existence of an assignment, the assignee is bound by the amendment if the assigned rights have not been fully earned by performance. If the assigned rights have been fully earned by performance, the assignee's consent to the amendment will be required for it to be bound thereby.

Chapter 8

Form and Formalities

§ 8:1   Introduction

The difference between "form" and "substance" in contracts is often a very subtle one. The way an idea is expressed can often affect its perceived meaning, so good lawyers take the form of a contract very seriously. The substance of an agreement is a collaborative effort among the lawyers and the business people; the reduction of that substance into a written contract is the province of the lawyers.

Some people may believe that lawyers pay too much attention to the form, the details, the typos, the so-called "nits." This may be true, but to use a cliché, the devil is in the details. Lawyers who have sweated over an interpretation issue that turned on a misplaced word, incorrect punctuation or a mistaken cross-reference (that is, any lawyer who has regularly worked with contracts for more than a few years) will be hesitant to dismiss anything as merely form over substance.

Our legal system today requires fewer formalities than at any time in its history. The concept of "forms of action," which dictated that a plaintiff failing to use the proper form of pleadings would lose its opportunity to proceed, has given way to a system where the substance of the pleadings rather than their form will determine whether the plaintiff has an actionable case. Similarly, in medieval England the transfer of an interest in real property was accompanied by the transferor's presentation to the transferee of a piece of turf, a tree branch or the like in order to signify delivery of seisin. See section 8:2.2.[1]

It would be a mistake, however, to think that all formalities can be dispensed with. There are a number of reasons why certain of them are of continued importance:

- some formalities are legally necessary

- many of the formalities described in this chapter are customary, and thus their absence may cause a reader to wonder whether the draftsperson knew what he was doing

- some formalities are followed because they make the contract easier to read—in other words, they promote the user-friendliness of the contract.

A good craftsman cares about both the appearance and utility of his work. Likewise, a good lawyer cares about the appearance as well as the substance of his work product. Rightly or wrongly, lawyers are often evaluated by third parties (including other lawyers) by the appearance of their work. Further, a draftsperson who cannot maintain internal consistency in an agreement, who fails to produce an accu-

---

1. At the beginning of the author's career, he often was required to prepare a collateral assignment from a form that started with the following statement: "KNOW ALL YE MEN BY THESE PRESENTS." After a while, he realized that this phrase was not legally necessary, and probably had a genealogy tracing back to the Middle Ages.

rate table of contents, or who produces an agreement with headings that are misleading, will often be the same lawyer who is unable to analyze issues completely and who fails to draft the parties' agreements clearly and effectively.

§ 8:2 Legal Requirements

Certain formalities are, in the instances described in this section, legally required.[2] For that reason, it is extremely important to employ them where necessary to ensure the effectiveness and enforceability of the contract. On the other hand, do not use them where not legally necessary; there is no need to complicate things with unneeded formalism.

§ 8:2.1 *Execution*

Every written contract must be signed, or "executed" by each party to the contract. This is an absolute requirement: failure to have the parties execute the written contract means that the contract has not been entered into and may not be enforced by the parties.

There are several wrinkles to this absolute principle. Although a written contract may not exist because one or more of the parties have not executed it, oral agreements may be valid and enforceable. There are a number of legal issues that arise in connection with determining the enforceability of oral agreements—including the statute of frauds and the rules of evidence—that are beyond the scope of this book. Suffice it to say that it is always preferable to have every agreement embodied in a signed writing.

Some contracts as a legal matter only require the signature of one party: for example, guarantees and security agreements. However, if the contract is nonetheless designed to be signed by both parties, the absence of either party's signature would raise significant doubts as to its enforceability.

What does it mean for a party to execute a contract? In the case of a person, the answer is obvious: he must sign his name at the end of the

---

2. Different jurisdictions may have specific requirements as to certain requirements or formalities that are not addressed here.

contract.[3] The answer is more complicated in the case of agreements being signed by corporations, partnerships, limited liability companies and other legal entities. A contract is executed on behalf of an entity by an individual who is properly authorized to execute the contract on its behalf. A basic due diligence function is determining that the person who signs for an entity has the authority to do so. In the case of a corporation this involves a review of the corporation's certificate of incorporation and by-laws and the resolutions of the board of directors authorizing the corporation to enter into the contract. Similar reviews are necessary in the case of other types of entities. The legal principle of apparent authority may be applicable, but the responsible lawyer will not rely on something as ephemeral as this; she will want to review the documentary chain of authority. In many transactions, legal opinions are required with respect to whether the agreements have been "duly executed."

[A]   Power of Attorney

An individual or entity may be authorized pursuant to a power of attorney to execute and deliver an agreement on behalf of another person or entity. This individual or entity is referred to as an "attorney-in-fact." The scope of the attorney-in-fact's authority must be clearly described in the power of attorney. Additionally, there are very specific legal requirements relating to powers of attorney that vary from state to state. In cases where an agreement is executed by an attorney-in-fact, the lawyer providing a legal opinion as to the due execution of an agreement, and the lawyer representing the other party, will each review the power of attorney carefully to make sure that it is itself enforceable. In the case of a power of attorney executed by an entity and not a natural person, all of the requirements of authorization discussed above must be satisfied.

---

3.   It is somewhat misleading to say that the signatures go at the end of the contract: they go at the end of the main text of the agreement, but usually before exhibits, schedules, annexes and other attachments.

[B]   Signature Blocks

There are conventions for the preparation of the signature blocks to be signed by the parties. For a natural person, a line with the person's name underneath is used:

_____

John K. Smith

For a corporate or limited liability signatory, the signature block will be set up to identify both the entity that is signing and the identity and capacity of the person actually signing for such entity.

ABC CORPORATION

By: _____
    Name:
    Title:

Note that the draftsperson should never fill in the "name" and "title" lines unless he is absolutely certain as to the individual who will sign the document on behalf of the entity; otherwise, hurried revisions will be required at closing if a different person shows up to sign.

If the signatory is a partnership, the signature block must reflect that the agreement is being executed by the partnership's general partner on behalf of the partnership. If the signing general partner is a natural person, the signature block can follow the format of the one seen above, with the person's name and title as general partner being indicated below the signature line. If the general partner is itself an entity, it complicates matters a bit. Here is how the signature block should look for a partnership whose general partner is a corporation:

ABC PARTNERS,
a limited partnership

By: ABC Incorporated,
its general partner

By: _____
    Name:
    Title:

This signature block tracks the chain of legal authority that permits the ultimate human signatory to execute the document on behalf of, and in a manner that binds, the entity that is a party to the agreement. In the above example, the individual is an officer who has been properly authorized (under the corporate general partner's certificate of incorporation, by-laws and board of directors' resolutions) to sign agreements on behalf of the corporate general partner. The corporate general partner, in turn, must be authorized under applicable partnership law and/or the partnership agreement to bind the partnership by executing agreements on its behalf.

The last and most complicated example, for purposes of this discussion, is a partnership the general partner of which is another partnership, which in turn has a corporate general partner. Here it is:

> ABC PARTNERS,
> a limited partnership
>
> By: ABC Partners II,
> a limited partnership,
> its general partner
>
> By: ABC Incorporated,
> its general partner
>
> By: _____
>   Name:
>   Title:

[C]   Original or Not?

Is it necessary to obtain an original execution copy of a contract, as opposed to a fax or photocopy showing the signatures of the parties? Many lawyers attach a talismanic importance to having an original signed copy of an agreement. The truth, however, is that possession of the signed original is important only in a few narrow circumstances. The first of these is when possession of the original signed document has independent legal significance. This is the case in the following instances:

- A negotiable promissory note, the possession of which can afford holder in due course status under the Uniform Commercial Code

- A negotiable document of title, possession of which gives the holder rights to the goods covered by the document

- A letter of credit, which often can't be drawn upon without delivery by the beneficiary of the original to the issuing bank

- A secured promissory note or a lease ("chattel paper" under the Uniform Commercial Code), the possession of which is effective to perfect a security interest

- An instrument or stock certificate, the delivery of which (together with an appropriate endorsement) constitutes a transfer of ownership

Signed originals are also required for certain agreements that must be publicly filed, such as mortgages. Also, having an original signature is helpful if the authenticity of the signature is in question. This is a relatively rare occurrence.[4]

It is customary at a closing for the parties to execute a sufficient number of copies of each agreement so that each party and its counsel can receive an original set. In most cases this is a reasonable practice, but there are circumstances when it can be taken to extremes. For example, in a syndicated bank financing involving 40 lenders, the borrower will object to signing 40 extra copies of every closing document.

§ 8:2.2 Delivery

A contract that has been executed by the parties is still not effective until it has been delivered. For delivery to occur, the parties must take steps indicating that they authorize the other parties to a contract to take possession of the signed contract and to treat it as effective. How is delivery evidenced? It can take a variety of forms:

---

4. It is incorrectly believed by some that the "best evidence rule" requires that a copy of an agreement may not be admitted into evidence. This is not the case. This rule requires an original to be submitted as evidence if it exists. If no original is available, a copy is admissible.

- Physical exchange of original signed agreements (this ordinarily occurs only in circumstances involving a single agreement).

- Delivery at a closing. This usually involves all of the contracts being executed and left on the closing table, and being deemed by the parties' agreement to be mutually and simultaneously delivered.

- Delivery by third party, such as a messenger, mail or delivery service.

- Delivery out of escrow. In a formal escrow, signed agreements are delivered to a third party (the escrow agent), which is authorized to deliver the agreements to the parties upon the satisfaction of specified conditions. An informal escrow is created where one party (or its counsel) delivers its executed agreement to the other party (or its counsel), on the understanding (preferably written) that the agreement is in escrow and may only be released upon the written or oral instructions of the signer (or its counsel).

- Delivery by fax. This is an increasingly common method, often employed by parties who cannot be present at a closing.

When *hasn't* delivery occurred? The most common situation where this question arises is at a closing. The execution of documents by the parties at a closing is a process that can be spread out over many hours or even days. The signatories execute the documents as they are finalized, after which the documents are placed in folders and left on the closing table. It is generally understood that each of these executed documents is not delivered until the moment in time when the parties mutually agree that the transaction is closed.

§ 8:2.3 Notarization

The vast majority of contracts do not as a legal matter require the signatures to be notarized, or "acknowledged." Certain contracts to be filed publicly, such as real estate conveyances and U.S. Patent and Trademark Office filings, require acknowledgments. Powers of attorney also typically require acknowledgments. While requiring a notarization may reduce the risk that the agreement will be signed fraudulently by some person other than the stated signatory, this is rarely a risk in large transactions.

§ 8:2.4   *Corporate Seals*

Corporate seals, like acknowledgments, are rarely a legal requirement, and are used most often in the context of agreements that require filing in the real estate records. Anyone can purchase a corporate seal, so the benefits of insisting upon a seal as a protection against fraud are almost nonexistent. If agreements are to be executed under seal, make sure that the seal exists and that it is brought to the closing. The best reason to resist any unnecessary requirement that agreements be executed under seal is that it introduces one more element to a closing that can go wrong—for example, where the seal apparatus is lost or forgotten.

§ 8:2.5   *Foreign Agreements*

All bets are off when it comes to the formalities that are required in connection with agreements governed by laws of jurisdictions outside the United States, and local counsel must be consulted. Many jurisdictions retain formalistic requirements that may strike American lawyers as quaint or archaic. For example, many German agreements must be read aloud from beginning to end (including schedules) by a notary, and some must be bound by a ribbon which is affixed to both the cover page and the back page with a waxed seal.

§ 8:3   Form: the Contract's "Package"

A 100-page agreement would be enforceable, as a strict legal matter, without a cover page, table of contents, paragraphs, sections or headings—in other words, 100 pages filled up solidly with words. There is no doubt, however, that such an agreement would be a nightmare for those having to work with it. Certainly a judge would not be favorably disposed toward the lawyer who created such an abomination.

Most of the issues described in this chapter may be avoided by the choice of a good precedent. A lawyer starting with a well-developed model for a stock purchase agreement won't have to spend much time making decisions regarding where and how to employ section headings, whether to employ whereas clauses, and so forth. Those decisions will already have been made by the creator of the form. However, the draftsperson should not be bound by the precedent as to these matters if the precedent is inadequate or if there is a good reason for going in a different direction. Furthermore, the commercial lawyer will often be faced with the assignment of drafting a contract from scratch. In such a case, a decision will need to be made as to each of the points covered in this section.

§ 8:3.1   *Letter Agreements*

A short agreement will often be in the form of a letter, addressed to one party from the other, and signed by the sender with a separate signature line for the receiving party. Agreements in this form are usually shorter and less formal than contracts not in letter form—although lengthy note purchase agreements used in the private placement of debt securities traditionally employ the letter format.

As with any other letter, a letter agreement will have a date at the top. This is the date that the letter agreement is signed by the sender, but will not necessarily be the date that it is signed by the recipient. If there is any reason why the recipient wants to make it clear that it signed the agreement on a date other than the date referred to at the top of the letter its signature block must have a line indicating the date of its signature, or alternatively the recipient can insert the date by hand beneath its signature.

Some letter agreements refer to the parties as "you" and "we." This makes it very difficult for the reader to remember who is who, and should be avoided in all but the shortest letter agreements. Define the parties in the normal fashion, as Seller, Borrower, Lessee, or by reference to the party's name: "ABC" for Alpha Binding Co., for example.

§ 8:3.2   *Title*

Most agreements have a title, for the same reason that anything else has a name: so we know what to call it. Because of their format, letter agreements do not usually have titles, but the parties will eventually start calling it something, even "the letter agreement." The naming of agreements is often taken care of by custom or by the precedent used to draft the agreement. A registration rights agreement is always called a registration rights agreement. An agreement to sell assets can be called an asset purchase agreement, a purchase agreement, an asset sale agreement, or a sale agreement. An agreement to provide revolving loans can be called a loan agreement, a credit agreement, a revolving loan agreement, or a revolving credit agreement.

An agreement's name should reflect its subject matter to decrease the likelihood of confusion in the future. If a contract among a corporation's shareholders covers a number of subjects including confidentiality, it would be a mistake to call it "Confidentiality Agreement." A lawyer looking for transfer restrictions might skip over a "Confidentiality Agreement," assuming that it does not deal with other issues; if the agreement is entitled "Stockholders Agreement," however, it signals the reader that it covers matters concerning the relationship among the stockholders, including transfer restrictions.

§ 8:3.3   *Cover Page*

Whether a contract has a cover page is a matter of style. When an agreement has a table of contents, it is customary to have a cover page so that the first page is not the table of contents. Short letter agreements usually do not have cover pages. A cover page may either refer solely to the name of the contract, or additionally recite the names of the parties and the date of the agreement.

§ 8:3.4   *Table of Contents*

Carefully crafted section headings and a good table of contents make an agreement easier for its users to work with. The table of contents allows the reader to see what subject matter is covered by the agreement and to find specific provisions with relative ease. The table of contents should also list all of the exhibits and schedules attached to the agreement.

If a provision warrants a separate section heading in the text, that section heading should be reflected in the table of contents. One well-known firm uses a form of credit agreement whose table of contents merely refers to "negative covenants" (a section of the agreement covering at least 20 pages), without identifying each one separately. As a result, a reader who wants to find a specific covenant is forced to flip through the entire 20-page section to find it; this is obviously inefficient. The goal must be to make the contract as user-friendly as possible.

A table of contents should not be inserted only at the time of execution; it should be included from the first draft, for the convenience of the parties as they review and negotiate successive drafts. If sections of the contract are deleted or added, the agreement should reflect such changes in the table of contents as they occur. Also, after the deal is closed check that the sections referred to in the table of contents actually begin on the pages that are specified for them. Many agreements have tables of contents that are misnumbered.

§ 8:3.5   Date

A contract must have a date. The agreement may provide that it becomes effective or that performance is required on a later date—but (except as described below) the date of the contract is the date that it is first executed and delivered.

The date of a contract is usually recited in the first paragraph. Sometimes the date is at the end of the contract with the signature lines. In a transaction which involves a number of related documents or a formal closing, all agreements and documents are usually dated the same date. Unless the closing date is known in advance with absolute certainty (this is rare), it is a good practice to leave the date blank, and fill it in only after the closing has actually occurred. Otherwise, the date in each document must be changed if the closing is delayed. (Some lawyers superstitiously believe filling in the dates too early in these circumstances may increase the likelihood of a delay.) Similarly, references in an agreement to other contracts that are to be dated the same date should refer to them as being "dated the date hereof." This avoids the need to refer to a specific date that will need to be filled in when the closing occurs.

A contract dated "*as of* December 31, 2000" may not have actually been entered into on that date. This device may be used where the parties don't want to fuss with putting the actual date of execution and delivery in the contract—for example, an employer sending an execution copy of an employment agreement to the employee on November 23 who expects that it will be signed by the employee within the next week may date the contract "as of November 30."

Sometimes an "as of" date is used to address a substantive concern. An example is where the parties to a contract wish to amend a provision requiring performance of an obligation by a date certain, say, December 31, 2000 and the obligation was not performed by that date. If the amendment extends the date for this performance to June 30, 2001, but the amendment itself is dated January 7, 2001, there would be a question as to whether the breach existed during the period from the date performance was required through the date of the amendment. One way to address this issue is to have the amendment explicitly provide for a waiver of this breach. On the other hand, neither party may want to acknowledge that a breach existed. An alternative approach is to date the amendment "as of December 31, 2000" so that the effect of the extension will be retroactive.[5]

Care must be taken where a contract is dated other than the date of execution and delivery, including where an "as of" date is used. If representations are made "as of the date hereof" or covenants are effective "from and after the date hereof," the lawyer must ensure that no technical problems ensue. For example, if a contract dated as of September 15 is actually signed by a party on September 30, and the contract contains a representation that the party "is in good standing in its state of incorporation on the date hereof," the representation would be breached by a failure to be in good standing on September 15, even if the problem was cured by September 30. Another example is a contract that provides for the payment of a fee or interest measured for a period "commencing on the date hereof"—if the contract bears an "as of" date, such a provision may not reflect the true intent of the parties because the measurement period will commence too late or too early. Also, the date of the conveyance of property may not be altered by the use of an "as of" date.

§ 8:3.6 Whereas Clauses

The "recitals" or the "preamble" are the paragraphs at the beginning of a contract that list the parties and recite the factual background of the contract. They are frequently referred to as "whereas" clauses because they take the form of one or more paragraphs starting

---

5. This technique may be ineffective to negate other ramifications of the existence of the breach (cross-default provisions, for example).

with the word "whereas" (usually capitalized), followed by a sentence such as : "Now, therefore, the parties hereto agree as follows." Often the whereas clauses are preceded by the heading "WITNESSETH." The words "witnesseth," "whereas" and "now therefore" are anachronisms and are not required for any legal reason.

The whereas clauses are not intended to have any substantive effect. Their purpose is to set the stage for the agreement, to give the reader an idea of what is going on. This is an important function in a contract that is just one component of a complicated transaction.

§ 8:3.7 *Headings*

The use of headings is another device not intended to have a substantive effect, but instead to make the agreement a more user-friendly tool. A heading should accurately reflect the contents of a provision, in a manner that will be useful to the reader. The headings should be sufficiently abundant so that the user can find provisions without too much effort. For example, a ten-page section of representations with 22 separate provisions will be difficult to use if the only heading is "representations" at the beginning. Instead, each separate provision should be identified with its own heading.

Sometimes one section of an agreement will have provisions covering two or more topics. The better practice here would be to create different sections, each with its own heading. If not, then it is important that the heading reflect the fact that multiple subjects are covered; otherwise the reader may be misdirected. For example, a single section which sets forth requirements as to both insurance and the maintenance of property should bear the heading "Insurance; Maintenance of Property."

There is often a boilerplate provision in the miscellaneous section to the effect that the headings are "for convenience of construction only and not intended to have any substantive purpose." See section 10:2.5.

§ 8:3.8   Section Numbering

The main purpose for employing a numbering[6] system is to make the contract easier to read and use. As described earlier, a 100-page contract written as a single paragraph without divisions or guideposts would be enforceable but almost impossible to use. Contracts often contain internal cross-references; these would be impossible without a numbering system. The key feature of an effective numbering system is consistency. Articles, sections, subsections, and sub-subsections should all be numbered consistently. Maintaining this numbering hierarchy forces the draftsperson to better organize the document and helps the reader follow the text.

§ 8:3.9   Organization of the Agreement

The manner in which the different parts of a contract are organized and ordered is an area where style and functionality come jointly into play. The draftsperson using a precedent to draft an agreement will not need to think about the organization of the agreement; it will be dictated by the precedent. But the lawyer who creates an agreement from scratch should give some thought to how it should be organized—in other words, which provisions go where. An agreement of any significant length should first be divided into large sections, the equivalent of chapters in a book. These are often referred to as "Articles" but can also be called "Sections." The provisions of an agreement should be divided into articles based on the purpose they serve. In many cases, each different article will cover a different type of building block provision—for example, representations will be contained in one article and covenants in another.

In most agreements the definitions appear immediately after any whereas clauses. The advantage of this is that the reader knows where to find them, since this is their traditional spot. The disadvantage is that someone reading the agreement from front to back can easily get bogged down in the definitions. Of course, there is nothing that stops the reader from postponing the definitions and moving to the other provisions (usually the best approach in reviewing an agreement, by

---

6. The term "numbering" is used to encompass the use not only of identifying numbers but also identifying letters.

the way). Where possible, the first article(s) appearing after the definitions should contain the operative provisions—i.e., the subject matter of the agreement. Then, the articles containing the building blocks are set forth. The last article in an agreement is usually the miscellaneous provisions. Sometimes a provision will not fit neatly into any of the agreement's articles. The draftsperson's first instinct in this situation is to add the provision at the end of the agreement, in the miscellaneous section. This is not necessarily a bad approach, but it suggests that when one is reviewing a contract, one ignores the miscellaneous section at one's own risk.

§ 8:4 Aesthetics

Contracts are the tangible embodiment of the transactional lawyer's work. Significant skill is required to structure and negotiate a transaction effectively, to counsel a client properly, and to bring the transaction to closing. But all of these are ephemeral; the written agreement is the distillation of all of this work. That, of course, is why it is critical that it be substantively correct and precise. That is also why most lawyers take extreme care to make sure that a contract's form and appearance are as pristine as its content. In addition to the elements of form, certain aesthetic considerations must be taken into account.

§ 8:4.1 Font

The lawyer should select a font that the reader will not notice. Traditional styles such as Times New Roman, Bookman, Century and Garamond all fall within this description. The size of the type used is also a consideration. In order to maximize the agreement's readability under normal circumstances, nothing smaller than 12 point should be used.

§ 8:4.2 Spacing

Agreements are almost always single spaced. Although this makes them somewhat more difficult to read, it is preferable to double spacing, which would double the length of documents, raising environmental and logistical concerns. On the other hand, there is no reason that the line spacing in an agreement shouldn't be set at 1.1, 1.2 or 1.3. This increment in spacing may reduce eyestrain.

§ 8:4.3   *Margins*

The margins should be set to leave ample space at the top, bottom and sides. A page with inadequate margins is unfriendly to the reader. The eye tends to get lost following a line of type that is too long. Narrow margins also make marking comments more difficult, and lead to a cramped markup that will be more challenging to follow.

§ 8:4.4   *Paragraphs*

There is almost nothing more daunting to the reader of an agreement than to confront an entire page of single-spaced text without paragraph breaks. Such a page is visually and psychologically difficult to get through. The antidote is simple: break up the text into smaller sections or paragraphs. In addition to making the document easier to read, this will make it easier to discuss and negotiate. It is much simpler to refer to a provision that is in the first sentence of the third paragraph on the page, for example, than to try to provide verbal directions to a provision that is buried in a full page of unbroken text.

Chapter 9

Building Blocks in Detail

§ 9:1   Introduction

In this chapter we look in detail at the way certain of the building block provisions are used in two different types of transactions: a bank loan and an acquisition of one company by another. Together, they provide an opportunity to explore a broad array of important contract provisions. Both transactions involve one party making a significant investment in another, but are quite different in terms of the nature of the business relationship that they create. The credit agreement creates contractual obligations that run between the parties for years, while under the acquisition agreement the business relationship ends (for the most part) at the closing. By examining the way that representations, covenants, conditions and remedy provisions are used in typical credit and acquisition transactions, the reader will develop a deeper understanding of the ways that these provisions are used to address particular business objectives and concerns.

First, however, this chapter will discuss a set of representations that are familiar to every practitioner who works with contracts, regardless of type.

§ 9:2   Enforceability Representations

Many contracts contain representations relating to facts that could affect the enforceability of the contract (referred to here as "enforceability representations"). Whether or not these representations are made is usually a matter of custom and negotiating leverage. In addition, where performance is only required from one party, usually only that party will make these (or any other) representations.

It is also important to understand the specific purpose of a subset of the enforceability representations: the representations regarding organization, power and authority and corporate or other action (sections 9:2.1 through 9:2.3 below). These representations go to the *capacity* of an entity (as opposed to a natural person) to enter into the contract. A corporation, limited liability company, limited partnership or other entity has not validly executed and delivered an agreement unless (a) it validly exists as an artificial legal person, (b) it has the legal power and authority to enter into the agreement and (c) all necessary organizational action has been taken to authorize the entity's entering into the agreement. Not only are these representations usually required of contracting entities, they are often the subject of legal opinions and closing conditions as well.

§ 9:2.1   *Organization*

> The Company is a duly organized and validly existing corpora-
> tion in good standing under the laws of the jurisdiction of its or-
> ganization and is duly qualified and authorized to do business
> and is in good standing in all jurisdictions where it is required to
> be so qualified and where the failure to be so qualified would
> reasonably be expected to have a Material Adverse Effect.

This representation goes to whether the party making the
representation has been properly organized, is validly existing as an
entity and is in good standing.[1] Due diligence for this representation
would include ordering a certified certificate of incorporation (or
analogous filing for a limited partnership or limited liability company) and a good standing certificate from the state where the entity is
organized. This representation is requested to avoid the risk that an
entity does not legally exist as an artificial person.

This provision often also covers the entity's good standing and
qualification to do business in states other than its state of organization. Failure to be so qualified in a state doesn't affect the entity's capacity to enter in the contract, but may impair its ability to appear in
the courts of that state to enforce the contract. Often this portion of
the representation is subject to a materiality qualification, as in the
above example.

§ 9:2.2   *Power and Authority*

> The Company has the corporate power and authority to (a) own
> its property and assets and to transact the business in which it is
> engaged and presently proposes to engage and (b) execute, de-
> liver and perform this Agreement.

An entity's ability to enter into and perform different kinds of contracts may be limited by its organizational documents or, in the case
of regulated entities, by statute or regulation. This representation is a

---

1.   An entity's being properly organized depends on whether all legal require-
     ments were properly followed in connection with its creation. Being validly
     existing goes to the *present* valid existence of the entity. This technical dis-
     tinction is often the subject of debate in the context of legal opinions, but
     not contract representations.

statement that there are no such restrictions on the party's ability to conduct its business or to execute, deliver and perform the contract. Enforcement of an agreement against an entity that lacks the legal right or power to enter into the agreement may be subject to an *ultra vires* defense. The due diligence required to ensure that this representation is made correctly is a review of the organizational documents and, if the party is a regulated entity, of all applicable statutes and regulations.

§ 9:2.3   *Necessary Action*

> The Company has taken all necessary action to authorize the execution, delivery and performance of this Agreement.

This is another representation that applies only to entities. It states that all actions required by its organizational documents and by applicable law in connection with the execution, delivery and performance of the contract by the entity have been properly taken. In the case of a corporation, this representation would be correct if the corporation's board of directors had duly adopted a resolution authorizing it to enter into the agreement. In the case of a limited or general partnership, a general partner must execute and deliver the agreement. The partnership agreement must be reviewed to determine whether other actions or consents may be required. If the general partner is itself an entity, there must be appropriate action taken by such entity. For example, if the general partner is a corporation, its board of directors must adopt a resolution authorizing its execution and delivery of the contract on behalf of the partnership, in its capacity as general partner.

Most limited liability company statutes provide a great amount of latitude to the organizers of an LLC as to how acts of the LLC may be authorized. The limited liability company agreement may grant this power to each member, a single member, a board of members, or one or more managers.

§ 9:2.4   *Due Execution and Delivery*

The Company has duly executed and delivered this Agreement.

This representation states, first, that the agreement has been properly *executed* by or on behalf of the party making the representation. In the case of an entity, it means that the agreement was signed by an officer or representative who was properly authorized to do so. To ensure that this representation is true, the lawyers should (a) review the organizational documents to ascertain whether there are any specific requirements relating to execution and delivery of contracts (for example, a requirement that certain kinds of contracts be signed by specific officers), (b) determine whether the officer or representative signing on behalf of the entity is authorized to do so, by inspecting the organizational documents and any authorizing resolutions, and (c) obtain evidence that the signer's signature is genuine, usually in the form of an incumbency certificate, in which the secretary (or other officer) of the entity certifies the authenticity of the signatures of the individual signers. See section 3:5.1[A].

The representation also covers due *delivery* of the agreement. An executed contract is not enforceable until it has been delivered by each of the parties. Deal-specific delivery requirements may exist. For example, in the case of an agreement signed by the parties and placed in escrow subject to the satisfaction of stated conditions, valid delivery of the contract would not occur until the conditions to delivery of the agreement out of escrow were satisfied.

§ 9:2.5   *No Conflict*

The execution, delivery and performance by the Company of this Agreement will not (i) contravene any applicable provision of any law, statute, rule or regulation, or any order, writ, injunction or decree of any court or governmental instrumentality, (ii) conflict with or result in any breach of any agreement to which the Company is a party or (iii) violate any provision of the Company's Certificate of Incorporation or By-Laws.

This is a representation that the execution, delivery and performance of the contract does not violate or conflict with other legal restrictions or arrangements to which the representing party is subject. It cannot be made if there are any provisions in the entity's organizational documents or other agreements that would prohibit, or impose conditions that have not been satisfied on, the execution, delivery or performance of the agreement. The representation also cannot be made if there are restrictions on the party's ability to execute, deliver or perform[2] the agreement under statutes, rules, regulations, judgments or orders. To ensure that this representation is correct requires a careful analysis of organizational documents, contracts and applicable laws, rules, regulations, judgments and orders. It should be obvious why this is a standard representation: the party receiving the representation wants to be certain that entering into the contract is not going to give rise to a conflict which could be the basis for litigation or worse.[3]

§ 9:2.6   *Governmental Approvals*

> No authorization or approval or other action by, and no notice to or filing with, any governmental authority or regulatory body is required for the due execution, delivery and performance by the Company of this Agreement, other than those that have been duly obtained or made and are in full force and effect.

This representation covers governmental approvals required in connection with the party's entering into the contract or performing under it. The representing party must determine whether any such approvals are required and, if so, obtain them. Examples of governmental approvals that may be required in connection with particular transactions include the following: Federal Communications Commission approval of a contract to sell a radio station; the passage of the necessary waiting period under the Hart-Scott-Rodino Antitrust Improvements Act in connection with certain mergers and acquisitions; and the receipt of a necessary zoning variance in connection with an agreement to purchase and develop real property.

---

2. It is possible for performance to be restricted even if execution and delivery are not. For example, a company enters into an agreement requiring it to do A, B and C. The company is subject to regulation prohibiting it from doing C. The regulation is not violated by the company executing and delivering the contract, nor is it violated when the company performs its A and B obligations. Because of the potential conflict created by its obligation to perform C, however, the company would not be able to make the representation.
3. See section 6:3.4[C], note 3.

The provision contains an exclusion for approvals "that have been duly obtained or made and are in full force and effect." Without this language, the representation would be untrue if necessary approvals had already been obtained. Of course, this representation may require exceptions on the date that an agreement is signed if approvals are required for performance (as opposed to execution and delivery). In this case, obtaining the approvals would be added as a condition precedent.

§ 9:2.7 Enforceability

> This Agreement constitutes the legal, valid and binding obligation of the Company enforceable against the Company in accordance with its terms, except to the extent that the enforceability thereof may be limited by applicable bankruptcy, insolvency, reorganization, moratorium or similar laws affecting creditors' rights generally and by equitable principles (regardless of whether enforcement is sought in equity or at law).

This representation states a legal conclusion that in part depends on each of the other representations discussed above. In other words, the enforceability of a contract may be impaired if a party isn't validly organized, if it doesn't have the necessary power and authority, if it hasn't taken the necessary organizational actions to enter into the contract, if the contract hasn't been duly executed and delivered, if the contract conflicts with other contracts to which it is a party or with its organizational documents or other legal requirements or if the contract requires governmental consents that aren't obtained. Additionally, the enforceability representation constitutes a conclusion that the necessary legal elements of a valid contract formation—consideration, mutuality, offer and acceptance and the like—are present, and that no other defenses to enforcement exist.

The qualification at the end is known as the bankruptcy and equitable principles exception. This exception recognizes that a contract may be wholly or partly unenforceable if the promisor is the subject of a bankruptcy proceeding, or may be modified by a court in the exercise of its powers of equity, notwithstanding that all enforceability requirements have been satisfied. Bankruptcy law provides, among other things, for the application of the automatic stay, which prevents enforcement of contract claims against the bankruptcy debtor except through specific procedures provided for under the Bankruptcy Code.

The representations discussed in this section are often the subject of legal opinions required as a condition precedent to the effectiveness or closing of the agreement in which they are contained. Since the subject matter of these representations consists primarily of legal conclusions, it is appropriate for these legal opinions to be requested. Whether or not these opinions are given is usually a matter of custom. For example, opinions are almost always provided by borrower's counsel in connection with a loan agreement, but are not usually required in connection with an employment agreement.

§ 9:3 Credit-related Provisions

Specific representations, covenants and remedial provisions have evolved to protect a party to a contract against the credit risk of its counterparty. Credit risk, the risk that the obligor will become financially unable to perform its payment obligations when required under the contract, is present any time a party has an ongoing contractual obligation to make payments to another party.

An understanding of the fundamental principles of bankruptcy law is necessary to understand credit risk. In a bankruptcy liquidation, the value of assets subject to liens goes first to satisfy the claims secured by those liens. Any excess value attributable to such assets plus the value of all unencumbered assets is shared ratably by all unsecured creditors. In a bankruptcy reorganization, where the debtor in possession keeps its assets, the value that each creditor is entitled to receive under the reorganization plan is based on the value that such creditor would have received in a liquidation.[4] So, it is easy to see why a creditor with a contractual claim against a debtor has an ongoing interest in the credit or financial health of the debtor. A financial failure by the debtor could result in its bankruptcy and the creditor's loss of all or a portion of its claim, depending on the existence and amount of other secured and unsecured claims and the value of the debtor's assets.

The magnitude of credit risk is a function of the amount that is at stake at any one time. Take a supply contract that requires the purchaser to pay for each shipment within 15 days of delivery. The con-

4. This is an extremely oversimplified description.

tract further provides that the seller is not obligated to make any shipments if payment for any previous shipment is in arrears. If the purchaser fails to pay for a shipment, the seller can limit its credit risk to the amount of that payment by not making any additional deliveries until the delinquent account has been settled. By allowing the seller to limit the credit risk, this type of arrangement is likely to result in the seller requiring fewer provisions in the contract relating to the purchaser's financial condition.

On the opposite end of the spectrum is a term loan agreement under which a loan is made at closing, which the borrower promises to repay in installments, with interest, over a stated term. Once the term loan is made, the money is gone—typically, having been spent by the borrower on capital assets or acquisitions. Before making the loan, the lender will have reached a conclusion that the borrower's financial condition over the term of the loan will enable it to meet its principal and interest obligations. However, the lender will add provisions to the contract that protect it against the borrower's financial deterioration. These may include provisions that (a) require the borrower to provide regular financial information, (b) restrict the borrower's ability to act in a manner that would make it less creditworthy, and (c) give the lender certain legal rights in the event that the borrower gets into financial (or other) trouble.

A well-made credit decision will take into account the separate financial characteristics of each entity that is part of the credit. Two critical rules[5] apply in this context:

- In a bankruptcy, separate legal entities are treated separately.

- A creditor with a claim against a company does not by virtue thereof obtain a claim against any of the company's subsidiaries, parents or sister companies.

Many businesses are comprised of more than one entity. A creditor making a credit decision as to a multiple-entity business will want a combination of covenants relating to the entities, covenants limiting intercompany transactions, and guarantees—herein called the "credit

---

5. These rules may not apply if there is a piercing of the corporate veil, either through the application of the bankruptcy principle of substantive consolidation or otherwise.

package"—that protects the creditor from the loss of the value on which its credit decision was based.

Let's work with an example: suppose a bank is making a loan to Company A, whose business is comprised of three divisions. The assets, liabilities and business of two of the divisions are in separate subsidiaries, with the third division being owned directly by Company A. The following chart illustrates the different levels of credit protection the bank can create by the use of loan documentation. In reading this chart, the basic rules of bankruptcy distribution discussed above must be kept in mind.

Least Protection

No covenants	The lender has no protection against actions of Company A and its subsidiaries that would reduce their creditworthiness.
No guarantees from subsidiaries	The lender has no claim against the subsidiaries. In the event of a bankruptcy, the only economic benefit to the lender of each subsidiary's business is the remaining value after satisfaction of the claims of such subsidiary's creditors (and the lender must share such value with other creditors of Company A).

Better Protection

Covenants applicable to Company A only	The lender is protected against Company A's directly-owned business (the division) becoming less creditworthy. Because the covenants don't apply also to the subsidiaries, there is no similar protection as to the subsidiaries' businesses.
No guarantees from subsidiaries	Same as above.

Better Protection

Covenants generally applicable to Company A and its subsidiaries	The lender is protected against actions by any of the entities that would result in loss of creditworthiness.

No covenants restricting intercompany transactions	The lender is not protected against transactions that result in value moving from Company A to its subsidiaries. Any such transaction impairs the lender's credit position because the lender has no recourse to the value transferred to the subsidiary.
No guarantees from subsidiaries	Same as above.

Better Protection

Covenants generally applicable to all entities	Same as above.
Covenants restricting intercompany transactions	The lender is protected against intercompany transfers of value.
No guarantees from subsidiaries	Same as above.

Best Protection

Covenants generally applicable to all entities	Same as above.
Covenants restricting intercompany transactions	Same as above; may not be necessary because of protection afforded by existence of guarantees.
Guarantees from subsidiaries	These provide a direct claim by the lender against the subsidiaries and their assets. As a result, the lender is more likely to permit intercompany transactions by which value migrates from one entity to another.

This demonstrates that a creditor is best protected by requiring guarantees from each entity that makes up its credit. The next-best protection is having covenants that prevent value from being transferred to a non-guarantor.[6]

The remainder of this section is a detailed discussion of the other most common credit-related representations, covenants and remedial

---

6. An additional and important method of credit enhancement is obtaining a lien on the assets of obligors and guarantors. This gives the creditor the benefit of the value of the collateral, to the exclusion of unsecured creditors.

provisions. These provisions are found in debt agreements but should also be included in any other agreement where credit concerns need to be addressed.

§ 9:3.1   *Representations*

A party entering into a contractual relationship involving credit risk will normally undertake financial due diligence before entering into the contract. This would include reviewing the debtor's business plan, financial statements and projections, reviewing the debtor's key contracts, analyzing the collection history of its accounts receivable and so forth. This due diligence is usually buttressed by credit-related representations which, taken together, provide a snapshot of the debtor's financial condition. Some of these credit-related representations are discussed below.

[A]   Financial Statements

> The audited consolidated balance sheet of the Debtor for the fiscal year ended December 31, 2001, the unaudited consolidated balance sheet of the Debtor for the fiscal period ended March 31, 2002, and the related consolidated statements of operations and cash flows of the Debtor for the fiscal periods ended as of said dates (which annual financial statements have been examined by Big Accounting Firm LLP, certified public accountants), present fairly in all material respects the financial position of the Debtor on a consolidated basis at the date of such financial statements and the results for the periods covered thereby. All such financial statements have been prepared in accordance with GAAP, consistently applied and subject, in the case of the March 31, 2002 financial statements, to normal year-end audit adjustments.

The purpose of this representation is to have the debtor stand behind the accuracy of its historical financial statements. Since financial statements are probably relied on by a creditor more than any other due diligence item in making a credit decision, this representation is extremely important. It will always cover the debtor's most recent annual financial statements, as well as the most recent monthly or quarterly financial statements. Because consistency of presentation is fundamental to the reliability of financial statements, the representation usually includes a statement that the financial statements have been prepared in accordance with generally accepted accounting principles (GAAP), consistently applied. The key statement is that the financial statements "fairly present the financial condition and results of operations" of the debtor. This statement is not true if the financial statements are incorrect.

Note the distinction between audited and unaudited financial statements. Typically, a company's annual financial statements are audited by certified public accountants who issue an auditor's report that states that the financial statements fairly present the company's financial position and results of operations in accordance with GAAP. Interim financial statements—those prepared on a quarterly, and sometimes monthly, basis—are usually not audited and are therefore, as the last sentence of the representation indicates, subject to being retroactively adjusted as a part of the year-end audit process.

[B]   Projections

> The financial projections attached hereto as Exhibit P have been prepared on a basis consistent with the Debtor's financial statements and are based on good faith estimates and assumptions made by the Debtor. On the date hereof the Debtor believes that the projections are reasonable and attainable, <u>provided, however,</u> that projections as to future events are not to be viewed as facts and the actual results during the periods covered may differ from the projected results.

This representation addresses projected financial information, as opposed to historical financial statements. Projections are predictions as to a party's financial condition and results of operations in the future, and therefore cannot be the subject of a representation that is expressed with the same level of certainty as a representation regarding historical financial results. The representation above is typical: the debtor states that it believes in the projections, and that the assumptions that went into the development of the projections were reasonable. The creditor could allege a breach of this representation by asserting that the debtor didn't actually believe, at the time the representation was made, that the projections were attainable; but the mere fact that the results set forth in the projections are not achieved would not by itself constitute a breach.

[C]   Material Adverse Change

> Since December 31, 2001, there has been no material adverse
> change to the business, assets, liabilities, financial condition or
> prospects of the Debtor and its subsidiaries, taken as a whole.

This is an extremely important representation from a credit standpoint. It is premised on the creditor's reliance on the debtor's financial statements, and constitutes assurance by the debtor to the creditor that nothing significant has happened to it or its financial position since the date of the financial statements. The date in this provision will always be the date of a set of financial statements reviewed by the creditor. There may be a discussion as to whether the date should be the most recent audited statements, or available subsequent unaudited statements. The creditor will usually prefer the date of the audited statements, since the accountants' audit provides it with a more certain baseline. The debtor may advocate the use of more recent audited statements, particularly if the trend of the business between the date of the unaudited and subsequent unaudited financial statements was negative. A material adverse change test is always easier to meet if the starting point is lower.

[D]   Litigation

> There are no actions, suits or proceedings pending or, to the
> knowledge of the Debtor threatened, against the Debtor or any
> of its subsidiaries that (a) relate to this Agreement or any of the
> transactions contemplated hereby, or (b) are reasonably likely to
> be determined adversely to the Debtor or such subsidiary, and,
> if so adversely determined, could reasonably be expected to
> have a material adverse effect.

Why should the existence of litigation be part of a credit decision? Because a judgment resulting from litigation becomes a financial claim that might interfere with the debtor's ability to satisfy its other financial obligations. In addition, a judgment can be converted into a lien on the debtor's assets. In an extreme case, a large judgment might trigger a bankruptcy filing by the debtor.

The litigation representation set forth above is typical. The first part addresses actions, suits and other proceedings that relate to the transaction pursuant to which the contract is being entered into. In other words, if there is any litigation at all related to the transaction it must be disclosed here.[7]

The second part of the representation relates to all other litigation (i.e., litigation *not* relating to the transaction). The above language limits the representation to litigation that satisfies two criteria. The first is that the litigation is reasonably likely to be adversely determined. Thus, if the debtor has been sued on a claim that it believes to be spurious, it may conclude that such claim is not reasonably likely to be adversely determined and therefore not covered by the representation. The second criterion is that the litigation is reasonably likely to have a material adverse effect if adversely determined. Even if the debtor believes it will lose the case, the litigation will not be picked up by the representation if the claim is for an amount of damages that is not material. This approach allows the debtor to make subjective determinations regarding the merits and materiality of the litigation. The other approach is to require the representation to be made "flat"—that is, draft the representation to cover *all* litigation. The benefit of this approach to the creditor is that there is no subjective element and therefore no possibility of a surprise. The problem is that it will result in the debtor having to disclose *all* litigation, and the creditor will then have to perform its own examination and draw its own conclusions as to the materiality of each disclosed item of litigation.

Note also that the representation as to threatened litigation is subject to a knowledge qualification. This is one of the few instances where such a qualification is generally accepted, on the basis that it would be unfair to hold a party accountable for a breach of this representation due to third party threats that aren't known to the debtor.

[E] Compliance with Law

> The Debtor and each of its subsidiaries are in compliance with all applicable statutes, rules, regulations, orders and decrees, except where the failure to be in compliance could not reasonably be expected to have a Material Adverse Effect.

---

7. This part of the representation is not strictly a credit-related provision. Even where there are no ongoing payment obligations, a contract party will want to be aware of all litigation relating to the contract itself or the related transactions.

This representation is designed to elicit disclosure of any violations of law or judicial orders or decrees. The material adverse effect qualifier is usually the only part of this representation that is negotiated. It may be resisted by the creditor on the basis that there shouldn't be *any* violations of law, material or otherwise. The debtor's counterargument is that the materiality standard does not deprive the recipient of the protection that it wants against violations of law that could result in some material reduction to the debtor's creditworthiness. Without a materiality qualifier the representation could be untrue as a result of some insignificant infraction. (See section 5:2.1.)

[F] Payment of Taxes

> The Debtor and its subsidiaries have paid all material taxes, assessments and governmental charges or levies imposed upon them or their income or profits, or upon any properties owned by them, prior to the date on which penalties attach thereto, except for any such tax, assessment, charge or levy being diligently contested in good faith and with respect to which reserves have been established in accordance with GAAP.

This reflects the creditor's general concern about the existence of claims against the debtor. Tax claims are a particular issue, because taxing authorities may obtain liens securing their claims that in certain circumstances may take priority over the creditor's.

There are two customary qualifiers in the above language. First, the limitation of the covenant to material taxes allows the debtor to make the representation despite a delinquency in the payment of an immaterial amount of taxes. Second, the provision allows the debtor to make the representation even if it has not paid taxes, so long as the debtor is contesting the validity of the tax and has entered on its books any reserve required by GAAP. Without this carveout, the debtor would be required to pay even wrongfully asserted taxes.

[G] True and Complete Disclosure

> All factual information (taken as a whole) delivered in writing by or on behalf of the Debtor to the Creditor for purposes of or in connection with this Agreement or the transactions contemplated hereby is true and accurate in all material respects and does not omit any material fact necessary to prevent such infor-

mation (taken as a whole) from being misleading in any material respect.

This representation is designed to counteract the principle of *caveat emptor,* that a contracting party is under no obligation to volunteer information not otherwise required to be disclosed by the agreement. It reflects the reality that even an exhaustive set of representations may not be effective to uncover some adverse fact that may be relevant to the creditor's credit decision. It is a difficult representation to object to, because doing so creates the impression that there is something to hide. This representation is often referred to as a "10b-5 representation" because it is modeled on the disclosure standard set forth in Rule 10b-5 under the Securities Exchange Act of 1934.

[H]   Other Representations

There are numerous other more specialized credit-related representations that regularly appear in credit-related documentation. These representations cover subjects such as environmental, ERISA and intellectual property matters. In addition, individual transactions often give rise to representations that are specially tailored to address specific risks and circumstances.

§ 9:3.2   *Affirmative Covenants*

Affirmative covenants in credit documentation are sometimes referred to as the housekeeping covenants: they require the debtor to do the kinds of things that good companies ordinarily do, such as pay its taxes, insure its operations, and so on. Accordingly, there is usually a limited amount of negotiation of these covenants.

[A]   Reporting Covenants

Just as the primary basis for a creditor's initial credit decision is to review the debtor's financial statements, the primary means for continued oversight of the credit is the regular review of financial statements over the life of the contract. This is less of an issue where the debtor is a public company whose quarterly and annual financial statements will be publicly available. A private company, on the other hand, has no obligation to deliver financial reports or other information to its creditors absent a contractual obligation to do so.

Interim Financial Statements

> The Debtor shall deliver to the Creditor, within (a) 30 days after the end of each fiscal month of the Debtor (other than the last fiscal month in any fiscal quarter), the consolidated and consolidating balance sheets of the Debtor and its subsidiaries as at the end of such month and the related consolidated and consolidating statements of income and retained earnings and of cash flows for such month and for the elapsed portion of the fiscal year ended with the last day of such month, in each case setting forth comparative figures for the corresponding month in the prior fiscal year, and (b) 45 days after the close of each fiscal quarter of the Debtor (other than the last fiscal quarter of the fiscal year), the consolidated and consolidating balance sheets of the Debtor and its subsidiaries as at the end of such fiscal quarter and the related consolidated and consolidating statements of income and retained earnings and of cash flows for such fiscal quarter and for the elapsed portion of the fiscal year ended with the last day of such fiscal quarter, in each case setting forth comparative figures for the corresponding quarter in the prior year, which shall be in reasonable detail and be accompanied by a certification by the chief financial officer of the Debtor that they fairly present in all material respects the financial condition of the Debtor and its subsidiaries as of the dates indicated and the results of their operations and changes in their cash flows for the periods indicated, subject to normal year-end audit adjustments.

There are several things to note here. The monthly and quarterly financial statements must be delivered 30 and 45 days, respectively, from the last day of the reporting period. These time periods are fairly standard, but may be subject to negotiation. (Under the securities laws, the time period for a public company to report its quarterly financial statements is 45 days.) Monthly statements are only required for the first two months in any quarter, and quarterly statements are only required for the first three quarters of a fiscal year. This is intended to avoid duplicative reporting, but is often negotiated (for example, by a party who wants to receive financial information as soon as possible).

The description of the financial statements to be delivered (here, a balance sheet, income statement, statement of retained earnings and cash flow statement) should conform to the financial statements that the reporting company actually produces. The above language refers to consolidated and consolidating statements—the former are combined for the reporting entity and its subsidiaries, while the latter are broken out separately for each entity in the group. There is a requirement for comparative statements, which show comparisons to the same financial statements in the corresponding period of the preceding year. The debtor is also required to deliver year-to-date statements—statements for the period commencing at the beginning of the present fiscal year end and ending with the period being reported on. Lastly, there is a requirement that the chief financial officer certify the financial statements as fairly presenting in all material respects the financial condition of the entities being reported on, subject to year-end adjustments required by the auditors.

Annual Financial Statements

> Within 90 days after the end of each fiscal year of the Debtor, the consolidated and consolidating balance sheets of the Debtor and its subsidiaries as at the end of such fiscal year and the related consolidated and consolidating statements of income and retained earnings and of cash flows for such fiscal year, setting forth comparative figures for the preceding fiscal year and (in the case of such consolidated financial statements) accompanied by a report by independent certified public accountants of recognized national standing as shall be reasonably acceptable to the Creditor, which report shall contain no going-concern or similar qualification and shall state that such statements fairly present in all material respects the financial condition of the Debtor and its subsidiaries as of the dates indicated and the results of their operations and changes in their financial position for the periods indicated in conformity with GAAP applied on a basis consistent with prior years.

Many of the same concepts apply to this covenant regarding annual financial statements as applied to the interim financial statements. The most important difference is that the annual consolidated financial statements must be audited by independent accountants; typically the consolidating numbers are not audited. The accountants' report must not contain any going-concern qualification, a statement that the accountants are unable to conclude that the company can survive as a going concern. The time by which the audited annual financial statements must be delivered (here 90 days, the time period applicable to public companies under securities laws) is longer than for the interim statements, due to the length of time it takes the accountants to complete their audit.

Projections

> Not more than 30 days after the commencement of each fiscal year of the Debtor, the Debtor shall deliver financial projections of the Debtor and its subsidiaries (on a consolidated basis) in reasonable detail for each of the four fiscal quarters of such fiscal year and on an annual basis for the next three fiscal years thereafter, as customarily prepared by management for its internal use setting forth, with appropriate discussion, the principal assumptions upon which such projections are based.

A creditor that is carefully monitoring its debtor's credit situation will, in many cases, want to receive not only the debtor's financial statements (which show its historical financial performance) but also its financial projections. Also known as a forecast or a budget, these set forth the debtor's best estimate as to its expected financial performance during the period(s) covered by the projections. Projections will often be on a monthly or quarterly basis for the first year, and annually thereafter. This covenant usually requires the assumptions on which the projections are based to be included with the projections and to be reasonable.

Compliance Certificate

> At the time of the delivery of its quarterly and annual financial statements, the Debtor shall deliver a certificate of its chief financial officer stating that no Default or Event of Default exists, or, if any such Default or Event of Default does exist, specifying the nature thereof, which certificate shall set forth detailed computations required to establish whether the Debtor was in compliance with the financial covenants for the periods covered by such financial statements.

The purpose of this covenant is to require the chief financial officer of the debtor to certify that there is no default,[8] and to provide calculations showing compliance (or non-compliance) with the financial covenants. Because most credit documents require the debtor to provide notice every time that a default occurs, this certificate may appear redundant. Most creditors, however, believe that a responsible financial officer will not sign a certificate without some investigation,

---

8. The distinction between "Default" and "Event of Default" is discussed in section 9:3.4, note 13.

and that the discipline of requiring such a certificate regularly improves the chances that problems won't be overlooked.

Notice of Default

> The Debtor shall deliver, within two business days of the occurrence of any Default or Event of Default, notice thereof specifying the nature and duration thereof and what action the Debtor intends to take with respect thereto.

Some would argue that this provision lacks teeth, inasmuch as the failure to comply with it results in a default at a time that another default already exists. The creditor's remedies are typically the same whether there is one default or a number of defaults. Notwithstanding this argument, this is a standard reporting covenant.

Notice of Litigation

> Within three business days of the commencement of, or the occurrence of any significant development in, any litigation or governmental proceeding or investigation pending against the Debtor or any of its subsidiaries that could reasonably be expected to have a Material Adverse Effect, the Debtor shall deliver notice thereof to the Creditor.

This covenant reflects the creditor's continuing interest in litigation affecting the debtor, because any judgment would represent a competing claim and possibly a competing lien. The material adverse effect standard will be the subject of negotiation: for a sizable company that is subject to hundreds of lawsuits annually, the standard is a sensible one for both debtor and creditor. As burdensome as it would be for the debtor to provide so many notices, it would be equally or more burdensome for the creditor to review and evaluate them all. For this reason, sometimes notice is only required of those proceedings where damages in excess of some stated dollar amount are claimed.

Other Information

> The Debtor shall promptly deliver such other information and documents (financial or otherwise) as may be reasonably requested by the Creditor.

This is a customary provision in most bank credit agreements; however, many debtors may find it objectionably open-ended. It illustrates the importance of information as one of the linchpins of the credit-monitoring process.

In addition to the foregoing reporting covenants, many agreements contain requirements as to reporting of other categories of information, most notably tax, ERISA and environmental.

[B]   Books and Records

> The Debtor will, and will cause each of its subsidiaries to, keep proper books and records in which full, true and correct entries in conformity with GAAP and all requirements of law shall be made.

Without proper and accurate bookkeeping, there is no ability to monitor a company's financial performance or to understand its financial condition at any point in time. This covenant gives the creditor a remedy in the event that the debtor fails to keep its books and accounts properly in accordance with GAAP. Of course, the typical covenants and representations regarding annual and interim financial statements would also be breached if the debtor's accounting practices failed to meet this standard. Without the books and records covenant, however, the creditor would have to wait until the next financial statement delivery, instead of having an immediate remedy.

[C]   Inspections

> The Debtor will permit, and will cause each of its subsidiaries to permit, upon reasonable prior written notice, representatives of the Creditor to visit and inspect any of the properties of the Debtor or its subsidiaries, to examine the books and records of the Debtor and its subsidiaries, and to discuss the affairs, finances and accounts of the Debtor and its subsidiaries with their respective employees, officers and independent accountants, all at such reasonable times and intervals as the Creditor may reasonably request.

This covenant goes hand-in-hand with the covenant that allows the creditor to request any information not specifically required to be delivered under the other covenants. This provision goes one step further, and permits the creditor to directly go through the debtor's books and records and discuss them with the debtor's officers and employees. Although seldom used, this right is an important one to creditors when there is a concern that there is either a systemic accounting problem or possible fraud.

[D]   Compliance with Law

> The Debtor will, and will cause each of its subsidiaries to, comply with all applicable statutes, regulations and orders of, and all applicable restrictions imposed by, all governmental bodies, domestic or foreign, in respect of the conduct of their business and the ownership of their property except for such non-compliance as would not reasonably be expected to have a Material Adverse Effect.

This is similar to the representation regarding compliance with law, but in this context it is an ongoing obligation rather than a mere statement of fact that is made at a particular point in time. For that reason, a materiality qualification is even more important here. Often there are also detailed covenants requiring compliance with specific bodies of law, such as ERISA and environmental law.

[E]   Maintenance of Insurance

> The Debtor will, and will cause each of its subsidiaries to, maintain at all times in full force and effect insurance with reputable insurance carriers in such amounts, covering such risks and liabilities, and with such deductibles and self-insurance as are consistent with normal industry practice. Such insurance shall name the Creditor as additional insured with respect to liability coverage and loss payee with respect to casualty coverage. All policies or certificates with respect to such insurance shall state that such insurance policies shall not be cancelled or materially changed without at least 30 days' prior written notice thereof by the respective insurer to the Creditor.

The need for this covenant from a credit-protection standpoint should be obvious. If the debtor incurs a significant uninsured loss, its credit is impaired to the extent of such loss, which must be paid for out of the debtor's cash flow. To prevent this, a creditor will often insist on a covenant requiring the maintenance of insurance. The above provision is relatively loose, in that there are no specific requirements as to the identity of the insurers or the insurance coverage levels; it merely requires the debtor to maintain insurance in accordance with normal industry practice. The insurance covenant can also be extremely detailed and specify types and minimum amounts of coverage, and minimum credit ratings of the insurance carriers. The latter approach is more typical in fixed asset financings, such as real estate and project finance transactions, where the credit decision is tied closely to the value of the debtor's property.

Several other important points regarding insurance are contained in this provision. There is a requirement that the creditor be named as "additional insured" in respect of liability insurance and "loss payee" in respect of casualty insurance. By being named as additional insured, the lender will be covered by the debtor's liability insurance to the same extent that the debtor is covered under the policy. For example, an adjoining landowner claiming damages due to a hazardous waste spill from a plant financed by a creditor may sue both the debtor and the creditor. With an additional insured endorsement, the creditor is insured to the same extent as the debtor. The covenant also requires that the creditor is named as loss payee under casualty insurance policies. As a result, any payment made by the insurer on account of damage to the debtor's property would be paid directly to the creditor. This provision is always required when the creditor has a security interest in tangible assets—it ensures that the creditor receives the cash proceeds of its collateral in the event it is damaged or destroyed.

The covenant also requires each policy to provide that it cannot be materially modified or cancelled without prior notice to the creditor. This goes one step further than having the debtor agree to this requirement: it creates an affirmative obligation on the part of the insurer. This gives a further level of assurance to the creditor that the insurance that was a part of its credit decision won't disappear or change in a way that is adverse to it.

[F] Payment of Taxes

By now, the reader may have detected a pattern: matters that are the subject of representations are also often the subject of covenants. The reason is that the representation states one or more facts in respect of a certain area of the debtor's business at closing, but without the covenant there would be nothing to prevent the debtor from making significant changes in that area after the closing. So, for example, the debtor that is current on all of its taxes at closing might, in the absence of a tax covenant of the type set forth below, thereafter build up tax arrears that could impair its creditworthiness.

> The Debtor will pay, and will cause each of its subsidiaries to pay, all material taxes, assessments and governmental charges or levies imposed upon them or their income or profits, or upon any properties owned by them, prior to the date on which penalties attach thereto, provided, however that neither the Debtor nor any of its subsidiaries shall be required to pay any such tax, assessment, charge or levy being diligently contested in good faith and with respect to which reserves have been established in accordance with GAAP.

Note also the difference in the wording of this tax covenant and the tax representation at section 9:3.1[F]. The covenant also requires the debtor to *cause its subsidiaries* to pay their taxes. Why doesn't the covenant directly require each subsidiary to pay its taxes? Because each subsidiary is not a party to the agreement; only the debtor is. The debtor does not have the legal power to bind its subsidiaries. On the other hand, it does have the power to agree to cause its subsidiaries to act in a specified way. In the case of the representation, in contrast, the debtor does have the power to make factual statements regarding its subsidiaries.

[G]   Corporate Existence

> The Debtor will do, and will cause each of its subsidiaries to do, or cause to be done, all things necessary to preserve and keep in full force and effect their existence and their material rights, franchises and qualifications to do business, except for rights, franchises and qualifications to do business the loss of which (individually or in the aggregate) would not reasonably be expected to have a Material Adverse Effect.

This is a relatively uncontroversial covenant that requires the debtor to maintain its corporate (or partnership or limited liability company) existence, and to maintain its qualification to do business where such authorization is required. As with the corresponding representation discussed above at section 9:2.1, the requirement to maintain qualification to do business is often subject to a materiality standard.

[H] Payment of Claims

The Debtor will, and will cause each of its subsidiaries to, pay all material claims against them when due and payable, except where the failure to pay such claims, individually or in the aggregate, would not reasonably be expected to have a Material Adverse Effect.

The failure by a debtor to pay its obligations as they become due is often the first sign of financial difficulty. If a debtor is having cash flow problems, its first reaction is often to "stretch the trade"—that is, to defer the payment of its accounts payable and other short-term obligations. This is why this provision is often included in credit documentation. The debtor, on the other hand, will argue that the provision prevents it from delaying payments either to address a bona fide dispute or some legitimate and unthreatening cash flow imbalance. The normal middle ground is to insert a material adverse effect qualification, as in the above example, and/or to exclude payments that are not made as a result of a bona fide dispute.

§ 9:3.3 *Negative Covenants*

Negative covenants are the primary battleground of credit documentation. Their purpose is to prevent the debtor from taking actions that may tend to worsen its credit; however, the negative covenants proposed by the creditor are often perceived by the debtor as overbroad and impairing the flexibility needed to take advantage of opportunities and to react to changing market conditions. The process of negotiating negative covenants involves finding an appropriate balance between the creditor's desire for control and the debtor's desire for autonomy and flexibility.

[A] Debt

The incurrence of additional debt is one of the primary ways that a debtor can make itself less creditworthy. The additional principal and interest payment obligations create further claims on the debtor's cash flow, making a liquidity problem more likely to occur. Furthermore, the additional debt represents another claim that will compete with the claim of the prior creditors in the event of a bankruptcy proceeding. Last, the existence of other debt means that there is another creditor with acceleration rights, the exercise of which could precipitate a financial crisis. These factors result in the inclusion of debt covenants in credit documentation for all but the most creditworthy debtors.

There are two basic types of debt covenants: maintenance covenants and incurrence covenants. Maintenance covenants are found most often in bank credit agreements and permit specified levels of debt to remain outstanding from time to time. Incurrence covenants are found most often in private and public offerings of debt securities, and permit the incurrence of additional debt if a specified financial test is satisfied, after giving pro forma effect to both the incurrence of the debt and the use of the proceeds thereof. Public and private debt indentures also usually permit the maintenance of debt under carveouts and baskets, in addition to debt that can be incurred under an incurrence covenant. The remainder of this discussion describes typical debt provisions in a bank credit agreement; however, many of the provisions are often also found in debt covenants in other agreements.

The starting point of any debt covenant is the definition of "debt" or "indebtedness." Here is a typical definition:

> "Debt" shall mean (i) indebtedness for borrowed money, (ii) obligations evidenced by bonds, notes or similar instruments, (iii) the deferred purchase price of assets or services but excluding trade payables incurred in the ordinary course of business, (iv) the face amount of all letters of credit and all drafts drawn thereunder, (v) all indebtedness of another Person secured by a lien on property, whether or not such indebtedness has been assumed, (vi) all capitalized lease obligations, and (vii) all guarantees of the obligations of another Person.

The purpose of this definition is to isolate those liabilities that another creditor will want to control. The foundation of the definition is actual borrowings (clause (i)) and obligations under instruments that are normally considered debt obligations (clause (ii)). The next general area is obligations that are incurred to finance the acquisition of property. Clause (iii) describes purchase money financing, in which the acquisition of an asset is financed by the seller's agreement to be paid the purchase price over time. Clause (vi) covers the obligations of the debtor under "capitalized leases," which are leases treated as a financing on the debtor's balance sheet—that is, the leased asset is recorded as being owned by the debtor and the lease payment obligations are treated as a liability. Note the exclusion of trade payables in clause (iii): trade payables are created when inventory or services are purchased on credit terms in the ordinary course of business. They are carried on a balance sheet as a current liability and typically not considered debt. Thus, financings of fixed assets through direct borrowing, purchase money financing or capitalized leases are treated as debt, whereas the ordinary financing of inventory or services is not.

Obligations under letters of credit (clause (iv)) are also normally treated as debt. A drawing under a letter of credit creates a reimbursement obligation to the issuing bank that is considered the functional equivalent of a direct borrowing from the bank. Clauses (v) and (vii) cover arrangements where the debtor provides credit support for a third party's obligations, either by pledging its assets or providing a guarantee.

Now that we have examined the definition, let's look at the body of a typical debt covenant:

> The Debtor shall not, nor shall it permit its subsidiaries to, create, incur, suffer to exist or permit any Debt, except:

The simplicity, and breadth, of this language demonstrates a basic paradigm of negative covenants: they generally start as a flat prohibition on a broadly-defined range of activities. The key to the negotiation of this and other covenants will be the provisions that follow the "except" at the end—the baskets and carveouts that allow the debtor room for certain types and amounts of debt during the term of the agreement. The following are some of the usual exceptions contained in debt covenants, though the types and amounts permitted will depend on the particular circumstances of the transaction and the credit status of the debtor.

Purchase Money/Capitalized Lease Obligations

Financing of assets by means of capitalized lease or purchase money financing will frequently be permitted, subject to separate or combined baskets permitting specified amounts of such financing to be outstanding at any time. The negotiation of these and other covenant baskets will often focus on whether the need for the requested amounts is reflected in the debtor's projections.

Existing Debt

Debt that exists at the time the credit agreement is entered into must be permitted or repaid. It is usually described on an attached schedule. This exception is not necessary if the covenant restricts only the creation or incurrence of new debt.

Let's examine the interplay between debt that is permitted by this exception and debt that is permitted by other exceptions. Assume, for instance, that a debtor has a $10 million capitalized lease in place on the closing date that is inadvertently omitted from the schedule of existing debt. If there is also a basket for up to $50 million of capitalized leases, there is no breach because $10 million of the basket can be utilized. If the debt had been scheduled, the basket would not have been unnecessarily diminished. This same issue arises in connection with any covenant, such as the lien and investment covenants, that permit items that exist at the time of closing.

Intercompany Debt

Companies and their subsidiaries often have a need to make loans to each other. Often this is a result of a parent borrowing under a credit facility and in turn lending to its subsidiaries to provide them with necessary working capital. Sometimes one entity will generate extra cash flow that is shared with its affiliates in the form of intercompany loans. Because these loans constitute debt, they must be specifically carved out of the covenant in order to be permitted. Such a carveout may be open-ended, or may be subject to a basket, most likely depending on whether the subsidiaries are part of the credit package by virtue of being covered by covenants and/or having guaranteed the debt (see section 9:3).

Intercompany Guarantees

Frequently, one member of a corporate group may be requested to guarantee the obligations of another member of the group—for example, a lessor may require a parent company's guarantee of its subsidiary's lease obligations, particularly where the parent is more creditworthy than the subsidiary. Accordingly, debt covenants will often permit this type of intercompany guarantee.

Subsidiary Debt

Sometimes it is anticipated that the debtor's subsidiaries will incur debt. This situation arises most often in the case of foreign subsidiaries whose financing needs are not provided for under the parent's credit facilities. Because debt of U.S. companies is usually not guaranteed by its foreign subsidiaries,[9] any debt incurred by a foreign subsidiary is structurally senior to a creditor of the U.S. debtor. This means that the foreign creditor has a claim to the foreign subsidiary's assets, in contrast to the parent company's creditor, which has no such claim. As a result, the parent company's creditor will want to restrict the amount of debt that can be incurred by its foreign subsidiaries.

Acquired Debt

Debtors that expect to make acquisitions may want a basket for debt existing at an acquired company that is not refinanced or paid off at the time of the acquisition. There are usually two reasons why an acquiror may want to leave such debt outstanding: (a) the debt may not permit, or may impose expensive penalties on, prepayment, or (b) the debt may have favorable economic terms that the acquiror wants to keep in place.

This carveout will require that the acquired debt was not created in anticipation of the acquisition transaction. This protects the creditor against the intentional creation of debt at the target before its acquisition.

General Debt Basket

Depending on the needs and credit of the debtor, there may be a general basket for permitted additional debt. Sometimes this basket will be limited to subordinated debt.

Refinancing Debt

This exception permits the refinancing and extension of maturity of other permitted debt. The usual language refers to the "refinancing, replacement or extension" of specified categories of debt. This provision is usually not applicable to debt permitted under a basket, because the nature of a basket permits the debt incurred thereunder

---

9. Guarantees of this type create taxable deemed dividends under Section 956 of the Internal Revenue Code and for this reason are usually avoided.

to be repaid and reborrowed, subject to the overall dollar cap. The categories of debt that are usually covered by the refinancing exception are debt existing at the time the agreement is entered into and other specific items of permitted debt. Often, this exception specifies that the refinancing, replacement or extension may not result in the increase in the principal amount of the debt. Additionally, there may be a requirement that the new debt may not have an earlier maturity or a shorter average weighted life[10] than the original debt. This prevents the refinancing from worsening the debtor's cash flow by creating more onerous repayment requirements. Sometimes there is a requirement that the terms of the new debt cannot be less favorable to the debtor than those of the debt being refinanced.

[B]   Liens

The interest of a creditor in restricting its debtor's ability to create liens on its assets is driven by the basic bankruptcy principle that secured creditors are paid prior to unsecured creditors, to the extent of the value of the encumbered assets. Thus, by prohibiting liens an unsecured creditor avoids coming behind a new secured creditor, and a secured creditor avoids having to share the value of its collateral.

A typical definition of "lien" is:

> "Lien" shall mean any mortgage, pledge, security interest, encumbrance, lien or charge of any kind, including any agreement to give any of the foregoing, any conditional sale or other title retention agreement, any financing or similar statement or notice filed under the Uniform Commercial Code or any similar recording or notice statute, and any lease having substantially the same effect as the foregoing.

This definition covers consensual liens such as mortgages (liens on real property), pledges (liens on securities) and security interests (liens on all other personal property), as well as all other liens and en-

---

10. "Average weighted life" tests the average due date of scheduled principal payments on a loan weighted by the amount of time such principal payments are outstanding. An amortization schedule that requires more principal payments to be made in later years will have a greater average weighted life than one that is front-end loaded.

cumbrances. Further, it includes the filing of all financing statements (the filing of which does not create, but merely perfects, security interests), and leases that have the effect of creating a lien. As with the debt covenant, the lien covenant usually prohibits the creation or existence of all liens that are not specifically permitted. Following is a discussion of frequently appearing carveouts to the lien covenant.

Tax Liens

There is customarily a limited carveout for tax liens. Because some tax obligations that are not yet due and payable result in inchoate liens, a customary exception to the lien covenant covers liens securing tax obligations that are not yet due and payable. Another typical exception permits liens in respect of taxes that are being contested by the debtor. Without this, a debtor would be required to pay when due all taxes that would otherwise give rise to a lien, even if it had a bona fide dispute as to the imposition of the tax.

Ordinary Course Liens

There are a variety of liens that arise in the ordinary course of business in commercial arrangements. For example, under the laws of some states (and under some leases) a landlord has a lien on property at the leased premises that secures unpaid rent obligations. Similar liens include those in favor of mechanics, materialmen, warehousemen and carriers. Sometimes the carveout specifies that obligations secured by the permitted liens cannot be overdue beyond some stated period of time, unless contested in good faith.

Workers Compensation Security Arrangements

State workers compensation, unemployment insurance and similar programs often require the employer to post security for its obligations. There must be a carveout to the lien covenant to permit such security.

Deposits

A variety of commercial arrangements require cash deposits. The most common example of this is the security deposit required in connection with a real estate lease. Deposits of this type fall under the broad definition of lien above, because the depositor is pledging its cash to secure its payment obligations. The typical lien covenant exception allows deposits in connection with leases, trade contracts, bids, performance bonds and insurance obligations.

Easements, etc.

There are a number of restrictions on real estate that arguably fall within the definition of "lien" that shouldn't trouble a creditor and are therefore excluded from the lien prohibition. The usual exception is along these lines:

> Easements, rights-of-way, restrictions, reservations, permits, servitudes and other similar encumbrances on real property that do not materially interfere with the ordinary conduct of business at the affected property.

Of course, if the affected real property is the subject of the transaction (as would be the case, for example, in a mortgage loan), these issues are negotiated much more closely.

Leases and Subleases

If the debtor anticipates leasing (as lessor) or subleasing (as sublessor) any of its property, there must be an exception for these activities. A lease or sublease creates an encumbrance (the interest of the lessee or sublessee) on the property of the debtor, so a carveout is required.

Capitalized Leases and Purchase Money Financing

To the extent the debt covenant permits the creation of capitalized leases or the incurrence of purchase money debt, there must be an equivalent carveout to the lien covenant to permit the liens securing these obligations. Generally speaking, a capitalized lease is treated as a secured financing for accounting and creditors' rights purposes. Thus, the leased asset appears on the lessee's balance sheet as an owned asset, and would be treated as part of the lessee's estate in a bankruptcy proceeding. A purchase money lender often takes a security interest in the asset being financed.

Permitted purchase money and capitalized lease liens may be subject to limitations. The exception may specify that the liens can't cover property other than the assets that are the subject of the financing (in other words, the debtor can't grant a lien to the financer of an item of equipment on any assets other than that item of equipment). Also, the provision may specify that the lien must be created at the time that the purchase money debt is incurred or the capitalized lease is entered into. This is to ensure that the lien is granted to facilitate the financing, not granted after the fact to assuage an insecure creditor.

Existing Liens

As with existing indebtedness, liens that are in place at the time that the agreement becomes effective are typically scheduled and permitted. Liens that secure refinancings, extensions and replacements of the debt that is secured by these liens will also be permitted, subject to a restriction that such liens cannot cover any new or additional property as a result of the refinancing, extension or replacement.

Liens Securing Acquired Debt

If the debtor is permitted by the debt covenant to assume or acquire debt in connection with acquisitions, there should be a corresponding carveout to the lien covenant to permit liens securing such indebtedness. There will usually be a requirement that the liens may not extend to any assets other than those originally covered by the lien—this protects against a blanket lien spreading to cover the assets of the other party to a merger transaction, for example.

Judgment Liens

In many states, a judgment that is docketed or delivered to the sheriff for execution results in a lien in favor of the judgment creditor on the judgment debtor's property located in that state. Without an exception for this type of lien, a borrower would be required to pay immediately any judgment entered against it, or risk being in breach of its lien covenant. For this reason, most lien covenants permit judgment liens, so long as the enforcement of the judgment is stayed within 30 or 60 days after its entry. Such a stay will occur when the judgment is appealed. Thus, under this provision the borrower will have 30 to 60 days to either pay or appeal the judgment. If the appeal is lost, the stay of judgment will be lifted and the judgment will have to be satisfied in order to avoid a breach of the covenant.

Precautionary Financing Statements

If the prohibition on liens includes the filing of any financing statements, there should be an exception for the filing of precautionary financing statements filed pursuant to section 9-505 of the Uniform Commercial Code. This section permits the lessor under an operating lease or a consignor under a consignment to file a financing statement as a precaution in the event that the lease or consignment is subsequently recharacterized as a secured transaction.

[C]   Asset Sales

Credit agreements restrict the debtor's ability to sell assets in order to prevent significant changes to the business on which the creditor's credit decision was made. Asset sales not contemplated by a debtor's business plan could indicate that the debtor is cannibalizing its property to make up for a cash flow shortfall. The asset covenant sale typically starts with a broad prohibition:

> The Debtor will not, and will not permit its subsidiaries to, sell, transfer, convey, assign, lease or otherwise dispose of any of their assets, except:

Following is a discussion of the most typical exceptions to the asset sale covenant.

Sale of Inventory

This is an essential exception for any company that sells merchandise. Often it is limited to sales of inventory *in the ordinary course of business*, which allows for normal sales but prohibits bulk sales and other extraordinary transfers.

Sales Subject to Debt Repayment

A creditor's resistance to the sale of productive assets is lessened when the cash proceeds of the sale are used to repay debt. Accordingly, there is often a basket for a certain amount of asset sales, if the net cash proceeds are used to permanently repay the debt. "Net cash proceeds" is usually defined as the total proceeds of the sale, after deducting the actual costs of the sale (including brokers', investment bankers' and lawyers' fees, sales commissions, debt payments required to be paid with such sale proceeds and tax costs). This basket may be limited to a maximum amount over the life of the agreement, a per annum amount, or an aggregate amount that does not exceed some stated percentage of the debtor's total assets. This provision often requires a specified percentage of the consideration for the sale to be in cash. The non-cash consideration will usually consist of a note (a "seller note") or other payment obligation. The creditor will want to maximize the portion of the sale consideration that is in cash and to minimize the non-cash consideration, which represents an exchange of operating assets for an investment (the investment by the debtor in the seller note) of uncertain quality.[11]

Sales of Assets that Are Replaced

Operating companies often sell equipment with an expectation of replacing it. One example of this is where existing equipment is traded in as new equipment is acquired. Accordingly, there is generally an exception for trade-ins and sales where the proceeds are used to acquire replacement equipment within some period of time. Sometimes the reinvestment requirement is not limited to the replacement of specific assets but refers to fixed or other assets that are "useful in the business of the debtor." This is an especially broad exception, particularly if it's not limited to fixed assets, in which case the debtor is able, for example, to sell real estate and use the proceeds to acquire inventory.

Dispositions of Obsolete Equipment

Another standard exception is one that permits the disposition of equipment that is obsolete, worn out or otherwise uneconomic. The creditor has no legitimate reason not to permit the debtor to dispose of assets that are no longer productive. Sometimes, this exception is open-ended, other times limited to an annual or overall dollar amount.

Sale of Specified Assets

If a debtor is expecting to sell certain property at the time that it enters into a credit agreement, it will ask for a carveout permitting those sales. Often the carveout will specify how the proceeds of these sales must be applied. Sometimes the creditor will want the carveout to specify a minimum sales price, but if the credit agreement is going to be publicly available (as an exhibit to SEC filings, for example), the debtor will resist this because of the negative impact disclosure would have on its ability to negotiate price with potential purchasers.

---

11. The debtor may not take back a seller note as partial consideration for an asset sale if it is subject to a covenant restricting investments that doesn't have an applicable exception.

Leases, Subleases and Licenses

Where the asset sale covenant is drafted very broadly, many transactions that are not typically thought of as "sales" are swept in. Among these are transactions in which the debtor leases or subleases out property as lessor or sublessor, or licenses intellectual property as licensor. In each of these cases, the debtor is transferring a partial interest in its rights to property. Such transfers, to be permitted, must be carved out of the covenant.

Intercompany Sales

There are several reasons why a debtor may want to have the flexibility to conduct sales among itself and its subsidiaries. One of the subsidiaries may be a marketing arm that sells product to customers that it in turn purchases from another subsidiary. One subsidiary may manufacture and sell raw materials that are used by the debtor in its manufacturing process. There may be a perceived need, for tax, operational or other purposes, to move fixed assets around among different members of a corporate group. The creditor's willingness to provide this flexibility will depend primarily on the credit status of the entities that would be permitted transferors and permitted transferees under such arrangements—in other words, are the subsidiaries part of the credit package by virtue of being covered by the covenants and/or having guaranteed the debt (see section 9:3).

Sale-Leasebacks

In a sale-leaseback, a fixed asset is sold to a third party, who simultaneously enters into a lease with the seller that gives the seller the right to the continued use of the asset in exchange for ongoing lease payments. This has the effect of generating immediate cash for the seller in exchange for the incurrence of a long-term payment obligation. As such, it is usually considered by creditors as the economic and functional equivalent of a borrowing secured by assets. Because sale-leasebacks are often used as a last-ditch means of generating cash by companies that are suffering cash flow problems, they are often prohibited or tightly restricted in credit documentation

There may be circumstances where companies that lease equipment are forced, for timing reasons, to purchase the equipment in anticipation of the lease being entered into. A useful provision to address this circumstance is a carveout for sale-leasebacks that occur within some relatively short period of time (say, 90 days) of the initial acquisition of the property. A creditor that otherwise would be willing to permit the lease of this equipment should be willing to permit such a sale-leaseback.

[D]   Restricted Payments

"Restricted payments" are typically defined as follows:

> Any (a) dividend payments on the equity interests of the Debtor or its subsidiaries, (b) other distributions on account of the equity interests of the Debtor or its subsidiaries, or (c) payment on account of, or setting aside any payment for, or establishment of a sinking fund for, the purchase, redemption, defeasance, retirement or other acquisition of the equity interests of the Debtor and its subsidiaries.

A creditor often looks negatively on restricted payments by its debtor: if the debtor is generating enough free cash to be making distributions to its equityholders, it should instead be using the cash to reduce its debt. Each dollar paid out to equity is a dollar reduction to the debtor's net worth and a dollar less that the creditor has recourse to. Accordingly, restricted payments are often the subject of very tight covenants.

Non-cash Dividends

Dividends paid in additional equity are usually freely permitted, since this type of dividend has no effect on the debtor's cash or other assets. On the other hand, dividends of property other than cash are usually restricted to the same extent as cash dividends.

Subsidiary Dividends

Dividends that are paid to the debtor or a wholly-owned subsidiary of the debtor are typically permitted, because the cash or other property that is dividended continues to be part of the consolidated assets of the debtor. On the other hand, a different issue is raised where a subsidiary is not wholly-owned. In such a case, a prorated amount of any dividend or other distribution must be paid to third-party shareholders. As a result, dividends of this type are looked on with disfavor by creditors.

Equity Buybacks

Stock bonus and other stock incentive plans offered to a company's management often require the company to repurchase the stock upon the death, resignation or termination of the employee. A restricted payments covenant will block such payments, unless a carveout permits them. To the extent these payments aren't fully permitted by the covenant, the document providing for such payments must provide for their nonpayment or deferral—otherwise the debtor may be forced to breach either its credit agreement or its stock plan.

Tax Distributions

Many partnerships and limited liability companies are not taxed as entities; instead, their partners or members are taxed directly on the entity income that is attributable to their equity interests in the entity. As a result, these entities typically make distributions in a minimum amount sufficient to cover their investors' income tax liabilities arising as a result of their investments. These distributions should be carved out of any restricted payments covenant. The creditor's normal antipathy to cash dividends should be overcome by the fact that if the debtor were structured as a corporation, these amounts would be payable directly by the debtor as taxes.

Indenture Restricted Payments Covenants

The restricted payments covenant that appears in debt indentures differs from the typical credit agreement covenant. Rather than being structured as a flat prohibition subject to carveouts, the indenture covenant permits restricted payments in an amount (the "restricted payments basket") determined by a formula. This basket is usually equal to 50% of the debtor's consolidated net income from the date of the indenture through the date of the restricted payment, plus 100% of the cash proceeds of new equity issuances, less the aggregate amount of all restricted payments previously made under the basket. Thus, the debtor's ability to pay dividends and make other restricted payments increases with its profitability. In addition, there are often specific baskets similar to those found in credit agreements.

[E]   Investments

Unlike dividends, which from a creditor's standpoint is money out the door, an investment potentially creates value that may strengthen the debtor financially and thereby inure to the creditor's benefit. Accordingly, investments are usually not proscribed as narrowly as restricted payments. On the other hand, the creditor will want to restrict investments that either represent a deviation from the debtor's business plan, involve excessive risk or result in cash or assets being removed from its credit package. A typical definition of investments includes:

> Any advance, loan, extension of credit or capital contribution, any purchase of any stock, bonds, notes, debentures or other debt or equity securities, and any purchase of assets constituting a business unit of any person.

The first thing to note is that the definition covers both debt and equity investments, and is written broadly so that loans and other advances are included in addition to debt securities such as bonds. The definition also picks up asset purchases that constitute a "business unit," since acquisitions can be effected by purchasing either the stock or assets of the target. Sometimes the provision will instead cover purchases of all or substantially all of the assets of any entity.

Investments in Subsidiaries

It is very common for a consolidated group to need to move cash among the constituent entities, in connection with normal cash management functions as well as for strategic reasons. The creditor's willingness to permit these investments will be primarily driven by the potential effect on its credit package. For example, a creditor may be relatively indifferent to an investment by one subsidiary that is a guarantor of the debt in another subsidiary guarantor. On the other hand, the creditor will view an investment in a subsidiary that is not a guarantor as an impairment of its credit package, because it results in cash moving to an entity against which it has no claim.[12] (See section 9:3.)

---

12.   An intercompany investment consisting of a loan or advance will also need to be permitted as debt under the debt covenant.

Investments in Joint Ventures

An investment by a debtor in a joint venture is usually looked at with disfavor by a creditor. Typically, an investor in a joint venture doesn't have the same level of control that it would exercise over a subsidiary. In addition, amounts invested in joint ventures are outside the credit package because a joint venture will almost never guarantee the debt of one of its investors. As a result, baskets for investments in joint ventures are usually the subject of significant negotiation.

Acquisitions

Tension arises in negotiating carveouts for acquisitions between the debtor's desire for freedom to make acquisitions based on its own business judgment and the creditor's desire to make its own determination on the merits of each proposed acquisition. The middle ground usually involves a basket with some additional bells and whistles. For example, a frequently occurring requirement is that the debtor demonstrate pro forma compliance with its financial covenants (or other specified financial ratios), after taking the acquisition into account.

Loans and Advances to Officers and Employees

Companies often make loans and advances to their officers and employees for travel expenses, relocation, and for other purposes. These must be carved out of the investment covenant, subject usually to an overall cap.

Bankruptcy Investments

A debtor may be issued securities in satisfaction of an outstanding claim against a customer or other person in a bankruptcy proceeding. A carveout for this type of investment is usually not subject to a dollar cap, because it is outside of the debtor's control.

Existing Investments

Any investments that exist on the closing date are usually scheduled and permitted under a separate carveout.

Cash Investments

As a matter of sound cash management, a company that has cash will want to invest it rather than have it sit idle. Therefore, a customary exception to the investment covenant is one that permits the investment of cash in liquid securities. This category of permitted investments usually includes the following short-term investments (referred to as "cash equivalents"): government securities, certificates of deposit and commercial paper, subject to minimum rating requirements.

[F]   Transactions with Affiliates

A creditor worries about transactions between the debtor and the debtor's affiliates because of the risk that the transaction will result in value escaping from the debtor. For example, the debtor could sell assets to its sole shareholder for a below-market price. This concern does not come up in the case of transactions with non-affiliates because it is assumed that in this circumstance the debtor will behave in an economically sensible way and obtain equivalent value. However, in the case of transactions with affiliates this same assumption isn't made, due to the possibility that the debtor's self-interest will be subordinated to its affiliates' needs. "Affiliate" is usually defined as a person or entity that directly or indirectly controls, is controlled by, or is under common control with the debtor, with "control" often defined as the power to vote 5% or 10% of the affiliate's equity interests. Under this definition, a company's affiliates include (a) its parent company, (b) investors owning the specified amount of voting equity, (c) its sister companies (companies that are owned by its parent company), (d) its subsidiaries and (e) entities in which it has the requisite voting equity investment (including most joint ventures).

The typical transactions with affiliates covenant is worded:

> The Debtor shall not, and shall not permit its subsidiaries to, enter into any transaction with its Affiliates, unless such transaction is upon terms no less favorable to the Debtor or such subsidiary than it would obtain on an arm's-length basis with a Person that is not an Affiliate.

The covenant does not prohibit affiliate transactions; it merely requires that such transactions have terms that are equivalent to those that would be obtained from an independent party. Sometimes, there is a requirement that affiliate transactions with a value above a stated dollar threshold must be specifically approved by the debtor's board of directors or an investment banking or valuation firm as being on arm's-length terms. Requirements of this type appear more frequently in agreements relating to high-yield and other debt securities.

[G]   Payment Restrictions Affecting Subsidiaries

Conceptually, this is one of the hardest covenants to grasp. A simple version of this covenant (referred to here as the "payment restrictions covenant") reads as follows:

> The Debtor shall not, and shall not permit any of its subsidiaries to, enter into any agreement restricting any subsidiary's right to (a) pay dividends or make other restricted payments to the Debtor or any other subsidiary, (b) sell, transfer or otherwise dispose of assets to the Debtor or any other subsidiary, (c) make loans or advances to the Debtor or any other subsidiary, or (d) repay any loans or advances made by the Debtor or any other subsidiary.

This covenant ensures that there is no impediment to the up-streaming of money to a debtor from its subsidiaries. This is important to a creditor, who wants to make sure there is a clear pathway for the subsidiaries' cash and other assets to be available to the debtor, if the debtor's financial condition requires it. One of the reasons that this covenant is confusing is that, unlike other covenants that restrict *actions*, this covenant restricts the existence of other *contractual provisions*. It restricts the ability of a debtor's subsidiaries to enter into certain transactions in a way that sometimes gets overlooked. In the case where a subsidiary is proposing to incur debt, for example, most lawyers will realize that such incurrence must be permitted under the debtor's debt covenant. But they sometimes forget that restrictions applicable to the subsidiary under its debt agreement must be analysed under this covenant as well.

Some of the typical exceptions to this covenant are the following:

Existing Restrictions

Existing payment restrictions must be permitted. Usually, they are required to be listed on a schedule. Similar restrictions in agreements that refinance or replace the scheduled agreements are commonly permitted as well, as long as the new provisions aren't more restrictive than the ones being replaced. Sometimes, the lender will insist that existing restrictions be eliminated. For example, if there are restrictions of this type in existing debt of a subsidiary of the debtor, the lender may require that the debt be paid off or amended at the closing.

Anti-assignment Provisions

Many contracts restrict the parties' ability to assign their rights under the contract. For contracts constituting "accounts," "chattel paper," "promissory notes," "payment intangibles," "letter of credit rights," or "healthcare insurance receivables," as defined in the Uniform Commercial Code, such provisions may not be enforceable. (See section 10:2.10.) To the extent the anti-assignment provision is in another type of contract and is enforceable, such a provision in a contract of a subsidiary runs afoul of the payment restrictions covenant because it prevents the subsidiary from transferring the contract, or its rights to receive payments under the contract, to its parent company or other subsidiaries. An exception for transfers to affiliates is often negotiated and avoids this problem. But since this exception may not always be available, there should be a carveout to the payment restrictions covenant that permits these restrictions.

Subsidiary Debt

Agreements governing debt are likely to contain all of the restrictions that are proscribed by the payment restrictions covenant. Thus, if it is anticipated that there will be a need for a subsidiary to incur its own debt, a carveout to the payment restrictions covenant will be useful. A creditor will only agree to this covenant if the assets and cash flow of the subsidiary are not part of its credit decision.

Secured Financing

Agreements governing secured financings prohibit the sale or other disposition of collateral. If a credit agreement permits the debtor and its subsidiaries to incur secured debt (for example, purchase money debt and capitalized leases), it must also contain a carveout to the payment restrictions covenant to permit the restrictions that will appear in such debt agreements.

Agreements to Sell Assets

Agreements for the sale of assets, for obvious reasons, prohibit the seller from selling the assets to someone else. Accordingly, the payment restrictions covenant should permit such prohibitions in asset sale agreements to which a subsidiary of the debtor is a party. (Of course the asset sale itself must also be allowed under the asset sale covenant.)

[H]   Amendments to Other Documents

This covenant restricts the debtor's ability to amend specified agreements and, often, its charter, by-laws or other organizational documents. The agreements covered by this restriction are those that the creditor feels are important to its credit decision. Sometimes, the covenant will apply to "all material contracts" but this is a difficult line to draw. Sometimes the covenant will only restrict amendments that "could reasonably be expected to be adverse to the creditor's interests." Under this standard, a modification to a debtor's charter that changes notice provisions for its annual meeting, for example, would be permitted, whereas a modification providing for the issuance of preferred stock with mandatory redemption provisions would not.

[I]   Mergers

This covenant will read something like this:

> The Debtor will not, and will not permit its subsidiaries to, liquidate or dissolve, consolidate with, or merge into or with any other entity.

The reason for the restriction on liquidation and dissolution is self-evident in the case of the debtor: the creditor wants to ensure that the debtor continues to exist as a legal entity as long as its credit obligations remain outstanding. The creditor's interest in preventing the dissolution or liquidation of subsidiaries is not as strong, particularly since a liquidation or dissolution of a subsidiary results in the subsidiary's assets being distributed to its direct parent, normally a good result for the creditor. Accordingly, there is often a carveout for voluntary liquidations and dissolutions of subsidiaries.

The restriction on mergers should dovetail with the investment covenant. If the investment covenant permits acquisitions in the form of stock and asset acquisitions, there should be an exception to the merger covenant permitting any such permitted transaction to be effected by merger as well.

[J]   Capital Expenditures

Capital expenditures are defined as expenditures that are required to be included as property, plant and equipment on the debtor's consolidated balance sheet. A debtor's projections will forecast how much it expects to spend on capital assets during the period covered by the projections. If the actual expenditures significantly exceed the forecasted amounts, there may be undue strain on the debtor's cash flow. Accordingly, many credit agreements limit the debtor's annual capital expenditures. These limits are usually set at the level of the debtor's projected capital expenditure needs, plus a negotiated cushion. Often, there is a carryover provision, which allows amounts that aren't used under one year's basket to be used in the subsequent year.

[K]   Financial Covenants

A key component of a credit decision is the debtor's projections. The amortization of the principal of a loan is often structured to match the debtor's projected cash flow. The total amount of debt permitted will be based on the sufficiency of the debtor's cash flow to cover interest and principal payments. In many cases, the overall capitalization (i.e., the mix of debt and equity) of the debtor will cease to make economic sense if the debtor's actual operating results fall significantly short of those that have been projected. Compliance by the debtor with all of the affirmative and negative covenants discussed above may prevent certain credit-impairing behavior, but they cannot protect the creditor from the debtor's operating results taking a nosedive.

Financial covenants allow the creditor to monitor the debtor's financial performance and to exercise remedies in the event that such performance falls below required levels. Each financial covenant measures one or more elements of the debtor's actual financial performance against projected levels (with negotiated cushions). If any area of the debtor's business subject to a financial covenant falls short of the required level, the covenant is breached, an event of default occurs and the creditor is entitled to exercise remedies. There are different types of financial covenants, some of which are tailored to a specific company or a specific industry. Discussed below are several of the most frequently recurring financial covenants.

Minimum EBITDA

EBITDA is an acronym for "earnings before interest, taxes, depreciation and amortization." It is computed by taking a company's net income for a particular period and adding back the amount of interest expense, tax expense, depreciation and amortization for such period, all of which, under GAAP, have been deducted in arriving at the net income figure. EBITDA is considered one of the most important measures of a company's operating financial performance.

A minimum EBITDA test requires the debtor to reach certain EBITDA levels at the end of specified periods. The test can look at EBITDA on a quarter-by-quarter basis, but it is much more common for the test to be on a "trailing four quarter" basis. This means that at the end of each quarter, EBITDA for the four-quarter period then ending will be measured. The difference between testing EBITDA (or any other measurement of financial performance) for one quarter instead of four quarters is that a one-quarter test is more volatile—one bad quarter can result in a breach, whereas with a four-quarter test bad quarters can be offset with good quarters.

Interest Coverage Ratio

This test measures the ratio of the debtor's EBITDA to its interest expense, over some specified period of time (again, usually four quarters). This is an important ratio, because it demonstrates the sufficiency of the debtor's cash flow to cover its interest payment obligations.

Fixed Charge Coverage Ratio

Similar to the interest coverage ratio, this measures the sufficiency of EBITDA to cover interest as well as other specified payments, usually including scheduled principal payments on debt, preferred stock dividends and capital expenditures.

Leverage Ratio

There are actually two different ratios that are called "leverage ratio." The first is the ratio of (a) debt to (b) debt plus net worth. This test measures leverage by determining what portion of the debtor's capital structure consists of debt. It is a so-called "balance sheet test" because it measures items on the balance sheet, which reflects a company's *financial condition* as of a particular time (as opposed to the

EBITDA-based tests discussed above, which are derived from the company's income statements and test *financial performance*). The other financial covenant referred to as a leverage ratio is the ratio of EBITDA to debt. In the same way that an interest coverage ratio looks at the level of cash flow that is available for the payment of interest, this leverage ratio measures the level of cash flow available to cover principal. It is a hybrid covenant, measuring an income statement item, EBITDA, against debt, a balance sheet item.

Net Worth

A company's net worth is equal to its assets minus its liabilities. Profits increase net worth, losses reduce it. A net worth covenant is designed to measure the changes to net worth over time as a result of profits and losses. It does this by measuring, at the end of each quarter, the debtor's actual net worth against an amount equal to the debtor's net worth at closing, plus 50% (usually) of net income in each quarter thereafter, less 100% of net losses in each such quarter. The effect of this approach is that the cushion built into the benchmark increases by 50 cents for each dollar of profits and shrinks by 100 cents for each dollar of losses.

§ 9:3.4   *Events of Default*

This section of a credit agreement has two distinct parts: first, a list of the events that constitute events of default, and second, a description of the remedies available to the creditor if an event of default occurs. We will not examine in detail all of the events of default that appear in credit agreements, but instead focus on the events of default relating to the building block provisions discussed in this chapter: representations and covenants.

Credit agreements provide that it is an event of default if one of the debtor's representations was not true when made. The theory is that the credit decision was based on the facts covered by the representations, and, if a representation turns out to be false, the creditor should be able to reverse its credit decision. Because representations are only made at specific points in time, an event of default is caused only if a representation was false at the time that it was made. Changes in facts or circumstances occurring after the date a representation is made cannot make the representation false retroactively. Frequently, an event of default does not occur unless a representation was untrue when made "in any material respect." Because the potential results of the occurrence of an event of default can be so significant, the materiality qualifier is an appropriate protection against a hair-trigger default.

The breach of a covenant will also constitute an event of default. Specified covenant defaults may be subject to negotiated grace periods, in which case the breach will not constitute an event of default unless it remains uncured for a specified number of days.[13] The purpose of the grace period (also referred to as a cure period) is to give the debtor the opportunity to return to compliance by fixing the problem that gave rise to the breach. Some grace periods are drafted to commence only after the debtor has knowledge of the breach.

A breach by the debtor of its representations or covenants results in an event of default because it signals an event or condition that could result in the creditor's wanting to reverse or modify its original credit decision. Without the remedies that are made available to the creditor upon the occurrence of an event of default, judicial remedies would be the creditor's sole recourse in the event of a breach.

The primary remedy for an event of default is acceleration of the debt, so that principal, accrued interest and all other obligations of the debtor under the credit agreement immediately become due and payable. In most cases, the debtor will be unable to pay the accelerated obligations (if it had that much cash on hand, it probably wouldn't have any loans outstanding). As a result, acceleration will precipitate a financial crisis, often bankruptcy. The other principal remedy is to terminate undrawn commitments. This means that the debtor's ability to borrow additional loans is eliminated. This may also put the debtor in a precarious position, particularly if its liquidity is insufficient without the availability of revolving loans. Because these remedies create such drastic consequences, more often than not the creditor will not actually exercise its remedies. Instead, it will use the threat of exercising its remedies to obtain concessions from, and obtain an increased level of control over, the debtor.

---

13. Many agreements characterize breaches that have not yet become "events of default," because required notices have not been given or required cure periods have not yet run, as "defaults." The existence of a default may trigger lesser remedies, such as the creditor's refusal to make additional advances.

§ 9:4 Acquisition-related Provisions

The remainder of this chapter is devoted to building block provisions included in agreements governing the acquisition by one entity of another.[14] Because acquisitions can be structured as either stock purchases, asset purchases or mergers, the building block provisions applicable to each will be examined. As was the case with the credit-related provisions discussed in section 9:3 above, the goal is not to provide an exhaustive overview or analysis of all the possible provisions and their variants that may arise. Instead, the discussion should provide the reader with a broad understanding of how some of the building block provisions are used to achieve the respective goals of buyers and sellers in the acquisition process.[15]

First a note about the fundamental difference between stock acquisitions and mergers, on the one hand, and asset acquisitions, on the other. In stock acquisitions, the target becomes a subsidiary of the buyer.[16] All of the assets and liabilities of the target continue to be its assets and liabilities (and will be included on the buyer's consolidated balance sheet). The same result occurs in a merger: in structures other than a merger directly with or into the buyer, the target becomes the buyer's subsidiary. In a merger between the target and the buyer, all of the target's assets and liabilities become the assets and liabilities of the buyer, by operation of law.

In an asset acquisition, on the other hand, only the assets specified in the acquisition agreement are sold to the buyer, and only those liabilities similarly specified become liabilities of the buyer. So, for example, if the buyer purchases the assets of a division of the seller, none of

---

14. There are special provisions that relate to the acquisition of public companies that are not addressed here.

15. Although both the buyer and the seller make representations and covenants, this chapter will focus exclusively on the representations and covenants made by the seller and the buyer's remedies for breach thereof.

16. Throughout this section, three parties will be referred to: the buyer, the seller and the target. Depending on the context, the "target" is the entity to be acquired by stock acquisition or merger, or the business unit the assets of which are to be acquired in an asset acquisition.

the liabilities associated with such business will travel with the assets, except to the extent specified in the acquisition agreement.[17]

§ 9:4.1   Representations

[A]   The Purpose of Representations

The representations made by a seller in an acquisition agreement consist of a series of statements about the target[18] intended to create an accurate picture of the target on which the buyer can rely in making its investment decision. The representations serve three basic functions. First, negotiation of the representations uncovers issues that may give rise to additional price negotiations or requests by the buyer for additional protections (such as promises by the seller to remedy a problem that is disclosed by the representations). Second, if a representation is untrue, it may give the buyer the right to terminate the transaction. Third, if the buyer discovers after closing that a representation of the seller was untrue when made, it may have an indemnification claim or a claim for breach of contract against the seller.[19]

The scope of the representations in an acquisition agreement is typically much broader than in credit documentation, because a buyer's need to understand all aspects of the business being acquired is much more extensive than a creditor's need to know facts that may affect its credit decision. The primary business term in any acquisition is price, which may be affected significantly by any issues or problems relating to the target. The buyer will also have operational and management considerations that require a close understanding of the business that it intends to acquire.

---

17. However, if a transfer is found to be fraudulent, or if a court imposes successor liability under certain theories such as the product-line exception, an asset purchaser might be held liable for the obligations of the seller, even if not assumed in the contract.

18. In addition to representations about the target and its business, the seller will be required to make enforceability representations as to itself and the acquisition agreement. See section 9:2.

19. See KLING AND NUGENT, NEGOTIATED ACQUISITIONS OF COMPANIES, SUBSIDIARIES AND DIVISIONS, 11-2–11-8 (2000) [hereafter, "Kling and Nugent"].

[B]   Representations and the Disclosure Process

A buyer's first step in determining the necessary facts to make its investment decision and inform its pricing analysis is the completion of its own due diligence. The representations force the seller to stand behind the information provided to the buyer in the due diligence process. They also tend to smoke out facts that may not have surfaced during due diligence.

The way that the negotiation of representations results in disclosure is as follows. The acquisition agreement, which is normally drafted by counsel to the buyer, will contain, for example, a representation that the target is not the subject of any litigation which could reasonably be expected to have a material adverse effect on the target. (Sometimes the material adverse effect qualifier will not be included in the first draft but will be added as a result of negotiation.) If the target does have such potentially material litigation, it cannot make this representation truthfully unless the litigation is carved out of the representation. This is typically done in the disclosure schedules that are attached to the acquisition agreement. By disclosing facts that are inconsistent with the representations in the disclosure schedules, the seller eliminates the buyer's ability to walk away from the transaction or to bring claims for breach or indemnification on the basis of the fact that is disclosed. The risk of the disclosed information is thus shifted from the seller to the buyer by virtue of disclosure. The buyer, on the other hand, receives information that allows it to make a fully-informed investment decision and to price the deal accordingly.

[C]   Timing of Representations

Representations are often made at the time that the acquisition agreement is signed, and again at the closing. In cases where there is a long gap between these two points in time, the facts represented to by the seller may change. Accordingly, there should be a mechanism allowing the seller to update its representations so as to be true at closing. The buyer, despite its interest in knowing all the relevant facts, will not want to be forced to close after the seller has disclosed unfavorable facts between signing and closing. This is usually addressed by allowing the seller to terminate prior to closing if additional facts are disclosed by the seller; often this right is conditioned on the additional disclosure being material or resulting in a material adverse effect on the target.

[D]   Representation Qualifiers

The scope of a representation will dictate the amount and detail of disclosure that must be made by the seller in order to make the representation true. Consider the following two variations of the same representation made in an agreement to acquire a large chemical company:

> Except as disclosed in the Disclosure Schedule, the Target and its subsidiaries are in compliance with all environmental laws, rules, regulations, orders and decrees.

> Except as disclosed in the Disclosure Schedule, the Target and its subsidiaries are in compliance with all environmental laws, rules, regulations, orders and decrees, noncompliance with which could reasonably be expected to have a material adverse effect on the Target and its subsidiaries, taken as a whole.

This hypothetical target and its subsidiaries regularly run afoul of environmental requirements. Sometimes the noncompliance is immaterial—the target cures the problem by performing routine and inexpensive remediation. Sometimes the issue is material, involving potentially significant fines and remediation costs. Under the first variation of the environmental compliance representation, the seller is required to disclose all violations, material or otherwise. Although preparing such a long schedule may be more work, the seller will be off the hook for all matters that are disclosed. The buyer, on the other hand, will have gotten more information than may be useful to it. In order to understand the potential exposure resulting from these environmental issues, it must understand and analyze every item disclosed on this long schedule.

On the other hand, if the second representation is used a burden is placed on the seller to differentiate between material and immaterial events of noncompliance. The result of this is twofold. First, failure by the seller to include any material violations will result in the representation being breached. Second, the buyer's review and analysis will be better focused, and the risk of the target's noncompliance with environmental requirements will be shifted to the seller only with respect to those matters that are disclosed.

In addition to materiality qualifiers, the other main device used by sellers to soften their representations is the qualification that a representation is made "to the best of the seller's knowledge." An example of this is the following:

> To the best knowledge of the Seller, the Target has good, valid and marketable title to the property it purports to own, free and clear of all encumbrances.

After the closing the buyer learns of an existing easement in favor of a state agency running through the center of the target's main operating facility, and the state's plans to exercise its rights under the easement in connection with a road-building project. The buyer will have recourse against the seller only to the extent that it can show that the seller knew about the easement.

The use of a knowledge standard may have a negative impact on the value of the seller's representations, and therefore is usually vigorously resisted by buyers. The issue for the buyer as to most representations is not whether adverse facts are known by the seller, but rather which party should bear the risk they represent. The use of a knowledge standard effectively shifts the risk of unknown problems from the seller to the buyer.

Following is a discussion of some of the representations most often made by the seller in acquisition agreements.[20]

[E]   Corporate Existence, Power and Authority

In a stock acquisition or a merger, the buyer will want to know that the acquired companies have all the necessary attributes of corporate existence. The language of this representation is as follows:

> Each of the Target and its subsidiaries (i) is a corporation duly organized, validly existing and in good standing under the laws of its state of incorporation; (ii) has full corporate power and authority to carry on its business as it is now being conducted and to own the properties and assets it now owns; and (iii) is duly qualified or licensed to do business as a foreign corporation in

---

20. For a more exhaustive discussion of acquisition agreement representations, see Kling and Nugent § 11.04. Enforceability representations (see section 9:2) will always be made by both the buyer and the seller; they are not discussed here.

good standing in every jurisdiction in which such qualification is required.

The only part of this that is likely to be negotiated is clause (iii). The impact of failing to be qualified in a particular state may be small; accordingly, this representation is often subject to a materiality qualification. Additionally, if the entity being acquired is some form of entity other than a corporation, the representation must be modified accordingly.

Note that the representation covers not only the target but also the target's subsidiaries, as the acquisition of a target with subsidiaries results in the acquisition of the subsidiaries as well. Consider an acquisition of a holding company, the only assets of which are the equity interests in a number of operating subsidiaries. An acquisition agreement that provides for representations only as to the entity that is being directly acquired (the parent holding company) will fail to provide the buyer with comfort as to the real guts of the business. Therefore, the buyer will always want representations that cover both the target and the target's subsidiaries.

[F]   Consents; No Violations

If an acquisition results in the target's violation of a legal or contractual requirement, the buyer may be purchasing a headache. For example, if the target has an important lease with a change of control provision that isn't discovered by the buyer until after the closing, the buyer may find itself with a landlord that has the right to terminate or renegotiate the lease. Or, the target could be in violation of a law or order because of the transaction and as a result be facing criminal sanctions or penalties. Obviously, no buyer wants to walk unknowingly into a situation like this, and therefore the following representation is standard.

> The consummation of the transactions contemplated hereby will not (i) conflict with or result in the breach of any provision of the certificate of incorporation, by-laws or similar organizational documents of the Target or any of its subsidiaries, (ii) require any filing with, or permit, authorization, consent or approval of, any Governmental Entity or other Person (including consents from parties to agreements to which the Target or any of its subsidiaries is a party), (iii) require any consent, approval or notice under, or result in a violation or breach of, or constitute (with or with-

out notice or the passage of time or both) a default (or give rise to any right of termination, amendment, cancellation or acceleration) under, any agreement to which the Target or any of its subsidiaries is a party, or (iv) violate any order, writ, injunction, decree, statute, rule or regulation applicable to the Target, any of its subsidiaries or any of their properties or assets.

The buyer will probably require, as a condition to closing, that the seller obtain any consents that are necessary to make this representation true. Sometimes a materiality qualifier is negotiated with respect to conflicts with agreements. For example, a target that is a retailer with 500 leased locations may have a handful of leases that contain change-of-control provisions that aren't waived. A materiality qualifier would prevent this situation from blowing up the deal.

[G]   Financial Statements; No Undisclosed Liabilities

This is an extremely important representation: the financial statements of the target are probably the single most crucial document to a buyer in making its investment decision. The representation will be similar in form and substance to that discussed above in connection with credit agreements (see section 9:3.1[A]). This representation may need to be significantly modified in the context of an asset sale or the sale of a subsidiary. If the acquisition involves all of the assets of a business that has its own financial statements, there is no issue: the seller will make the normal representations with regard to these financial statements. If, however, the assets being sold are the assets of a division or a subsidiary of a larger business, it is likely that separate financial statements with respect to the business represented by these assets will not exist. In this case, the representation will have to be tailored to cover the financial information that was actually delivered to the buyer in its due diligence. So, for example, if such financial information was not audited by accountants, no representation can be requested as to the existence of an audit.

[H]   Material Adverse Change

The buyer protects itself against target problems or financial deterioration after the date of the financial statements by getting a representation that there has been no material adverse change after the statement date. Thus, if the target's sales had fallen significantly since the period covered by the financial statements delivered to the buyer, the seller fails to disclose this as a material adverse change at its own risk.

[I]   Books and Records

In many cases, the effectiveness of the buyer's due diligence will depend on the soundness of the target's books and records (including accounting records, minute books and stock transfer records). Therefore, the seller will be expected to make the following representation:

> The books of account, minute books, stock record books and other records of the Target and its subsidiaries are complete and correct in all material respects and have been maintained in accordance with sound business practices, including the maintenance of an adequate system of internal controls. The minute books of the Target contain accurate and complete records of all meetings of, and corporate action taken by, the shareholders of the Target and its board of directors and all committees thereof.

[J]   Title to Assets

> Except for inventory sold in the ordinary course of business, the Target and each of its subsidiaries has good, valid and marketable title to all the properties and assets that they purport to own (tangible and intangible) free and clear of all Encumbrances.

This representation will be worded differently depending on whether the transaction is an asset purchase or a stock purchase. In an asset deal, the seller will make this representation as to the assets that are being sold to the buyer. In a stock deal or a merger, the representation will be made with respect to the assets that are owned by the target and each of its subsidiaries.

A buyer is trying to mitigate two important risks by asking for this representation: first the buyer's plans to operate the acquired assets may be impaired by a claim or encumbrance. For example, trademarks might be subject to a long-term license agreement that would prevent their use by the buyer, or an encumbrance may represent an economic cost that should be factored into the purchase price. If, for instance, as a result of disclosure under this representation the buyer learns that a plant of the target is subject to a $1 million mechanics' lien, the buyer will probably require either a corresponding reduction to the purchase price or satisfaction of the lien by the seller as a condition to closing.

[K] Capitalization

This representation will be required in stock acquisition and merger transactions. Since in each of these transactions the buyer is acquiring the target by acquiring the target's shares directly (or indirectly, in the case of certain mergers), it is important for the buyer to fully understand the characteristics of these shares.

> The authorized capital stock of the Target consists of _____ Shares of common stock (of which _____ shares are issued and outstanding) and _____ shares of preferred stock, par value $___ per share (of which ____ shares are issued and outstanding). All the outstanding shares of the Target's capital stock have been duly authorized and validly issued and are fully paid and non-assessable. Except as set forth above, (i) there are no shares of capital stock of the Target authorized, issued or outstanding; (ii) there are no existing options, warrants, calls, preemptive rights, subscriptions or other rights, agreements, arrangements or commitments of any character, relating to the issued or unissued capital stock of the Target, obligating the Target to issue, transfer or sell or cause to be issued, transferred or sold any shares of capital stock, or other equity interest in, the Target or securities convertible into or exchangeable for such shares or equity interests, or obligating the Target to grant, extend or enter into any such option, warrant, call, preemptive right, subscription or other right, agreement, arrangement or commitment; and (iii) there are no outstanding contractual obligations of the Target to repurchase, redeem or otherwise acquire any capital stock of the Target.

The buyer's overriding concern is to ensure that it is acquiring 100% of the voting and economic interests in the target. This goal could be defeated if there are shares owned by someone other than the seller, if there are options, conversion rights or preemptive rights pursuant to which third parties may be able to obtain shares or if there are voting agreements relating to such shares. The existence of present or future minority shareholders may affect buyer's view as to the appropriate value of the transaction or whether the potential nuisance of dealing with other shareholders makes the deal undesirable. The buyer will also want to know the details of any preferred or other non-voting stock, because such securities raise a potential economic (as opposed to control) issue. If the buyer expects to have the target pay dividends or make distributions to it, the existence of other classes of capital stock that would be required to share therein will be significant. Outstanding preferred stock may have dividend requirements that have to be satisfied before common dividends may be paid. The provisions of the preferred stock may give the holders thereof veto power over specified transactions or contain other contract-like provisions that may be adverse to the buyer's interests.

[L]   Litigation, Full Disclosure, Etc.

Acquisition agreements contain a number of representations that are similar to, and serve the same purpose as, certain of the representations discussed above in the context of credit agreements. These include representations regarding litigation (section 9:3.1[D]), compliance with law (section 9:3.1[E]), and full disclosure (section 9:3.1[G]).

[M]   Other Representations

The typical acquisition agreement will also contain a number of additional representations regarding specific aspects of the target's business. They will often be tailored to the specific transaction. These representations may cover, among other matters, the following:

- Environmental matters—has the target complied with all applicable rules and regulations? Are there any pending or threatened claims relating to environmental matters? Have all relevant environmental activities been disclosed?

- Accounts receivable—how timely are they being paid? Are there disputes with customers?

- Inventory—have all necessary writedowns and reserves been taken on the books?

- Real property—have all appropriate title documents been delivered to the buyer? Are there any condemnation or similar proceedings pending or threatened? Are any properties under lease?

- Leases—have they all been disclosed? Are there any defaults under any leases?

- Contracts and commitments—have all material items been disclosed? Are there any defaults? Do employment agreements provide for severance payments? Do any agreements provide for the payment of liquidated damages in the event of breach or termination?

- Insurance—is the property of the target properly insured? Are there any unsettled insurance claims outstanding?

- Employee benefit plans—have they all been disclosed? Will any plans be terminated as a result of the acquisition, and, if so, at what cost?

- Tax matters—has the target filed all tax returns and paid all taxes? Are there any disputes with any taxing authority?

- Intellectual property—are all items disclosed? Are there any disputes with respect to ownership or use? Are there any third-party infringement claims? Have all actions been taken to maintain validity and effectiveness?

- Labor matters—are there any strikes or labor problems? Has the target complied with all applicable labor laws?

§ 9:4.2   Covenants

Unlike covenants imposed on a debtor by a creditor (see sections 9:3.2 and 9:3.3), which tend to regulate a broad range of business activities, covenants under an acquisition agreement impose requirements that generally relate only to the transaction itself. They can be distinguished by the period of time that they cover: some apply during the period between signing and closing and others apply after closing. The pre-closing covenants, as a general rule, require the seller to take actions that will either facilitate the closing or will prevent the target's business from being changed or impaired in any meaningful way. The buyer's recourse for a breach of the seller's covenants are (a) termination by the buyer of the acquisition agreement (if the breach occurs and is discovered before closing), (b) action by the buyer against seller for breach of contract, or (c) indemnification, to the extent provided under the agreement.

[A] Interim Operations of the Target

A recurring theme in acquisition documentation is the buyer's interest in protecting itself against changes that would result in the target's being a different company in some sense from the one the buyer initially decided to acquire. The seller is required to bring down its representations at the time of the closing; however, the buyer typically requires more: it will want to curtail certain activities between signing and closing that the buyer considers detrimental to its potential investment in the target. This covenant will generally prohibit the target and its subsidiaries from engaging in activities outside the ordinary course of business during the period from the signing of the acquisition agreement through the closing date. Often, this general restriction will be supplemented by a number of specific restrictions on the target and its subsidiaries doing any of the following:

- changing accounting practices
- amending its organizational documents
- creating subsidiaries
- amending or terminating material contracts or insurance policies
- incurring or prepaying debt
- changing compensation levels or modifying benefit plans
- entering into new leases or licensing agreements
- entering into material contracts
- paying dividends
- entering into transactions with affiliates
- making investments
- issuing or selling capital stock
- making capital expenditures
- disposing of assets
- settling claims or litigation

The tension in negotiating this covenant is between the buyer's interest in tightly restricting the target's behavior in order to preserve its value, and the seller's (and the target's) interest in having an adequate amount of operating flexibility. This tension increases in direct correlation to the expected length of time between signing and closing.

There are a number of methods to soften these covenants to satisfy the need for flexibility. First, the parties can exclude transactions in the ordinary course of business that are consistent with past practices. This approach works as long as the target has a demonstrable track record as to the activity at issue that the buyer understands and is comfortable with. A second approach is to permit the restricted action up to a negotiated level. This is appropriate as to actions that can be quantified—for example, a restriction on entering into new supply contracts can apply only to contracts that involve payments in excess of some specified dollar amount.

[B]   Actions Relating to the Closing

The buyer's obligation to purchase will be subject to a number of conditions precedent that must be satisfied by the seller. If the seller fails to satisfy any of these, the buyer will be able to walk away from the transaction. Why, then, does the buyer need a covenant requiring the seller to do its best to cause such conditions to be satisfied? Because, without this covenant, the seller would be able to get out of the transaction without cost merely by failing to satisfy these conditions (unless the buyer was willing to waive them). This covenant allows the buyer to assert a breach of contract claim against a seller that has failed to diligently pursue closing.[23]

> Prior to the Closing, the Seller shall use its reasonable best efforts to take all actions, and to do all things necessary, to consummate the Closing as promptly as practicable.

In many cases, this general language will be supplemented by specific requirements as to particular closing conditions. For example, if a governmental permit is required, the buyer may propose a provision

---

23.   This issue runs both ways: the seller will also want to be able to drag a reluctant buyer to the altar. Accordingly, this covenant is often written to apply to both parties.

not only requiring the seller to use its best efforts to obtain the permit, but also requiring the seller to file its application for the permit by a specific date.

[C]   Notification of Certain Matters

The buyer will want to be made aware of any new facts or developments arising prior to closing that are pertinent to its investment decision. This is addressed by the following covenant:

> The Seller shall promptly supplement or amend the Disclosure Schedule with respect to any matter arising after the date of this Agreement that, if existing or occurring on the date of this Agreement, would have been required to be included on the Disclosure Schedule. No supplement or amendment of the Disclosure Schedule pursuant to this section shall be deemed to cure any breach of representation hereunder.

When new facts arise or are discovered after the signing date that would have originally been disclosed under the seller's representations, the seller is obligated to disclose them under this covenant. If the facts existed on the signing date and their omission resulted in the representation's being incorrect, the buyer will usually have the right to terminate the agreement. In other words, the buyer can't be forced to close in the face of facts that could have affected its original investment decision. The seller may argue that this covenant is not really necessary: the new facts will prevent the seller from satisfying the closing condition that it bring down all of its representations. This will allow the buyer to terminate the transaction. The buyer, however, doesn't want to be kept in the dark as to adverse facts or developments while the seller is furtively trying to make them go away. Particularly when there is a long gap between signing and closing, the buyer will want the ability to evaluate the situation when it arises, not at a much later date.

[D]   Post-closing Covenants

The perfect acquisition transaction ends in a neat closing and a happy buyer and seller who shake hands, go their separate ways and never speak to each other again. Unfortunately, this ideal is seldom, if ever achieved. Often, there are post-closing purchase price adjustments. There may be loose ends that must be tied up, such as closing conditions that were converted into post-closing covenants. There may be a transitional period during which the seller is required to continue to provide services to the target. In addition, there are certain common post-closing covenants. Following is a brief discussion of some of these.

Confidentiality

As a result of their due diligence the buyer and the seller may have obtained confidential information relating to the other. Under a confidentiality provision each party agrees to maintain the confidentiality of non-public information. There are a number of customary exceptions to the confidentiality obligation, including:

- Confidentiality need not be maintained for information that is made public through no fault of the covenanting party.

- Confidential information may be shared with counsel, accountants and other advisors in connection with the transaction.

- Information may be disclosed if required by process of law (subject to the other party being given notice and an opportunity to obtain a protective order blocking public disclosure of the information).

Covenant Not to Compete

A buyer will often want to ensure that the seller does not start up a new business to compete with the business that it just sold to the buyer. This is accomplished by the inclusion of a covenant not to compete in the acquisition agreement. Broad covenants not to compete are carefully scrutinized by the courts, so it is important to narrowly describe the scope of the restricted business and the duration and geographical coverage of the covenant.

Anti-poaching Covenant

Both the seller and the buyer may have an interest in protecting against the other party hiring away its employees. This covenant protects against that behavior.

§ 9:4.3　　*Conditions Precedent: Chickens, Eggs and Big Fat Moments in Time*

Most acquisition agreements are signed well in advance of the actual closing. As a result, the conditions precedent to closing are the subject of careful scrutiny and negotiation. If the buyer isn't careful in negotiating the conditions, it may be forced to purchase a company that is less attractive than the one it thought it was getting or be subject to an action for damages by the seller. By the same token, the seller will do its best to avoid conditions that are so open-ended that the buyer will be able to walk on the basis of some technicality. Both parties will want to protect themselves against unforeseen risks that may be triggered by the consummation of the acquisition—for example, claims by third parties for tortious interference.

The obligation of each of the buyer and the seller to close is subject to a different (although in some respects overlapping) set of conditions. If each of the conditions to the seller's performance isn't satisfied, the seller is not required to close (unless it chooses to waive the unsatisfied conditions). The same is true for the buyer if the conditions to its performance are not satisfied. From the perspective of the parties' lawyers, the conditions of both parties fall into two categories: those that the lawyers can help to satisfy and those completely outside of the lawyers' control. Once an acquisition agreement is signed, the lawyers will begin to work towards the closing of the acquisition. Each lawyer will take primary responsibility for certain items that must be delivered to get the opposing party to perform. For example, the conditions to the seller's performance will include delivery to the seller of the buyer's certified charter and by-laws, board resolutions and one or more officer's certificates: buyer's counsel will be responsible for producing these. At the same time, the seller's counsel will have responsibility for similar documents with respect to its client that must be delivered to the buyer. Each lawyer will review the items prepared and delivered by the other. Notwithstanding the occasional skirmish, the preparation for the closing is essentially a collaborative effort.

What happens if a closing condition isn't satisfied? There are several potential results:

- The closing does not occur
- The closing is delayed until the condition has been satisfied

- The failure of the condition to be satisfied is waived in exchange for a concession (such as an adjustment to the purchase price)

- The condition is converted into a covenant to be performed after closing

- The condition is waived

Questions of timing are often the subject of intense focus. Imagine two boys involved in the swap of baseball cards where neither will give up possession first; the exchange can be consummated only with a simultaneous snatch and release. Commercial and corporate transactions are, in essence, no different. The seller will not risk delivering title to the assets without receiving payment. The buyer does not want to pay before delivery. In a simple acquisition this is generally addressed without much fuss through the mechanics of closing. Each closing document is executed and placed on the closing table. Included among these will be the key documents for transferring title: stock certificates and stock powers, in the case of a stock deal; bills of sale and other transfer documents in the case of an asset deal; and a signed merger agreement, in the case of a merger. When the parties and their counsel are in agreement that all conditions have been satisfied (or waived) other than the payment of the purchase price, the buyer instructs its bank (usually over the phone) to wire transfer the purchase price to the seller's bank account. At that point, the parties will agree that the transaction is closed. This is a modest fiction: at that point, the seller will not have yet received the money, because wire transfers are not instantaneous. The parties will generally mill about the closing room until the seller's bank acknowledges receipt of the wire.

As transactions become more complicated, with a greater number of parties, more steps and more payments to be made, the mutual suspension of disbelief inherent in the scenario described above becomes harder to sustain. Frequently, one of the parties will insist that its performance must be the last step in the closing process, leading to a metaphysical discussion that practitioners refer to as the chicken-and-egg debate. Eventually, the parties will inevitably get comfortable with the (also metaphysical) notion that all the steps are occurring simultaneously in a "big fat moment in time."

The remainder of this section examines some specific acquisition agreement conditions.

[A]   Payment and Transfer

The primary condition to a buyer's performance is the seller's transfer to it of the acquired assets or stock. The primary condition to a seller's obligation to effect such transfers is the buyer's payment of the purchase price and delivery of any non-cash consideration.

[B]   Legal Impediments

Neither party will want to close if doing so violates a law or a court order. Both parties' performance will therefore be conditioned on there being no statute, rule, regulation order, decree or injunction that prohibits the consummation of the closing. The buyer will also seek a separate condition that there are no pending governmental proceedings that could impair the acquired business or the buyer's ownership thereof—for example, antitrust proceedings that may result in the buyer being forced to divest part of the acquired business. In addition, neither party will be willing to close if any required governmental approval is not delivered.

[C]   Litigation

Each party will want to have its performance of the acquisition agreement conditioned to some extent on the absence of litigation relating to the transaction itself. No one wants to close a transaction under a cloud of litigation. The issues arising in the negotiation of this condition are usually the materiality level of the litigation and how and by whom such materiality is quantified. Without a materiality qualification, the existence of any litigation as to the transaction, no matter how spurious, will give each of the parties a free walk. This is of particular concern if one of the transaction parties is a public company, given the possibility of strike suits.

The buyer will also want a condition relating to litigation affecting the target. The buyer will want the right to assess litigation against the target seeking money damages or injunctive relief that could be disruptive or harmful to the target's business. The mechanism to provide for this is a condition to the buyer's performance that there is no litigation against the target. Often this condition will be subject to a materiality qualification.

[D]   Representations

The buyer will not be required to close unless the seller's representations are true on the closing date.[24] Without this condition, the buyer could be forced to acquire a target that is substantially different from the one described in the seller's original representations. True, the buyer may have an indemnification claim or a claim for breach of contract, but most buyers will not willingly purchase damaged goods and the right to bring a lawsuit.

An often-negotiated issue is whether the condition requires the representations merely to be "true and correct" or "true and correct in all material respects." The seller will make all of the usual arguments in favor of the materiality standard. The buyer will argue that certain of the representations already are subject to a materiality standard. According to the buyer, the addition of a general materiality standard to the condition will have two improper results: the representations that were originally made flat will become subject to materiality, and the representations that were originally made with a materiality standard will become subject to two materiality standards (with whatever mysterious effect that may have).

[E]   Performance of Covenants

Another condition to the buyer's performance will be compliance by the seller with all of its covenants. As discussed above, the covenants applicable to the seller prior to closing generally prevent actions that could result in significant changes to the target. If the seller has breached one of these covenants the buyer will be able to walk away from the deal, but in most circumstances this will not be the result. Unless the harm to the target is extremely significant, the failure of the condition to be satisfied will instead give rise to a negotiation, most often relating to a purchase price adjustment.

[F]   Officer's Certificate

The seller will be required to deliver a certificate signed by one of its officers stating that (i) its representations in the acquisition agree-

---

24. The remainder of the discussion of conditions precedent will, for simplicity's sake, address only conditions to the buyer's performance.

ment are true and correct at closing, and (ii) it has performed all of its covenants in the acquisition agreement. While this seems duplicative of the conditions discussed in sections 9:4.3[D] and [E] above, there is a technical but important difference. If no certificate is delivered, there is no actual bring-down of the representations and no statement that all of the covenants have been satisfied at closing to provide the basis for an indemnification claim by the buyer. On the other hand, if the representation and covenant conditions are omitted and only the condition requiring the officer's certificate is included, the buyer will be forced to close if the officer delivers the required certificate, even if the buyer is aware of representation or covenant breaches. A further benefit of getting an officer's certificate, in this as well as other circumstances, is that an individual officer will be likely to investigate the correctness of the statements in a certificate that he is required to sign.

[G]   Financing

The inclusion of a financing condition permits a buyer to terminate the transaction if it is not able to obtain financing for the purchase price. The seller who accepts this condition to the buyer's performance assumes a potentially large risk of non-closure. Often, one of the seller's primary criteria in choosing a buyer is whether the buyer has the financial ability to close. A seller may even be willing to accept a lower purchase price in exchange for greater certainty of closing. Conversely, a buyer lacking the financial ability to consummate the acquisition that enters into an acquisition agreement without a financing out, also assumes a significant risk. If the closing fails due to the buyer's inability to pay, the buyer will be subject to a claim by the seller for damages.

In some cases, the seller may be willing to accept a financing condition if at the time the acquisition agreement is signed there is some indication that the buyer has a reasonable expectation of lining up the financing. This usually involves the delivery by the buyer of a financing commitment from a third party, indicating the third party's agreement to provide all or a portion of the necessary financing. The seller and its counsel will examine any such commitment carefully: the more conditions there are to the commitment, the less comfort will be obtained by the seller.

[H] Legal Opinions

A legal opinion is a letter by a lawyer setting forth legal conclusions regarding his client and the transaction documents to which the client is a party. The primary subjects of legal opinions delivered in connection with transactions are similar to those that are covered by the "enforceability representations" (see section 9:2). Legal opinions are requested to assure the opinion recipient that the necessary legal due diligence relating to these representations has been undertaken. Some also view the opinion as something akin to an insurance policy: if the statements made by the lawyer in an opinion turn out to be false, a claim may be asserted against the lawyer. Such claims are subject to a negligence standard, however—the statements made by lawyers in legal opinions do not give rise to strict liability if determined to be wrong.

Whether or not opinions are delivered as a condition to closing a particular transaction is a function of custom and negotiating leverage. In acquisition transactions, the trend has been away from the use of opinions. Of course, opinions may be requested to provide comfort as to a particular legal issue in a transaction.

§ 9:4.4   *Remedies*

The remedies that are available to a party under an acquisition agreement are usually the following:

- Termination of the agreement in the event of the other party's breach of representations or covenants

- Indemnification from the other party for its breach of representations or covenants

- An action for damages resulting from the other party's breach of representations or covenants (unless the agreement provides that indemnification is the sole remedy)

- An action for damages resulting from the other party's failure to close notwithstanding the satisfaction of all of the conditions precedent to its performance

Only the first two of these, which are explicitly provided for in the agreement, will be discussed here.

[A]   Termination

The remedy of termination is relatively straightforward: if one party breaches its representations or warranties, the other party may terminate the agreement. This remedy is available only before the closing of the acquisition, since its primary effect is to prevent the closing from occurring. This may raise a question as to the need for this remedy, given that the breach will also cause the failure of a closing condition. But most agreements provide for an outside date for the closing to occur, and without a termination provision a party would have to wait for that date before it could assert the other's breach as a basis for ending the agreement. The termination provision allows the party to walk away immediately upon the discovery of a breach by the other party.

[B]   Indemnification

Indemnification is usually the sole remedy for breaches of an acquisition agreement that occur or are discovered after closing.[25] Although the indemnification provisions are generally mutual, the vast majority of indemnity claims are by the buyer against the seller and relate to the breach by the seller of representations or covenants relating to the target. In other words, the typical indemnification claim is based on a buyer that has received, in its view, damaged goods. Other indemnification claims may seek compensation for out-of-pocket expenses incurred as a result of the other's breach. Indemnification may also be provided for specific claims without regard to the existence of a breach. For example, a seller may agree to indemnify a buyer against all liability and attorneys' fees in connection with a specified litigation to which the target is a party at the time of the closing.

Here is the basic indemnification provision by a seller in favor of a buyer:

---

25. As additional features are introduced to a simple acquisition, additional remedies may be added as well. If a part of the purchase price is to be paid by the buyer over time, breach by the buyer may result in the seller having the right to accelerate such obligations, for example.

> The Seller shall indemnify and hold harmless the Buyer from and against all losses, damages, penalties, disbursements, costs and expenses (including without limitation attorneys' fees and expenses) incurred by the Buyer as a result of any breach by the Seller of any of its representations or covenants under this Agreement.

What is the difference between a buyer asserting a claim for indemnification under this provision and asserting a claim for damages in an action for fraud or breach of contract? First, a party's right to indemnification may be subject to negotiated limitations. Second, the type of damages provided for in an indemnification provision may be different from those available in a legal proceeding—for example, attorney's fees might not be awarded to the plaintiff in a contract action. Having said this, the inclusion of indemnification provisions does not avoid the need for the indemnitee to prove the breach and its damages.

There are a number of techniques to limit exposure under an indemnification provision. The first is a basket, which is similar to an insurance deductible. The indemnitee may not receive indemnity payments except to the extent its indemnity claims exceed a stated dollar amount. In addition, sometimes any claim beneath a specified dollar amount will neither give rise to an indemnity claim or count against the basket. Another negotiated approach in this context may be that indemnity claims are not paid until they aggregate a stated dollar amount, at which point they are all paid. Sometimes a buyer will agree to cap the maximum aggregate amount of indemnity payments that it is entitled to receive. These provisions often contain detailed procedures with respect to claims for indemnification for legal claims. The basic rule is that the indemnitor, being responsible for paying a judgment or settlement in respect of a claim against the indemnitee, is entitled to control the defense of such claim, including the selection of counsel.

Chapter 10

Miscellaneous Provisions; Miscellaneous Thoughts

§ 10:1   Introduction

At the end of all long contracts is the "Miscellaneous" section, where everything that doesn't fit neatly elsewhere is collected. Last minute agreements are often tucked in there as well. As with contracts, so with this book. This last chapter covers the customary provisions included in contract "miscellaneous" sections. It also is the collection area for stray points that didn't find a useful place elsewhere in the book.

§ 10:2   The "Miscellaneous" Sections

This part of a contract often contains provisions that are neither operative provisions, representations, covenants, conditions, definitions nor remedial provisions. There are two basic categories of provisions included in this section: provisions that relate to the enforcement, amendment and interpretation of the contract (most of these are often considered boilerplate), and provisions that are specific to the transaction but that don't fall neatly into any of the other sections. For this reason, a lawyer reading a contract skips the miscellaneous provisions at her and her client's risk; sometimes important items are buried there.

§ 10:2.1   *Choice of Law*

This provision states that the contract is to be interpreted and enforced under the law of a particular jurisdiction. A common formulation of this is the following:

> This Agreement and the rights and obligations of the parties hereunder shall be governed by, and construed and interpreted in accordance with, the laws of the State of _____.

This is the most important of the miscellaneous provisions and should never be omitted from any contract, no matter how short or informal. It specifies that all substantive legal issues arising in connection with the enforcement or interpretation of the contract are to be resolved by looking to the law of the chosen jurisdiction. Without this provision, any dispute regarding a contract will most likely also involve a dispute over the law governing the contract. Anyone who has taken a conflict of laws class knows the complexity of the issues that can be involved in a judicial determination of this issue.

Let's look at two examples illustrating the potential importance of this provision:

- A Massachusetts finance company and an individual resident of Ohio enter into a loan agreement governed by New York law. The bank lends the individual $200,000 under the loan agreement, at an interest rate of 18%. The borrower files for bankruptcy and asserts usury as a defense against the bank's claim. The bankruptcy judge applies New York usury law, which prohibits loans to individuals of less than $250,000 bearing interest at greater than 16% per annum. The lender's entire claim against the borrower is voided. If the law of Ohio had been selected as the governing law of the loan agreement, the usury defense would not have been available to the borrower.

• The seller under a long-term supply contract asserted a claim against the buyer for breach; the dispute lingered for a while and the parties went their separate ways. Four years later, seller was acquired and the acquiror determined that the seller's claim was meritorious. Unfortunately, the statute of limitations had run under Arkansas law, which was the governing law of the contract. If the parties had selected the law of Virginia, the state where the buyer was located, the claim would still be enforceable because the statute of limitations there for contract claims is six years.

What law should be selected to govern a contract? In some cases the answer is self-evident. A contract relating to the conveyance or lease of real estate is almost always governed by the law of the state where the property is located. A contract between two individuals who are residents of New Jersey should probably be governed by the laws of New Jersey. A shareholders agreement among shareholders of a Delaware corporation will often be governed by the law of Delaware. In many cases, the correct choice of law is much less obvious. Most states will enforce the parties' choice of its law as the governing law of a contract only if there are sufficient contacts with that state. The contact requirement may be satisfied, for example, if one or more parties is incorporated or resident in that state, the contract involves property located in the state, or payments are to be made from or into the state. The failure to ensure that there are sufficient contacts to support the contractual choice of law can have unpleasant consequences. The party that would benefit from the application of another state's law may argue that the choice of law was invalid and that the law of a different state should be applied based on common-law choice of law principles.

The law that is most often chosen in large corporate and financing transactions is New York law. There are three reasons for this. First, New York has a well-developed body of case law regarding commercial issues and a judiciary experienced in these matters. Second, many of the prominent players in this arena—investment banks, banks, corporations and law firms—are based in New York. Last, New York has a statute[1] that permits contracting parties to select New York law as the governing law regardless of the existence or sufficiency of any contacts with New York. It is easy to choose New York law knowing that a New York court will enforce this choice of law. (On the other hand, a court outside of New York may entertain arguments that under *its* owns laws, the choice of New York law was improper.)

Sometimes a governing law provision will refer to a state's laws "without regard to any choice of law rules thereunder." The purpose of this is to avoid having the application of that state's choice of law rules result in a different state's laws being chosen to govern the contract. For example, if State A's law requires the application of the laws of the state with the most significant contacts, it is possible that a court looking at a contract governed by State A's law may decide that State B's law should be applied because there are greater contacts with State B. If the language referred to above is included in the governing law clause, this possibility is avoided.[2]

§ 10:2.2   *Consent to Jurisdiction*

This provision is designed to ensure that a dispute regarding the contract will be heard in a particular court or the courts of a particular state. This is achieved by having the parties agree that they are subject to the personal jurisdiction of such courts. Sometimes this provision is drafted to provide that the jurisdiction to which the parties consent is the exclusive jurisdiction to litigate issues arising under the contract. The risk of this approach is that it forecloses each of the parties from obtaining possible strategic advantages by bringing suit elsewhere.[3] For this reason it is usually more customary to state that the consent to jurisdiction is nonexclusive.

Frequently there is also an agreement by the parties that service of process in any litigation may be made by mail sent in accordance with

---

1.   N.Y. GEN. OBLIG. LAW § 5-1402. The transaction must be for at least $250,000; certain exclusions apply.
2.   In contracts governed by New York law or the law of a state with a statute similar to the New York statute discussed in the preceding paragraph this language is refined as follows: "without regard to any choice of law rules thereunder except GOL Section 5-1402".
3.   In addition, a provision for exclusive jurisdiction may be unenforceable.

the notice provision of the contract. This improves the likelihood that parties will not be able to assert any procedural defects in the manner by which service is effected. These provisions also frequently contain a waiver of the parties' right to assert that a proceeding in the specified jurisdiction is in an improper or inconvenient forum.

§ 10:2.3   *Waiver of Jury Trial*

Commercial contracts routinely provide for a waiver by the parties of their right to a trial by jury in connection with any litigation associated with the contract. Most sophisticated parties would prefer to avoid the extra uncertainty that is often associated with having a jury be the trier of fact. On the other hand, an individual entering into a contract with a bank or other large institution may prefer to know that a dispute will be heard by a jury of his peers. This is exactly why the bank or institution wants a waiver of jury trial, and, unfortunately for the individual, it is invariably the institution that drafts the contract.

Waivers of jury trial are usually binding on both parties. This is done to counteract the concern that the waiver of jury trial may not be upheld by a court that determines the waiver was obtained as a result of greatly unequal bargaining power. Jury trial waivers are also often written in block capital letters in order to satisfy the requirement imposed by some jurisdictions that such waivers be conspicuous.

§ 10:2.4   *Counterparts*

A counterparts provision states that the contract may be executed separately by the parties—in other words, the signatures of the parties do not need to be on the same piece of paper. This is an extremely useful provision in the current age of virtual closings where signatories may be spread around the globe. These situations involve the parties signing signature pages separately and returning them by fax or mail to the lawyers, who then attach them to the contract when the closing occurs. These are separate "counterparts." If faxed signatures are anticipated, it is also useful (though perhaps not a legal necessity) to add a statement that signatures delivered by fax are effective.

§ 10:2.5   Headings

This section provides that headings are included for reference purposes only and are not to be given any substantive effect. This is to prevent the parties from making arguments based on headings that are incorrect or badly written. For example, suppose that a contract contains a provision under which Party A waives all rights of setoff. The provision does not include a similar waiver by Party B. The provision's heading, however, is "Waiver of the Parties' Rights of Setoff." Without the provision specifying that headings are to be substantively ignored, Party A could argue, based on this heading, that Party B has waived its right of setoff.

§ 10:2.6   Severability

This section states that if a provision in the agreement is found to be legally prohibited or unenforceable, the offending provision is "severed" from the rest of the agreement which otherwise continues to operate as originally written. Otherwise, there is a risk that a court may throw out the baby with the bathwater and refuse to enforce the entire contract.

§ 10:2.7   Integration Clause

This clause provides that the agreement is the entire and exclusive agreement between the parties with respect to its subject matter. This clause prevents the parties from arguing that there are side agreements or understandings that are not set forth within the four corners of the agreement. This may be extremely important in the event of a dispute. Its absence opens the door to the introduction of evidence that the parties had other agreements that superseded or modified the contract in question, which creates an opportunity for much mischief. Of course, if there *are* such other agreements, they should be explicitly excluded from the effect of the integration clause.

§ 10:2.8   No Implied Waivers

A party may contend that a waiver granted by another party should be broadly interpreted to cover events and circumstances other than those to which it was originally addressed. A similar argument can be made that a party's actions or inactions create an implied waiver. For example, a lessee that obtains the lessor's waiver of a requirement that the lessee file its October maintenance report, may argue that it may also skip the delivery of the November report. Or, an employee who has repeatedly failed to deliver his tax returns to the employer as required by his employment agreement, may take the position that by not complaining about the non-delivery, the employer has waived the requirement. To prevent arguments like these, it is customary to include a provision like the following:

> No failure to exercise and no delay in exercising any right or remedy hereunder shall operate as a waiver thereof. No waiver or consent hereunder shall be applicable to any events, acts or circumstances except those specifically covered thereby.

This provision makes it clear that any waivers must be given in writing and will be construed narrowly.

§ 10:2.9   Amendments

This section describes the requirements for entering into amendments, consents and waivers. This section should *always* require amendments, consents and waivers to be in writing.[4] Different contracts have different requirements as to which of the parties must execute and deliver an amendment, consent or waiver. Sometimes it is the "party or parties to be charged" that must sign, which requires the signature of the parties that are negatively affected by the amendment, waiver or consent. The difficulty with this approach is that it may not always be clear which parties are negatively affected. Accordingly, it is generally preferable to require all of the parties to sign each amendment, waiver and consent (see Chapter 7).

§ 10:2.10   Assignment

In many cases the provision governing whether and under what conditions the parties may assign their rights under the agreement is found in the miscellaneous section. The primary exception to this is agreements where assignability is one of the key substantive issues, such as partnership agreements and shareholder agreements. There

---

4.   However, this requirement may be unenforceable under many states' laws.

are three kinds of assignment that may be covered by these provisions.

[A]   Novation

A complete assignment involves the replacement of one of the contract parties by another person or entity that assumes all of the assigning party's rights and obligations under the contract.[5] This form of assignment (technically referred to as a "novation") is found, for example, in real estate leases, where the lessee can be replaced under the lease by assignment. Another example is in a syndicated credit agreement, where lenders usually have the right to assign their rights to be repaid in respect of outstanding loans and to delegate their obligations to make additional loans. In this type of assignment, the assignee becomes a party to the agreement and the assignor usually ceases to be a party (although certain rights and obligations—for example indemnities—may continue). If the assignor assigns and delegates only a part of its interest under the contract, it will continue to be a party with respect to its retained interest.

The right to create a novation is often subject to conditions or the consent of the other parties to the contract. In the case of a lease, for example, the lessor is not going to agree in advance that the lessee can assign the lease to anyone: the lessor will want to ensure, for example, that the credit of the assignee is not any worse than that of the assignor and that the assignee is not going to use the premises for undesirable purposes. Therefore, the assignment section of the lease will set forth criteria that must be satisfied before a novation may be effected.

[B]   Absolute Assignment of Rights

An absolute assignment (e.g., a sale) by a party of its rights under a contract results in the assignee being entitled to receive the benefits of the contract that would otherwise have been paid to or performed for the benefit of the assignor. The assignor continues to be responsible for its performance under the contract.

Article 9 of the Uniform Commercial Code, revised in 1999, renders many contracts' anti-assignment provisions unenforceable. A

---

5.   Many provisions relating to assignments don't clearly distinguish between assignment of rights and delegation of duties.

party may assign its rights under these contracts notwithstanding any prohibition on such assignment or any provision that an assignment results in a termination, defense or default.[6]

[C]   Collateral Assignment of Rights

Another type of assignment is a collateral assignment. A party granting a security interest in its rights under a contract has entered into a collateral assignment of the contract, in other words, has given its secured party the right to foreclose on its interest in the contract if it defaults on the secured obligations.[7] Here's an example: Company A grants to its banks a security interest in its rights under an acquisition agreement pursuant to which Company A is acquiring all of the assets of Company B from Company C. Two years after the acquisition, Company A is in financial distress, in part due to environmental problems associated with Company B's assets. Company A has potentially valuable claims against Company C under the indemnification provisions of the acquisition agreement. After Company A defaults on its bank debt, the banks have the right to foreclose on their security interest in the acquisition agreement, selling Company A's rights thereunder (including the indemnification claims) to a third party for value.

§ 10:2.11 *Costs and Expenses*

Many contracts specify how the parties' costs and expenses relating to the transaction are allocated. Even if each party is to be responsible for its own costs and expenses, it is not a bad idea to state that fact in order to avoid any possible disputes. Where one party

---

6.   UCC § 9-406(d). Absolute assignments of so-called "payment intangibles" (rights to receive monetary payments), promissory notes and certain other rights are also permitted notwithstanding such prohibitions or provisions, but the assignee's rights are limited. UCC § 9-408. Anti-assignment provisions as to certain types of "general intangibles" not involving the payment of money are still enforceable. UCC § 9-109.

7.   Revised Article 9 also affects the enforceability of anti-assignment clauses as they relate to collateral assignments. Anti-assignment clauses are ineffective as to accounts, chattel paper, payment intangibles and promissory notes (UCC § 9-406), and are ineffective as to certain types of general intangibles not for money due but in this case are subject to limitation of the secured party's rights (UCC § 9-408).

agrees to reimburse another for all or a part of its transaction expenses, several issues tend to be negotiated. First is whether only reasonable costs will be covered. The party with the reimbursement obligation wants to impose some limit on the other party's ability to run up unlimited expenses on its ticket. Sometimes a cap on these costs will be negotiated. In other cases, only certain categories of expenses will be reimbursable.

§ 10:2.12   Indemnification

Indemnification is an agreement to pay or reimburse another party's expenses, losses, damages and costs. Many transactions involve some form of indemnification. In most acquisition agreements, the indemnification provision is one of the primary battlegrounds. (See 9:4.4[B].) In credit agreements, on the other hand, indemnification provisions in favor of the lender are customary but seldom negotiated extensively.

The typical language of an indemnification provision is the following:

> Party A indemnifies Party B for and against all liabilities, losses, damages, penalties, actions, judgments, costs, expenses or disbursements of any kind or nature that may be imposed on, incurred by, or asserted against Party B, in any way relating to or arising out of Party B's execution, delivery or performance of this agreement or the consummation of the transactions contemplated hereby.

Let's examine the description of the indemnified amounts: all "liabilities, losses, damages, penalties, actions, judgments, costs, expenses or disbursements." This litany is a classic example of the propensity of legal writers to use every available synonym. This type of list is traditional, however, so it would be inadvisable to shorten it. Exactly what does all of this mean? Let's assume the quoted language appears in an agreement pursuant to which Party B operates a deep-sea drilling rig owned by Party A. There are a list of things that would potentially be covered by this indemnification provision:

- Fines or penalties assessed against it as a result of its performance under the agreement.

- Judgments arising in connection with its performance—for example, a judgment granting damages to a landowner whose property is harmed by a spill emanating from the rig.

- The legal fees and expenses incurred by Party B in defending itself against any claim arising in connection with the agreement or its performance thereunder.

What if the oil spill described in the second point above was Party B's fault? Should Party B be entitled to indemnification for this from Party A? Most indemnification provisions address this type of concern by excluding costs that result from the indemnitee's bad behavior, such as its gross negligence or willful misconduct. See section 5:6.5 for a more thorough description of this exclusion.

§ 10:2.13   *Further Assurances*

> The parties agree to do such further acts and things and to execute and deliver such additional agreements and instruments as may be reasonably necessary to give effect to the purposes of this Agreement and the parties' agreements hereunder.

The further assurances clause addresses one of the transactional lawyer's primal fears: that he forgot to tie down some loose end. By adding this provision, the lawyer gains some measure of comfort that unforeseen matters will be appropriately addressed. It is not a panacea, however. While it is likely to work in relation to minor or ministerial acts that are squarely within the parties' expectations and do not significantly impact either parties' position, it may be ineffective to address an unresolved issue which will result in a meaningful economic or other cost to one of the parties. Take, for example, a real estate lease that required a security deposit to be paid by the tenant in escrow to the landlord's attorney. If two weeks after the closing the landlord asks the tenant to sign a short escrow agreement to evidence this arrangement, the tenant would normally consent. If, on the other hand, the escrow agreement provided that interest on the escrowed funds is paid over to the landlord, the tenant will object. If the landlord points to the further assurances clause and reminds the tenant that during the negotiations there was some discussion of the landlord getting this interest, a pliable tenant may go along. The tenant could, on the other hand, just as easily take the position that the discussions regarding interest never made it into the lease because there was never an agreement on that point, and that therefore the language in the further assurances clause about agreements "reasonably necessary to give effect to the purposes of this Agreement and the parties' agreements hereunder" is inapplicable.

§ 10:3   Miscellany

Don't confuse "principal" and "principle." "Principal" is (a) the amount of a debt obligation, (b) the person instructing an agent, or (c) a synonym for "primary." "Principle" is a theory or idea.

The word "hereby" is often used unnecessarily. In the phrase "Seller hereby agrees," the word "hereby" can be eliminated with no loss of meaning. On the other hand, using "hereby" as an alternative to "by this agreement" is acceptable:

> Seller will not enter into any contracts that restrict its ability to consummate this Agreement and the transactions contemplated hereby.

It is common to see inconsistent provisions in different agreements that are entered into as a part of a single transaction. A frequently occurring example is in the case of a secured financing. The parties first negotiate the credit agreement. Then the security documents arrive, and they contain boilerplate that is inconsistent with fully negotiated provisions in the credit agreement, such as insurance and tax covenants. There are three ways to address this (in declining order of desirability): (a) Delete the inconsistent boilerplate. (b) Modify the boilerplate to exactly match the negotiated provision. (c) Include a provision that in the event of inconsistent provisions, the credit agreement controls.

Under a negative consent clause, a party that fails to object to a specified action by a stated time is deemed to have consented. The party advocating this approach (a) seeks certainty that a decision will be made by a specified date, and (b) fears that the forgetfulness and inertia of his counterparty may result in the consent not being given. The response of the counterparty, more often than not, is: "You want certainty? Fine, but we'll specify that no response by the cut-off time means that consent is denied."

Lawyers tend to be especially clumsy in the use of prepositions. This is particularly true when there is a series of prepositional phrases. For example:

> The Company will use reasonable efforts to ensure that there is <u>no theft or damage to</u> the inventory.

To check the grammar of this sentence, the draftsperson should imagine that there are two separate sentences, one addressing "theft" and the other "damage." By doing this, it is easy to see the error:

> The Company will use reasonable efforts to ensure that there is no theft to the inventory.

Of course, the proper prepositional phrase is "theft of" not "theft to." The sentence should be rewritten:

> The Company will use reasonable efforts to ensure that there is no theft of or damage to the inventory.

Beware of covenants that restrict a party's activities and also restrict the party from entering into an agreement to engage in the restricted activity. Consider, for example, a contract for the sale of a building that prohibits the seller from (a) selling any building fixtures and (b) agreeing to sell any such fixtures. Because the part of the covenant described in clause (b) is relatively unusual, the seller may forget that it is there and enter into another contract to sell a refrigeration unit located in the building. Subsequently realizing his mistake, the seller concludes he hasn't breached the first contract because the sale under the second contract is explicitly conditioned on receipt of consent of the building buyer to the sale of the refrigeration unit. The seller is wrong: he has breached the covenant in the first agreement.

The phrase "any and all" is inelegant, as in the following sentence:

> The Company waives any and all rights to object to the transfer of the Shares.

Would the waiver be less effective if it applied to "all rights" instead of "any and all rights"? Could an argument be made that the waiver of all rights was not effective as to any particular right? No, on both counts.

If a time limitation in a proposed contract seems too tight, it probably is too tight. Try to provide for more time with one of the following approaches:

- Convince the other side that the inevitable extension requests will be annoying and time-consuming.

- Build in an automatic extension if the required action isn't completed on time, as long as diligent efforts were made to meet the first deadline.

- Provide that consent to an extension request will not be unreasonably withheld.

- Where an extension request must be consented to by more than one party, designate one such party to provide a consent that will bind all of the parties.

Occasionally lawyers forget that there are limitations on the ability of contracts to create private law between the parties. Many legal requirements—such as the margin regulations and securities law registration requirements, to name but two examples—can't be waived or ignored because the parties agree to do so. It is also often a mistake to assume that parties can contract their way around property law requirements. An agreement between Party A and Party B stating that Party A is the owner of Blackacre does not make that statement true. A court, for example, could determine that the transaction between Party A and Party B is actually a secured financing and therefore Party B doesn't own Blackacre but merely has a mortgage on it.[8]

Avoid defining the same thing in two different ways in the same contract (as in "Xerxes, Yeoman and Zeus, Inc. shall be referred to herein as 'XYZ' or the 'Company'"). This merely creates confusion.

The concept of a majority is precisely described as "more than 50%." Using "51% or more" may seem close enough, until you are faced with a situation where the actual tally is 50.1%.

Be careful when making global changes. Think about unanticipated consequences. For example, a global change of the word "securities" to "certificates" could result in a reference to the "Securities Act of 1933" being changed to the "Certificates Act of 1933."

What is the effect of including one provision in a contract that requires that something be "satisfactory" to one of the parties and another provision that requires that something else be satisfactory to that party "in its sole discretion"? This type of inconsistency permits an argument to be made that the first determination is subject to some standard other than "sole discretion," such as "reasonable discretion." This illustrates the potential effect of careless inconsistency.

---

8. A riddle attributed to Abraham Lincoln: If you call a dog's tail a leg, how many legs does the dog have? Four: calling the tail a leg doesn't make it a leg.

Sometimes a party with negotiating leverage may impose on the other party an onerous provision, without any particular reason for doing so. This approach can often backfire. For example, a group of lenders may insist on a level of financial reporting that is unusually detailed—for example, a requirement that the borrower provide daily reports of sales and collections. A provision like this can come back to haunt the lenders if they have no real expectation of reviewing this information. First of all, it will require the borrower to devote human resources that would be better spent on more productive tasks. More importantly, the agent bank will be charged with knowledge of all the information delivered to it under this requirement even if it doesn't actually review the material. That fact could create unanticipated exposure to the other banks in the syndicate.

Or take the example of a merger agreement that prohibits the target from entering into contracts valued at $10,000 or more prior to the merger. The other party has not done itself any favors by imposing this restriction if the dollar threshold is unreasonably low in light of the target's business. The result will be a constant stream of requests from the target for waivers, which will become an administrative burden for both parties. Be careful not to put something in the contract just because you can: there should be a real need.

Words like hereof, thereunder, hereinafter, whereby and the like are widely criticized as one of the features of bad legal writing, or "legalese."[9] Admittedly, overuse of these words is to be avoided. On the other hand, these terms, when used properly, can be useful and precise signposts for the reader. They almost always result in fewer words being used. The phrase "as contemplated hereby," rewritten to avoid the prepositional indicator, would be "as contemplated by this agreement."

---

9. The author was once reviewing a contract with another lawyer from his firm and a client. The client scoffed at a provision that included the phrase "subject to this Agreement and the Pledge Agreement and the restrictions hereunder and thereunder." "Why do you lawyers always have to write like that?" the client asked. "You should be glad," said the other lawyer: "We usually write 'hereunder, thereunder and everywhereunder.'"

Here are some technical consistency points to be on the lookout for:

- If a term is defined with the word "the" (for example: the "Investor"), each reference in the agreement to that defined term should also be preceded by "the." The converse is also true: if the party is defined as "Investor," references should be to "Investor," not "the Investor."

- Be consistent in referring to schedules and exhibits. Don't refer in one spot to "Exhibit 1," in another spot to "Exhibit 2 attached hereto" and in another to "Exhibit 3 hereof."

- "Shall" and "will" are synonymous, but choose one and stick with it.

- Even if an agreement's notice provision requires all notices to be in writing, confusion may result if some references to notices specify that they are to be in writing, and others don't.

- Internal cross-references can either use the word "hereof" (as in, "to the extent permitted by Section 5A hereof"), or not. Be consistent.

- The format of definitions should be the same. If the first definition reads "Affiliate means . . .," do not draft the next definition as "Applicable Margin *shall* mean. . . ."

- Some agreements underscore internal cross-references to other sections of the agreement, or to schedules and exhibits. If you do this, do it consistently.

- Make sure that margins and spacing are used consistently throughout the document. Cutting and pasting from other documents can result in the inadvertent use of different fonts and formats.

- In referring to dollar amounts, use words or numbers consistently (i.e., $3 million or $3,000,000).

- Either follow all written references to numbers with a parenthetical reference to the numeral (e.g., "fifteen (15) days") every time, or don't do it at all.

- Be attentive to the use of the terms "the date hereof," "the date of the execution and delivery hereof," "the closing date" and "the date of effectiveness hereof." The failure to be precise and consistent with these references may create substantive as well as style problems.

- Be consistent in the use of serial references. In the phrase "Buyer shall not (a) pay any dividends, (b) redeem any shares or (c) investments in joint ventures shall be limited to $500,000," clause (c) should be harmonized as follows: "make investments in joint ventures in an amount exceeding $500,000."

General carveouts or baskets can be used to permit activities for which specific carveouts or baskets are also available. For example, take an asset sale covenant that has a $10 million basket for sales of obsolete equipment and a $20 million basket for any asset sales. The clients used up the $10 million basket last year; they now come to you asking whether they can sell an additional $2 million of obsolete equipment. The answer is yes, to the extent there is room in the $20 million general basket.

Some favorite typos (all of which illustrate that spell-check only goes so far):

- The Buyer waives its clams against the Seller.

- This agreement has been duly authorized by the Board of Deviators.

- XYZ CORPORATION

  By: _____
  Name: Samuel Doe
  Title: Vice President and Treasure

- All other instruments securing the indebtedness hereunder are hereby made part of this Note and the provisions of such instruments are deemed inappropriate herein.

———————————

Pay careful attention to whether modifiers apply to the items they are meant to modify, and be sure that they don't apply to items they are not meant to modify. Note the ambiguity in this provision:

> The Subsidiary shall not enter into new real property leases or acquire any real estate if its Leverage Ratio exceeds 3.00/1.00.

It is not clear whether the Leverage Ratio requirement applies to each of the restrictions. If it is intended to apply only to real estate acquisitions, the sentence can be clarified by flipping the restrictions and numbering them:

> The Subsidiary shall not (a) acquire any real estate if its Leverage Ratio exceeds 3.00/1.00, or (b) enter into new real property leases.

Alternatively, if the test is to apply to both restrictions, the use of "in either case" clarifies things:

> The Subsidiary shall not enter into any new real property leases or acquire any real estate if, in either case, its Leverage Ratio exceeds 3.00/1.00.

———————————

"Without duplication" is a handy phrase when there is a concern about double-counting or overlaps. For example, let's say the parties want to quantify all of an entity's liabilities, as disclosed on its most recent balance sheet, plus all of its obligations with respect to certain leases that are listed on a schedule. It is not clear whether any or all of the scheduled lease obligations are included as liabilities on the balance sheet. The following language does the trick:

> The sum (without duplication) of (a) all liabilities of the Company set forth on its December 31, 2001 balance sheet, plus (b) all obligations of the Company under the leases set forth on Schedule M.

Glossary*

ACCELERATION CLAUSE: A provision in an executory contract pursuant to which all obligations are accelerated and due irrespective of the stated time for performance (e.g., outstanding debt obligations becoming immediately due and payable if an event of default occurs).

ACCOUNT: *See* "Account Receivable."

ACCOUNT PARTY: *See* "Letter of Credit."

ACCOUNT RECEIVABLE: The right to receive payment for property sold, leased, licensed or services provided. Also referred to as an "account" or a "receivable."

ACCRETION: The growth of a payment obligation over time at an agreed-upon rate. For example, the principal amount of a zero coupon note accretes from the original discounted price for which it is issued to its face amount at maturity. *Compare* "Cash Pay," "Compounding" and "Payment in Kind."

ACQUISITION: A transaction in which all or a controlling portion of the equity, or substantially all of the assets, of a business are acquired.

ACQUISITION AGREEMENT: An agreement pursuant to which an acquisition is effected, either in the form of a stock purchase agreement or an asset purchase agreement.

ADDITIONAL INSURED ENDORSEMENT: A provision in a liability insurance policy giving third parties (most typically lenders to, or investors in, the named insured) protection under the policy. *Compare* "Loss Payee Endorsement."

AFFIRMATIVE COVENANT: *See* "Covenant."

---

*   As is the case with defined terms in contracts, many of the definitions in this glossary include terms that are also separately defined.

AGENT: The entity (often a financial institution) that acts as agent on behalf of a group of principals (most often a syndicate of lenders under a credit agreement).

AGREEMENT IN PRINCIPLE: *See* "Letter of Intent."

AMENDMENT: An agreement that changes the provisions of an existing contract, adds new provisions and/or deletes existing provisions.

AMENDMENT AND RESTATEMENT: A form of amendment in which the entire agreement being amended is set forth in full, with the amended terms being incorporated therein.

AMORTIZATION: (a) The scheduled repayment of the principal amount of a loan. (b) Under GAAP, a periodic reduction of earnings representing the diminution in value of intangible assets. *Compare* "Depreciation."

ANTI-ASSIGNMENT CLAUSE: A provision that prohibits, restricts or requires consent to the assignment of a party's rights or to the delegation of a party's obligations under an agreement.

ANTI-DILUTION PROVISION: A provision that protects a party entitled to the issuance of equity interests (e.g., under a warrant or an option) against events that would cause such equity to become less valuable in comparison to other equity interests (for example, the issuance of stock at below fair market value).

ANTI-LAYERING PROVISION: A provision in a subordinated debt agreement prohibiting the creation of additional debt that is senior to that subordinated debt but junior to senior debt.

ARM'S LENGTH: Used to describe a transaction that is at least as favorable as one that would have been entered into with a person that is not an affiliate.

ASSET-BASED LOAN: A revolving loan that is limited in amount by a formula measured by stated percentages of certain of the borrower's accounts receivable and/or inventory. *See* "Borrowing Base."

ASSET PURCHASE AGREEMENT: An agreement to acquire assets, typically all or substantially all of the assets, or all of the assets comprising a separate business unit, of another entity.

ASSET SALE COVENANT: A covenant restricting a party's ability to sell, transfer or otherwise dispose of its assets.

ASSIGNEE: *See* "Assignment."

ASSIGNMENT: The transfer by one party (an "assignor") to another party (an "assignee") of rights under a contract between the assignor and a third party. *Compare* "Novation" and "Participation Agreement."

ASSIGNMENT AND ACCEPTANCE: An agreement pursuant to which a lender in a syndicated credit agreement assigns all or a portion of its loans and/or commitments to another person.

ASSIGNOR: *See* "Assignment."

ATTORNEY-IN-FACT: A person who is authorized by a power of attorney to take legal action on behalf of the signer thereof.

AUDIT: In its most general sense, a careful review of a part of a business. An audit of financial statements by certified public accountants results in the accountants rendering an opinion that the audited financial statements fairly present the party's financial position as at the date of the financial statements and the results of its operations and changes in its financial position for the period of such financial statements, in accordance with generally accepted accounting principles.

AUTOMATIC STAY: The Bankruptcy Code prohibition against the exercise of contractual and other legal rights and remedies against a bankruptcy debtor.

BANKRUPTCY-REMOTE ENTITY: An entity that is subject to restrictions under contracts or its organizational documents that make it unlikely that the entity will become the subject of bankruptcy proceedings.

BASIS POINT: One one-hundredth of one percent (.01%).

BASKET: (a) An exception to a restrictive covenant, which permits a certain amount of the restricted activity. An example of a basket under a covenant restricting the incurrence of debt would be an exception permitting up to $10 million of outstanding purchase money debt. (b) A provision in an acquisition agreement excluding indemnity claims below a specified dollar amount.

BELT AND SUSPENDERS: Descriptive of a contract provision that is unnecessary because its subject matter has already been covered in another provision or document.

BENEFICIAL OWNERSHIP: Descriptive of an indirect interest in property. For example, an agent may be the "record owner" of property on behalf of its principal, who is the "beneficial owner." The concept of beneficial ownership is also applicable to the relationship of a parent company and a second-tier subsidiary: the parent is considered the beneficial owner of the shares of the second-tier subsidiary. Also called "equitable ownership."

BENEFICIARY: *See* "Letter of Credit."

BILL OF SALE: A document that transfers title to personal property.

BLACKLINING: The marking of a document to illustrate changes made from a previous version. Also referred to as "redlining."

BLANKET LIEN: A lien on all of a person's existing and future property.

BOILERPLATE: Contract provisions that are standard and in most cases not heavily negotiated.

BOND: A long-term debt security.

BORROWER: *See* "Credit Agreement" and "Debt Security."

BORROWING BASE: The amount of a borrower's accounts receivable and inventory that is eligible to be borrowed against in an asset-based loan facility. *See* "Asset-Based Loan."

BREACH: Failure by a party to perform a contractual obligation, or the making of a false representation.

BREAKAGE PROVISION: A provision requiring a borrower to compensate a lender for its economic losses resulting from an early repayment of a loan or a failure to borrow a loan that has been requested. *Compare* "Make-Whole Provision" and "Prepayment Penalty."

BREAK-UP FEE: A fee payable to a purchaser if the seller terminates an acquisition agreement in order to consummate a transaction with another purchaser.

BRING-DOWN: (a) The repetition of a representation subsequent to the date it was originally made. (b) A supplemental search of public records (for example, offices where financing statements are filed and secretary of state corporate records) to determine whether any changes have occurred since a previous search.

BUSINESS INTERRUPTION INSURANCE: Insurance protecting against lost income or profits resulting from an interruption of business.

CALL: A right to purchase a specified asset in the future at a set price. *Compare* "Put."

CALL PREMIUM: An additional amount required to be paid by an issuer to redeem debt securities prior to their maturity.

CALL PROTECTION: A provision which prohibits or restricts the early redemption of a debt security.

CAPITALIZED LEASE: A lease as to which the leased asset appears as an asset, and the lease obligations appear as a liability, on the balance sheet of the lessee. It usually constitutes a "security agreement" as defined in Article 1 of the Uniform Commercial Code. Also known as a "financing lease." *Compare* "Operating Lease."

CARVEOUT: A specific exception to a restrictive covenant. An example of a carveout to a covenant restricting liens would be an exception permitting mechanics' liens.

CASH COLLATERAL: Cash or cash equivalents that are deposited to secure an obligation.

CASH PAY: A term describing securities on which dividends or interest are paid in cash. *Compare* "Accretion," "Compounding" and "Payment in Kind."

CASUALTY LOSS: A loss to tangible property as a result of physical damage, such as fire or storm.

CHANGE OF CONTROL PROVISION: A provision pursuant to which a change in the voting control of a party (usually by reference to a change in the ownership of a stated percentage of voting shares or a significant change in the composition of the board of directors or other governing body) gives rise to a remedy such as termination of the contract or acceleration of indebtedness.

CLAWBACK: A provision requiring a payment previously made to be returned.

CLOSING: The satisfaction of the conditions precedent to either (a) the effectiveness of an agreement or (b) some action to be taken under an agreement or agreements (e.g., the funding of a loan or the transfer of title to real estate).

CLOSING CHECKLIST: A list of closing documents used to keep track of the status and satisfaction of conditions precedent.

COLLATERAL AGENT: A representative for other parties who in the case of a grant of a lien is the secured party and who may exercise the rights of a secured party.

COLLATERAL ASSIGNMENT: A type of security agreement in which the collateral consists of rights under one or more contracts.

COMFORT LETTER: (a) A letter from a parent company to a creditor of its subsidiary, informing the creditor that the parent is aware of the subsidiary's obligations to the creditor and that its normal policy is to ensure that its subsidiaries pay their obligations as they become due. A comfort letter is not enforceable as a guaranty. (b) A letter from certified public accountants stating that they have reviewed specified financial statements or reports, without engaging in audit procedures.

COMMERCIAL LETTER OF CREDIT: *See* "Letter of Credit."

COMMITMENT: (a) An obligation arising under a commitment letter. (b) A lender's obligation to make loans under a credit agreement.

COMMITMENT LETTER: An agreement to enter into a transaction, based on a summary of terms, and subject to completion of documentation and satisfaction of other conditions. Most often provided by lenders committing to a debt financing transaction. *Compare* "Proposal Letter" and "Letter of Intent."

COMPOUNDING: A method of interest accrual on a debt obligation, in which the accrued amount of interest is periodically added to the principal amount of the obligation instead of being paid in cash. *Compare* "Accretion," "Cash Pay" and "Payment in Kind."

CONDITION: *See* "Condition Precedent."

CONDITION PRECEDENT: A requirement that some action be taken before a contractual obligation is performed or is enforceable. Also referred to as a "condition."

CONFORMED COPY: A copy of a contract (a) which has been updated to reflect changes made in a subsequent amendment, or (b) in which the actual signatures have been replaced by the names of the signatories typed in the signature spaces (and usually preceded by "/s/").

CONSENT: An agreement by a party to permit a contractually prohibited action.

CONSENT AND AGREEMENT: An agreement under which Party A acknowledges that Party B's rights under its contract with Party A have been assigned to Party C, and under which Party A may agree that Party C has certain notice, cure and enforcement rights with respect to the assigned contract.

CONSENT SOLICITATION: A request for consent from the holders of debt securities to the amendment of the debt securities.

CONSOLIDATED: A method of financial reporting in which the financial condition and operating results of a parent company and its subsidiaries are combined.

CONSOLIDATING: A method of financial reporting in which the financial condition and operating results of a parent and each of its subsidiaries are separately reported.

CONSTRUCTION LOAN AGREEMENT: An agreement to make loans used to finance the construction of a building or other project. It provides for multiple drawdowns, each of which is subject to the satisfaction of conditions relating to the construction process ("milestones").

CONTRIBUTION AGREEMENT: An agreement under which multiple guarantors of the same claim agree to contribute their pro rata share of any payments made under the others' guarantees.

CONTROL AGREEMENT: An agreement pursuant to which an entity maintaining a deposit account or securities account agrees that it will honor certain instructions of a third party purchaser that is not the owner of the securities account or deposit account. As defined in the Uniform Commercial Code, a "purchaser" includes a secured party.

COUNTERPARTY: Another party to a contract, used primarily in the context of hedging agreements.

COUPON: The interest rate on a debt security. *Compare* "Zero Coupon."

COVENANT: A provision that obligates a party to either take (an "affirmative covenant") or refrain from taking (a "negative covenant") an action, or which requires the maintenance of some defined measure of financial performance (a "financial covenant").

COVENANT NOT TO COMPETE: An agreement not to engage in, or acquire an entity that engages in, activities that compete with the business of the recipient of the covenant.

CREDIT AGREEMENT: An agreement under which one or more parties (the "lenders") provide credit facilities (revolving loans, term loans, swingline loans and letter of credit facilities) to another party (the "borrower"). *Compare* "Debt Security."

CREDIT ENHANCEMENT: *See* "Credit Support."

CREDIT FACILITY: *See* "Credit Agreement."

CREDIT RATING: The rating given to a specific debt issue by a rating agency (e.g., Moody's or Standard & Poor's). These ratings are based on the creditworthiness of the issuer of the debt.

CREDIT RISK: The risk that a person will be financially unable to pay its obligations as they become due.

CREDIT SUPPORT: Any arrangement under which a creditor receives another source of repayment for a claim, such as a guarantee or pledge of assets by a third party or a letter of credit. Also known as "credit enhancement."

CREDITOR: A party that is owed money by another party (the "debtor").

CROSS-ACCELERATION: A provision in an agreement (usually a debt agreement) providing that it is a default by a party if its other debt has been accelerated.

CROSS-DEFAULT: A provision in an agreement (usually a debt agreement) providing for a default if a party is in default under another agreement.

CROSS REFERENCE: A reference in one provision of an agreement to another provision. Example: "Proceeds of sales permitted under this section 2(a) shall be applied in the manner set forth in section 3(b)."

CURE PERIOD: *See* "Grace Period."

CURRENCY RISK: Risk arising from the potential change in rates of exchange between two currencies. A business that has income in dollars and debt obligations payable in pesos has currency risk, to the extent the value of the dollar drops in relation to the value of the peso.

CURRENCY SWAP: A hedge agreement pursuant to which two parties agree to make specified payments to each other which take into account currency exchange rate fluctuations.

CUSHION: Extra room in a provision requiring a measurement. For example, a covenant limiting a company's annual capital expenditures to $12 million, when the company projects $10 million of capital expenditures, includes a $2 million cushion. *Compare* "Haircut."

DEBENTURE: A debt security.

DEBT INCURRENCE TEST: A provision in a debt agreement permitting the issuer to incur additional debt to the extent it satisfies a financial test.

DEBT: *See* "Indebtedness."

DEBT COVENANT: A covenant restricting a party's ability to incur or maintain indebtedness.

DEBT SECURITY: A security representing debt of the issuer. A debt security is functionally similar to a bank loan, but the nomenclature is different: A lender makes loans to a borrower under a credit agreement. An issuer sells debt securities to an investor or note purchaser pursuant to an indenture or a note purchase agreement. *Compare* "Credit Agreement."

DEBT SERVICE: Scheduled payments of principal and interest on indebtedness.

DEBTOR: (a) A party that owes money to another party (the "creditor"). (b) A person or entity that is the subject of a bankruptcy proceeding. (c) A person that has granted a security interest under the Uniform Commercial Code.

DEED: An agreement pursuant to which an interest in real property is conveyed.

DELIVERY: Delivery of an executed contract by one party to the other parties in a manner demonstrating such party's intent to be bound.

DEMAND REGISTRATION RIGHT: The right of a holder of securities to cause the issuer to register the securities under the Securities Act of 1933.

DEPRECIATION: Under GAAP, the charge to earnings over time representing the diminution in value of fixed assets. *Compare* "Amortization."

DERIVATIVE: An agreement creating an obligation to pay that is determined by reference to one or more external benchmarks, such as published interest or currency exchange rates or the trading price of one or more equity issues. *See* "Hedge Agreement."

DIRECT ORDER OF MATURITY: *See* "Inverse Order of Maturity."

DISCOUNT: A reduction to the stated amount of a payment or an obligation. A debt security is sold at a discount when the purchase price paid for the debt security is less than its face amount. *Compare* "Par," "Premium" and "Zero Coupon."

DOCUMENTARY LETTER OF CREDIT: *See* "Letter of Credit."

DOLLAR FOR DOLLAR: A phrase used to indicate that an adjustment to one amount will be the same as an adjustment to another. Example: "The escrow amount will be reduced *dollar for dollar* by the amount of each purchase price adjustment."

DRAG ALONG RIGHT: A right granted by one securityholder ("Holder A") to another ("Holder B") to include Holder A's securities in a sale by Holder B of its securities.

DRAWDOWN: A funding of a loan or equity investment (also called a "takedown").

DROP-DEAD DATE: A date specified in an agreement on which one party has the right to terminate the agreement if the other party has not satisfied or waived certain conditions by such date.

DUE DILIGENCE: An examination of a business or a portion thereof in connection with a proposed transaction.

DUE DILIGENCE OUT: A condition giving a party the right to terminate an agreement if it is not satisfied with the results of its due diligence.

EARN-OUT: Consideration for an acquisition that is paid to the seller after the closing only if certain financial performance goals are satisfied by the target.

EBITDA: Earnings before the deduction of interest, tax expense, depreciation and amortization. EBITDA is considered a key indicator of a company's profitability and is used in many financial covenants.

ENFORCEABILITY: A contract is enforceable if a court would enforce it either by granting monetary damages or equitable relief.

ENGAGEMENT LETTER: An agreement under which a professional or professional firm (e.g., an accounting firm, an investment bank or a financial advisory firm) is retained.

ENTITY: An organization that is recognized as a legal person, including a corporation, a general partnership, a limited partnership, a limited liability company, and a trust.

EQUAL AND RATABLE CLAUSE: A provision found in a debt financing agreement requiring that the debt obligations under that agreement be secured to the same extent that other future obligations may become secured.

EQUITABLE OWNERSHIP: *See* "Beneficial Ownership."

EQUITY: An investment in an entity, such as common stock, entitling the investor to a share of the entity's profits and enterprise value after the satisfaction of creditors' claims.

ERISA: The Employee Retirement Income Security Act of 1974. This federal legislation governs pension, retirement and other employee benefit plans, and is often the subject of representations and covenants.

ESCROW: An arrangement in which two or more parties deliver documents, money or property to a third party (the "escrow agent"), which agrees to deliver such documents, money or property in a specified manner upon the satisfaction of certain conditions.

ESCROW AGENT: *See* "Escrow."

EURODOLLAR INTEREST RATE: *See* "LIBOR."

EVENT OF DEFAULT: An event, act or condition that allows a party to exercise remedies under a contract, such as acceleration of debt under a credit agreement.

EXCULPATION CLAUSE: *See* "Hold Harmless Provision."

EXECUTION: The signing of a contract.

EXECUTION COPY: The final draft of an agreement, without draft lines, and often marked "Execution Copy" on the front page to identify it as such.

EXECUTORY CONTRACT: A contract in which substantial performance by one or more parties is still required.

EXHIBIT: An attachment to a contract which is usually a form of another agreement or document. *Compare* "Schedule."

FACE AMOUNT: The stated principal amount of a debt security.

FACTORING: A transaction in which a party (the "debtor") sells its accounts receivable to a second party (a "factor"). Typically, the factor has the right to sell an account receivable back to the debtor if payment thereunder is not received for reasons other than the financial inability to pay on the part of the obligor on the account receivable (e.g., a dispute over the quality of the goods sold).

FAIRNESS OPINION: An opinion of an independent financial expert as to the fairness of a transaction. A fairness opinion is often required as a condition precedent to merger and acquisition transactions.

FEE MORTGAGE: A mortgage on owned property.

FIDUCIARY OUT: *See* "No Shop Clause."

FINANCIAL COVENANTS: Covenants that test levels of financial performance. Common examples are the ratio of debt to EBITDA, the ratio of interest expense to EBITDA, and the ratio of debt to equity.

FINANCIAL STATEMENTS: Tables showing a person or entity's financial condition as at a particular time and the results of its operations for a specified period. The different types of financial statements include a balance sheet, an income statement (also called a statement of profits and losses), a statement of changes in equity and a statement of cash flows.

FINANCING LEASE: *See* "Capitalized Lease."

FINANCING OUT: A condition in an acquisition agreement allowing the acquiror to terminate the agreement if it is unable to obtain financing for the transaction.

FINANCING STATEMENT: A form describing the personal property in which a security interest is granted, which is filed with state and/or county officials pursuant to Article 9 of the Uniform Commercial Code in order to perfect the security interest.

FIXED RATE: *See* "Interest Rate."

FLEX PROVISION: A provision in a commitment letter or debt financing agreement permitting the initial lenders to change the structure, pricing or other terms if necessary to achieve a successful syndication. Also referred to as a "market flex provision."

FLOATING RATE: *See* "Interest Rate."

FORCE MAJEURE CLAUSE: A provision that excuses a failure to perform resulting from "Acts of God" and other circumstances outside the non-performing party's control.

FORBEARANCE: *See* "Standstill Agreement."

FORECLOSURE: A sale by a secured party of collateral, the proceeds of which are used to satisfy the secured obligations. *See* "Security Interest."

FRAUDULENT CONVEYANCE: A transfer made without fair consideration when the transferor is insolvent or is rendered insolvent thereby. Such a transfer may be set aside pursuant to federal and state law (e.g., Section 548 of the Bankruptcy Code).

FROZEN GAAP: A provision specifying that changes to GAAP after the date of the agreement are ignored for purposes of financial calculations.

FUNDED DEBT: A term usually defined as indebtedness with a maturity of one year or more.

FUNDS FLOW MEMORANDUM: A memorandum setting forth the details of each payment to be made at a closing.

FURTHER ASSURANCES CLAUSE: A provision requiring the parties to take such further actions as may be necessary to achieve the results contemplated by the contract.

GAAP: *See* "Generally Accepted Accounting Principles."

GENERALLY ACCEPTED ACCOUNTING PRINCIPLES: The rules of accounting employed by certified public accountants. Also referred to as "GAAP."

GOLDEN PARACHUTE: *See* "Severance Agreement."

GOVERNING LAW PROVISION: A contract provision specifying which jurisdiction's law governs the interpretation and enforcement of the contract.

GRACE PERIOD: A period of time during which a party can cure a breach before it gives rise to a remedy. Also referred to as a "cure period."

GRANT CLAUSE: (a) Generally, a provision pursuant to which an interest in property is conveyed. (b) The provision in a security agreement pursuant to which an owner of property (the "debtor") grants a security interest in the property to a creditor (the "secured party").

GROSS: *See* "Net."

GROSS-UP PROVISION: A provision requiring the amount of a payment to be increased in order to protect the recipient against specified reductions to such payment. For example, a tax gross-up requires a payor to increase a payment such that the net amount received by the payee, after any required tax payment or withholding by it, will be the amount that the payee would have received had no tax payment or withholding been required.

GUARANTEE (ALSO SPELLED GUARANTY): (a) An agreement under which a party (the "guarantor") agrees to be liable for the payment or performance of the obligations of another person. (b) The act of providing such a guarantee.

GUARANTEE OF COLLECTIBILITY: A guarantee that can be enforced only after the creditor has exhausted its remedies against the primary obligor.

GUARANTEE OF PAYMENT: A guarantee that may be enforced against the guarantor whether or not remedies have been enforced against the primary obligor.

GUARANTOR: *See* "Guarantee."

HAIRCUT: A reduction to an amount. For example, a seller who agrees to a reduction in the purchase price is said to be "taking a haircut." *Compare* "Cushion."

HAIR TRIGGER PROVISION: A covenant that is likely to be breached or a remedial provision that is likely to be triggered.

HEDGE AGREEMENT: A derivative agreement that protects against financial risks. The most common example of hedge agreements are interest rate swaps and currency swaps.

HELL OR HIGH WATER: A term describing an obligation that is unconditional. A "hell or high water lease" is a lease in which the lessee is required to make its rent payments regardless of any circumstances, including the complete loss of the leased property.

HOLD HARMLESS PROVISION: A provision under which one party agrees not to assert a claim against another party. Also called an "exculpation clause."

HOLDING COMPANY: An entity that owns only equity interests in other entities. *Compare* "Operating Company."

HYPOTHECATION AGREEMENT: A type of security agreement under which a security interest is granted by a "debtor" who is not an "obligor" (as such terms are used in Article 9 of the Uniform Commercial Code) as security for the obligations of a third party, not the obligations of the party granting the security interest.

IMMEDIATELY AVAILABLE FUNDS: Describing a manner of payment that gives the payee immediate access to the funds. Payment by check is not a payment in immediately available funds, because the check is subject to collection. Payment by wire transfer is a payment in immediately available funds.

IN ADVANCE: *See* "In Arrears."

IN ARREARS: Payment accruing over a period of time that is paid at the end of such period. For example, interest that accrues during a month and that is paid at the end of the month is paid in arrears. Payment "in advance" is the opposite.

INCORPORATION BY REFERENCE: Where a provision in Contract A deems a provision in Contract B to be part of Contract A.

INDEBTEDNESS: A term appearing most often in debt covenants and financial covenants that describes certain long-term liabilities. This term is usually defined to include borrowings, purchase money debt, capitalized leases, reimbursement obligations in respect of letters of credit, and sometimes guarantees and hedge agreements. Also referred to as "debt."

INDEMNITY/INDEMNIFICATION: A promise by one party (the "indemnitor") to reimburse another party (the "indemnitee") for certain costs, damages or losses, or to pay them directly.

INDENTURE: An agreement governing the issuance of debt securities. The parties to an indenture are the issuer of the debt securities and a representative for the holders of the securities (an "indenture trustee"). Indentures are most often used in the context of public debt offerings and sales of debt securities under Rule 144A.

INDENTURE TRUSTEE: *See* "Indenture."

INTEGRATION CLAUSE: A contract provision stating that the agreement represents the entire agreement between the parties. Its purpose is to supersede prior and contemporaneous agreements and to exclude parol evidence. Also known as a "merger clause."

INTELLECTUAL PROPERTY: Copyrights, patents, trademarks and trade secrets.

INTERCREDITOR AGREEMENT: *See* "Subordination Agreement."

INTEREST RATE: The rate of interest required to be paid on the outstanding principal amount of a debt obligation. Interest rates are either "fixed rates," which are set when the debt is first incurred and don't change over the term of the debt, or "floating rates" which are based on benchmarks that change from time to time, such as LIBOR or the prime rate. Floating interest rates usually include an additional percentage (called the "spread" or "margin") that is added to the applicable benchmark.

INTEREST RATE RISK: The risk that interest rates may fluctuate over time. For example, loans that are subject to a floating interest rate create interest rate risk for the borrower, because its interest payments may increase if interest rates go up.

INTEREST RATE SWAP: A hedge agreement pursuant to which two parties agree to make payments to each other, based on the calculation of different interest rates applied to a notional amount.

INVERSE ORDER OF MATURITY: A phrase used in loan prepayment provisions indicating that a prepayment reduces the final amortization payments. This is favorable to the lender because it shortens the maturity of the debt and unfavorable to the borrower because there is no short term reduction of its amortization payments. "Direct order of maturity" means the opposite.

INVESTMENT COVENANT: A covenant restricting a party's ability to invest in, or make loans or advances to, another person.

IPSO FACTO CLAUSE: A remedial provision providing that a contract is automatically terminated upon a party's filing of a bankruptcy petition. These clauses are generally unenforceable under Section 365(e) of the Bankruptcy Code.

ISDA: (a) The International Swap Dealers Association. (b) The standard printed form of swap agreement, promulgated by the International Swap Dealers Association.

ISSUER: A party that issues debt or equity securities. *See* "Debt Security."

ISSUING BANK: *See* "Letter of Credit."

JOINT AND SEVERAL LIABILITY: A contractual arrangement whereby two or more parties are each responsible for the full amount of the same obligation.

JUDGMENT CREDITOR: A party entitled to payment of money from another party pursuant to a judgment or decree.

JUNIOR: *See* "Priority."

LEASE: An agreement pursuant to which an owner of real or personal property (the "lessor") grants the right of use and/or possession of such property to another party (the "lessee"), in exchange for the payment of rent. *See* "Capitalized Lease" and "Operating Lease."

LEASEHOLD MORTGAGE: A mortgage on a lessee's interest under a lease.

LEGAL DESCRIPTION: A detailed description of the boundaries of a parcel of real estate that conforms with local law requirements relating to the recording of real estate interests.

LEGAL OPINION: *See* "Opinion."

LENDER: A party that makes a loan. *See* "Credit Agreement" and "Debt Security."

LESSEE: *See* "Lease."

LESSOR: *See* "Lease."

LETTER AGREEMENT: An agreement in the form of a letter from one party to another.

LETTER OF CREDIT: A three-party arrangement involving a bank (the "issuing bank"), the bank's customer (the "account party") and a creditor of the account party (the "beneficiary"). At the account party's request, the issuing bank issues a letter of credit to the beneficiary, pursuant to which the issuing bank agrees to pay the account party's obligation to the beneficiary when due, upon presentation by the beneficiary of specified documents to the issuing bank. Upon such payment, the account party is obligated to reimburse the issuing bank, typically under a "reimbursement agreement." A "standby letter of credit" is a letter of credit that can be drawn by the beneficiary if the account party fails to make a specified payment to the beneficiary. A "trade letter of credit" (also known as a "commercial letter of credit" or "documentary letter of credit") can be drawn by the beneficiary in payment for goods sold by the beneficiary to the account party.

LETTER OF INTENT: A written expression of interest or intention to enter into a transaction. A letter of intent typically does not create a binding obligation to consummate the transaction, but the letter may have enforceable provisions relating to confidentiality, disclosure, exclusivity and other features of the parties' actions relating to the proposed transaction. Also called an "agreement in principle." *Compare* "Commitment Letter" and "Proposal Letter."

LIBOR: The London Interbank Offered Rate. An interest rate based on the rate paid by banks to obtain dollar deposits in the London interbank market.

LICENSE AGREEMENT: An agreement pursuant to which an owner of intellectual property (the "licensor") permits another party (the "licensee") to use such intellectual property in a specified manner.

LICENSEE: *See* "License Agreement."

LICENSOR: *See* "License Agreement."

LIEN COVENANT: A covenant restricting a party's ability to create liens on all or a specified portion of its assets. Also called a "negative pledge clause."

LINE OF CREDIT: An arrangement under which a lender indicates its willingness to make loans to a borrower from time to time up to a stated maximum outstanding amount, but without any commitment to do so.

LIQUIDATED DAMAGE CLAUSE: A provision under which one party makes a specified payment to the other party upon the occurrence of certain events.

LOSS PAYEE ENDORSEMENT: A provision in a casualty insurance policy that requires payments thereunder to be made to a specified third party (most often, a secured creditor of the insured). *Compare* "Additional Insured Endorsement."

MAC: *See* "Material Adverse Change Clause."

MAKE-WHOLE PROVISION: A provision setting forth a formula for compensating a lender for lost income on a loan that is prepaid before its stated maturity. *Compare* "Breakage Provision" and "Prepayment Penalty."

MANDATORY PREPAYMENT: *See* "Prepayment."

MARGIN: *See* "Interest Rate."

MARKET: An adjective used to indicate that a term is in keeping with market standards, as in "it isn't market for a party to be indemnified against its own gross negligence."

MARKET FLEX PROVISION: *See* "Flex Provision."

MARKET OUT: A condition precedent that is satisfied only if there has not been a material adverse change in the financial markets.

MATERIAL ADVERSE CHANGE CLAUSE: A representation, condition precedent or event of default that is based on whether a party's condition has deteriorated to a material extent.

MATERIAL ADVERSE EFFECT: A term used to modify contract provisions on the basis of whether a particular event, act or circumstance results in a change that is both material and adverse to a party or a party's position.

MATURITY: The date on which a debt obligation becomes due.

MERGER AGREEMENT: An agreement to effect a merger of two entities.

MERGER CLAUSE: *See* "Integration Clause."

MERGER COVENANT: A covenant restricting a party's ability to enter into merger transactions.

MILESTONES: Required levels of performance contained in a contract. *See* "Construction Loan Agreement."

MORTGAGE: An agreement pursuant to which a lien on real property interests is granted by the owner or lessee thereof (the "mortgagor") in favor of its creditor (the "mortgagee").

MORTGAGE SATISFACTION: A recordable instrument pursuant to which a mortgage is released.

MORTGAGEE: *See* "Mortgage."

MORTGAGOR: *See* "Mortgage."

MUTATIS MUTANDIS: A phrase used when a provision from another contract is being incorporated by reference, indicating that such other provision is deemed to be modified as necessary to fit the context.

NATURAL PERSON: An individual, as opposed to a legal entity.

NEGATIVE COVENANT: *See* "Covenant."

NEGATIVE PLEDGE CLAUSE: *See* "Lien Covenant."

NET: After deduction of other amounts. An amount before any such deduction is the "gross" amount.

NON-RECOURSE: A secured obligation is non-recourse to a person when the person is not personally responsible for the obligation and the creditor's only remedy is to proceed against the collateral for the obligation; no damage claim is available if the collateral is not sufficient to satisfy the debt. A typical example is a real estate financing where the lender has a lien on the property but no separate claim against the owner if the value of the property isn't sufficient to satisfy the loan. Note that the non-recourse nature of an obligation may be disregarded under Section 1111(b) of the Bankruptcy Code.

NO RAID CLAUSE: A provision in an acquisition agreement or a letter of intent in which one or both parties agree not to solicit or hire the other's employees.

NO SHOP CLAUSE: In an acquisition agreement or a letter of intent, a provision under which a publicly-held target is prohibited from soliciting or negotiating a competing offer. There is usually a "fiduciary out," which permits the target to engage in the prohibited actions if failure to do so would result in the breach of the fiduciary duties of the target's board of directors or similar governing body.

NOTE: *See* "Promissory Note."

NOTIONAL AMOUNT: An amount used in a computation, the only function of which is as a basis for the computation. The most common use is in interest rate swaps, where the amount of payment is computed by applying a specified interest rate to a notional amount. In contrast, the principal amount of a note is also the basis for the calculation of interest, but is *not* a notional amount because the principal must be repaid.

NOVATION: An assignment by Party A of its rights and delegation of its obligations under an agreement to Party B, such that Party B becomes a party to the agreement and Party A ceases to be a party.

OBLIGEE: *See* "Obligor."

OBLIGOR: A party that owes payment or performance to another party (the "obligee").

OPERATING COMPANY: An entity that owns operating assets. *Compare* "Holding Company."

OPERATING LEASE: A lease as to which the leased asset appears as an asset on the lessor's balance sheet, and which does not give rise to a liability on the lessee's balance sheet. Also known as a "true lease." *Compare* "Capitalized Lease."

OPINION: A written statement of legal conclusions as to elements of a transaction, provided by one party's lawyer to the other party. An opinion is often required as a condition precedent to the closing of a transaction. Also referred to as a "legal opinion."

OPTIONAL PREPAYMENT: *See* "Prepayment."

OUT: A condition precedent that, if not satisfied, gives a party the right to terminate the contract or certain of its obligations.

PAR: The face amount of a debt security. A debt security that is trading "below par" is trading for less than its face amount. *Compare* "Discount," "Premium" and "Zero Coupon."

PARI PASSU: A term that indicates that two or more claims against a single obligor have the same level of priority. *Compare* "Priority."

PARTICIPANT: *See* "Participation Agreement."

PARTICIPATION: *See* "Participation Agreement."

PARTICIPATION AGREEMENT: An agreement pursuant to which one party transfers to another (the "participant") an interest (the "participation") in the first party's rights under another contract with a third party (usually a debt financing agreement). There is no direct contractual relationship between the participant and the third party. *Compare* "Assignment."

PAYEE: *See* "Promissory Note."

PAYMENT IN KIND: A feature of a security whereby dividends (in the case of an equity security) or interest (in the case of a debt security) are paid in the form of additional securities of the same type. Also called "PIK." *Compare* "Accretion," "Cash Pay" and "Compounding."

PAYOFF LETTER: A letter from a lender specifying the amount of outstanding principal and interest on a loan that must be paid for the loan obligations to be completely satisfied. Payoff letters are often required in connection with refinancings. A payoff letter relating to secured debt typically includes an agreement by the lender to release its liens when the loan obligations are satisfied.

PAYOR: *See* "Promissory Note."

PER ANNUM: Per year. Used in the designation of interest rates, as in "8% per annum."

PERFECTION: The legal steps necessary to make a security interest in property subject to the Uniform Commercial Code enforceable against third parties. For example, a security interest in most inventory is perfected by filing a financing statement in the filing office of the jurisdiction where the debtor is located, in accordance with the applicable Uniform Commercial Code.

PERFORMANCE: The satisfaction of contractual obligations.

PERSON: Usually defined in contracts to include both natural persons and entities. References to "person" in this glossary have this meaning.

PIGGYBACK REGISTRATION RIGHT: The right of a security-holder to cause the issuer to register its securities under the Securities Act of 1933, in connection with a registration of other securities of the same type.

PIK: *See* "Payment in Kind."

PLEDGE AGREEMENT: A type of security agreement pursuant to which a security interest is granted on instruments or securities, including equity interests and notes.

POISON PILL: *See* "Rights Agreement."

POWER OF ATTORNEY: A document pursuant to which the executing party grants authority to a named person (the "attorney-in-fact") to take specified legal action on the executing party's behalf.

PREAMBLE: *See* "Recitals."

PRECEDENT: A form or existing agreement which is used as the starting point for drafting a new agreement.

PREFERENCE: A payment or other transfer made by a person prior to such person's bankruptcy that is required to be returned to its bankruptcy estate under Bankruptcy Code Section 547.

PREMIUM: An increase to the stated amount of a payment or an obligation. A debt security is sold at a premium when the purchase price paid therefor is more than the face amount. *Compare* "Discount," "Par" and "Zero Coupon."

PREPAYMENT: Payment of all or part of a loan or debt security prior to its scheduled maturity. A prepayment may be made at the borrower's or issuer's option, or a mandatory prepayment, involving a prepayment required as a result of specified events or circumstances. *See* "Redemption."

PREPAYMENT PENALTY: A penalty imposed on the prepayment of a loan. *Compare* "Breakage Provision" and "Make-Whole Provision."

PRESENT VALUE: The value of a future payment, reduced by an amount (expressed as a percentage, the "discount") that reflects the time value of money.

PRICING GRID: A provision pursuant to which interest rates, fees or other payments are adjusted based on a party's credit rating or financial condition.

PRIORITY: (a) The status of one security interest having a claim to collateral that is superior to another security interest in the same collateral. (b) The status of one creditor having a claim against a common obligor that is superior to another creditor's claim. In each case, the superior security interest or claim is referred to as "senior," the other as "subordinated" or "junior." *Compare* "Pari Passu."

PRIVATE PLACEMENT: An issuance of securities that is exempt from the registration requirements of the Securities Act of 1933 under Section 4(2) thereof because it does not involve a public offering.

PRO FORMA: (a) The adjustment of existing financial statements or levels of financial performance to reflect an event or transaction not otherwise taken into account. (b) A financial statement as so adjusted.

PROJECTION: An estimate of financial condition and financial performance for future dates and periods of time.

PROMISSORY NOTE: An instrument executed by one party (the "payor") pursuant to which the payor promises to pay to the holder (the "payee") a specified principal amount at a specified time or times, together with interest computed at a specified rate. Also referred to as a "note."

PROPOSAL LETTER: A letter outlining the terms of a proposed transaction that is not a commitment. *Compare* "Commitment Letter" and "Letter of Intent."

PRO RATA: Apportioned based on relative amounts. For example, lenders in a syndicated loan facility are required to lend their pro rata share of each loan—that is, the lender that has committed to 50% of the facility must advance an amount equal to one-half of the loan. "Ratably" and "ratable" express the same concept.

PROVISO: A clause commencing with the words "provided" or "provided, however" that contains an exception to the concept it follows.

PURCHASE MONEY DEBT: Debt the proceeds of which are used to acquire specified assets. A promissory note issued to the seller of assets (a "seller note") is a form of purchase money debt. Also referred to as "purchase money financing."

PURCHASE PRICE ADJUSTMENT: A provision in an acquisition agreement pursuant to which the purchase price is adjusted after closing, usually by comparing the target's financial condition at closing with its financial condition as of the date of its financial statements delivered to the acquiror prior to closing.

PUT: A right to sell a specified asset in the future at a set price. *Compare* "Call."

RATABLE: *See* "Pro Rata."

RATINGS TRIGGER: A provision providing for contract termination or some additional benefit to one party (e.g., an increase in interest rates or a requirement that collateral be provided) if the credit ratings of the other party are reduced to specified levels.

REASONED OPINION: An opinion that sets forth the reasoning behind the legal conclusions set forth therein.

RECEIVABLE: *See* "Account Receivable."

RECITALS: The prefatory paragraphs of an agreement that describe the parties and the circumstances of the transaction. Also known as "whereas clauses" or the "preamble."

RECORD OWNERSHIP: *See* "Beneficial Ownership."

RECORDING TAX: A tax imposed on the recording of a deed, lease, mortgage or other agreement in the real estate records.

REDEMPTION: Purchase by an issuer of its debt or equity securities from the holder thereof. A redemption of a debt security is analogous to the prepayment of a loan. *See* "Prepayment."

REDLINING: *See* "Blacklining."

REFINANCING: A financing the proceeds of which are used to pay in full and terminate an existing financing.

REGISTRATION RIGHTS: The right of a holder of securities to have the securities be registered under the Securities Act of 1933.

REIMBURSEMENT AGREEMENT: *See* "Letter of Credit."

RELEASE: An agreement by a party to terminate a claim against another party or portion of a lien on another party's assets (if a lien on all collateral is released, it is referred to as a "termination").

RENT: A payment made by a lessee under a lease.

REPRESENTATION: A provision in which one party makes a statement of fact as of a particular point in time to be relied on by another party.

RESTRICTED PAYMENT: A term used in indentures and other debt agreements that includes dividends, equity repurchases and redemptions, other distributions on equity, and sometimes investments.

RESTRICTED PAYMENTS COVENANT: A covenant restricting a party's ability to make restricted payments.

RESTRICTED SUBSIDIARY: *See* "Unrestricted Subsidiary."

REVOLVING LOAN: A type of debt financing involving loans that can be borrowed, repaid and reborrowed.

RIGHTS AGREEMENT: An agreement giving the shareholders of a public company the right to acquire additional shares at a discount if there is a change of control, intended to repel hostile takeovers. Also called a "shareholders' rights plan" or a "poison pill."

ROYALTY: A payment made by a licensee under a license agreement.

SAVINGS CLAUSE: A provision that prevents another provision in the agreement from violating the law or another agreement. For example, a usury savings clause states that a floating rate of interest may not exceed the applicable usury rate.

SCHEDULE: An attachment to a contract which usually sets forth factual material. *Compare* "Exhibit."

SECOND-TIER SUBSIDIARY: A subsidiary of a subsidiary.

SECURED PARTY: *See* "Security Interest."

SECURED TRANSACTION: A transaction (usually a debt financing) in which obligations are secured by the grant of a security interest.

SECURITY AGREEMENT: An agreement pursuant to which a security interest is granted.

SECURITY INTEREST: A conditional interest in personal property granted by an obligor (the "debtor") to its creditor (the "secured party") to secure the payment of the debtor's obligations. After default by the debtor, the secured party has the right to sell the property (a "foreclosure") and apply the proceeds in satisfaction of the secured obligations. The term "security interest" as defined in the Uniform Commercial Code also includes (a) certain leases and (b) the sale of certain notes and contracts (e.g., chattel paper, accounts and payment intangibles).

SELLER NOTE: *See* "Purchase Money Debt."

SENIOR: *See* "Priority."

SETOFF PROVISION: A provision permitting Party A to satisfy a claim owed to it by Party B by cancelling an obligation owed to Party B by Party A. The most typical example is a bank that is owed money by a borrower applying amounts in a deposit account of the borrower in satisfaction of such obligation.

SEVERANCE AGREEMENT: An agreement requiring an employer to provide compensation and/or other benefits to an employee who is terminated. Sometimes referred to as a "golden parachute."

SHAREHOLDERS' RIGHTS PLAN: *See* "Rights Agreement."

SIDE LETTER: An agreement intended to modify or supplement another agreement that is entered into at the same time. If the agreement being modified or supplemented has an integration clause, the side letter may not be enforceable.

SIGNATURE PAGES: The pages at the end of a contract where the parties sign.

SOLVENCY OPINION: An opinion of an independent financial expert as to the solvency of a party to a transaction, after giving effect to that transaction. This is often required as a condition precedent to financing transactions. *See* "Fraudulent Conveyance."

SOURCES AND USES: A table showing the sources of funds being used in a transaction, and the uses to which such funds are applied.

SOVEREIGN IMMUNITY: The right of a sovereign entity to be immune from being sued for its actions.

SPECIAL PURPOSE ENTITY: An entity that is prevented by contract or its organizational documents from conducting business except for specified activities. It is often a bankuptcy-remote entity. Also referred to as a "special purpose vehicle."

SPECIAL PURPOSE VEHICLE: *See* "Special Purpose Entity."

SPREAD: *See* "Interest Rate."

STANDBY LETTER OF CREDIT: *See* "Letter of Credit."

STANDSTILL AGREEMENT: (a) An agreement in which a party (usually a creditor) agrees not to exercise its contractual rights against another party. Also referred to as a "forbearance." (b) An agreement in which a party agrees not to acquire stock or otherwise seek to gain control of a public company.

STIPULATED LOSS VALUE: A term used in a lease describing the amount to be paid by the lessee to the lessor in the event of a casualty loss to the leased property.

STOCK PURCHASE AGREEMENT: An acquisition agreement providing for the sale of all or a portion of the stock of a corporation. If the target is not an entity that issues stock (e.g., a limited partnership or a limited liability company), the agreement will be named accordingly.

STRUCTURAL SUBORDINATION: Where Creditor A is subordinated to Creditor B by virtue of not having a claim against a party who does have an obligation to Creditor B. Example: Both Creditors A and B have loans to Party X. Party X's subsidiary has guaranteed Creditor A's loan but not Creditor B's. Creditor B is structurally subordinated to Creditor A in relation to the subsidiary. *Compare* "Subordination Agreement."

SUBORDINATED: *See* "Priority."

SUBORDINATION AGREEMENT: An agreement between two parties having claims against, or liens on the assets of, the same debtor, in which the parties agree on the relative priority of such claims or liens. Also known as an "Intercreditor Agreement." *Compare* "Structural Subordination."

SUBROGATION: The right of a guarantor that has made payment under a guarantee to step into the shoes of the creditor receiving such payment and to enforce the obligations in respect of which such payment was made against the obligor.

SUBSIDIARY: An entity, the majority of the voting equity of which is owned by another entity (the "parent").

SUPPLEMENTAL INDENTURE: An amendment to an indenture.

SWINGLINE: An arrangement in a syndicated revolving loan facility in which a single lender makes revolving advances to the borrower in smaller amounts, and on shorter notice, than would otherwise be available.

SYNDICATION: The process by which a loan or investment is divided up among a group of lenders or investors (the "syndicate"). A syndicated loan agreement is one in which the loans are made by a number of lenders, each of which is responsible to fund its pro rata share of the loans.

SYNTHETIC LEASE: A lease that is treated as an operating lease for accounting purposes (i.e., neither the leased asset nor the lease liability appears on the lessee's balance sheet), but the lessee is treated as the owner of the leased property for tax purposes.

TAG ALONG RIGHT: A right of one securityholder to have its securities included in a sale of the same securities by another securityholder.

TAKEDOWN: *See* "Drawdown."

TARGET: The entity that is acquired in an acquisition.

10-B5 REPRESENTATION: A representation stating that all other representations in an agreement, taken together, do not contain any material misstatement and do not omit to state any material fact necessary in order to prevent such representations from being misleading.

TERM SHEET: A summary of terms outlining a proposed transaction. Term sheets are often attached to commitment letters or letters of intent.

TICKING FEE: A fee paid for a financing commitment that accrues at a per annum rate prior to closing.

TITLE INSURANCE: Insurance against the existence of adverse claims to real estate.

TITLE SEARCH: A search of the real estate records determining whether there are any recorded encumbrances or adverse claims to real estate.

TRADE LETTER OF CREDIT: *See* "Letter of Credit."

TRANCHE: A term used to distinguish different loan facilities provided under the same loan agreement. Different tranches may, or may not, have different maturities, amortization schedules and interest rates.

TRANSACTIONS WITH AFFILIATES COVENANT: A covenant restricting a party's ability to enter into transactions with its affiliates.

TRUE LEASE: *See* "Operating Lease."

TRUE SALE: A sale transaction that cannot be recharacterized as a financing in the seller's bankruptcy proceeding—i.e., the sold assets will not be treated as assets of the seller's bankruptcy estate.

TURNING PAGES: The process in which clients and/or counsel go through an agreement (or comments thereto) page-by-page.

ULTRA VIRES: Descriptive of an act by an entity that is (a) outside its statutory powers, (b) not permitted under its organizational documents, or (c) not properly authorized by its board of directors or similar governing body.

UNDER WATER: When a stock option's exercise price is greater than the market value of the underlying shares, it is said to be "under water."

UNDERWRITER: A financial institution that agrees to purchase debt or equity securities in order to resell them in a public offering.

UNDERWRITING AGREEMENT: An agreement pursuant to which an underwriter agrees to purchase debt or equity securities from the issuer or seller thereof in order to resell them in a public offering.

UNRESTRICTED SUBSIDIARY: In a debt agreement, a designated subsidiary of the borrower or issuer that is not subject to the agreement's covenants or representations. All other subsidiaries are called "restricted subsidiaries."

UPSTREAM GUARANTEE: A guarantee by a subsidiary of its parent's obligations. This type of guarantee presents potential fraudulent conveyance concerns, because in most cases the subsidiary receives no benefit for providing the guarantee.

VENDEE: A seller of goods.

VENDOR: A buyer of goods.

WAIVER: An agreement to give up or delay the time for performance of a contractual right.

WAIVER OF SOVEREIGN IMMUNITY: A provision under which a sovereign entity waives its right to assert sovereign immunity.

WATERFALL PROVISION: A provision providing for the application of specified funds to different purposes in a specified order.

WHEREAS CLAUSE: *See* "Recitals."

WORKING CAPITAL: A company's current assets (receivables, inventory and cash) less its current liabilities.

WORKING CAPITAL ADJUSTMENT: In a purchase agreement, an adjustment made to the purchase price if the target's working capital at closing is greater or less than a projected level.

WORKOUT: A restructuring of debt obligations outside of bankruptcy.

ZERO COUPON: A type of debt security that is issued at a discount to its face amount, and that is not interest-bearing. The principal amount of the security accretes from the original purchase price amount to the stated principal amount, at maturity. *Compare* "Discount," "Par" and "Premium."

Index

F

J

K

L

M